Asymmetries in Dialogue

Asymmetries in Dialogue

Edited by
Ivana Marková and Klaus Foppa

HARVESTER WHEATSHEAF
BARNES & NOBLE BOOKS

First published 1991 by
Harvester Wheatsheaf,
66 Wood Lane End, Hemel Hempstead,
Hertfordshire, HP2 4RG
A division of
Simon & Schuster International Group

First published in the United States of America in 1991 by
Barnes & Noble Books
8705 Bollman Place
Savage, Maryland 20763

© 1991 Individual chapter authors and editors

All rights reserved. No part of this publication may be reproduced, stored in a retrieval system, or transmitted, in any form, or by any means, electronic, mechanical, photocopying, recording or otherwise, without the prior permission, in writing, from the publisher.

Typeset in 10/12 pt Century Schoolbook
by Witwell Ltd, Southport

Printed and bound in Great Britain by
BPCC Wheatons Ltd, Exeter

British Library Cataloguing in Publication Data

Asymmetries in dialogue.
 I. Marková, Ivana   II. Foppa, Klaus
 410

 ISBN 0-7450-1029-6
 ISBN 0-7450-1031-8 pbk

Library of Congress Cataloging-in-Publication Data

 Available from the publisher
 ISBN 0-389-20980-5

1 2 3 4 5   95 94 93 92 91

Contents

Preface vii
1. Asymmetries in dialogue: some conceptual preliminaries   *P. Linell and T. Luckmann* 1
2. Asymmetries of knowledge in conversational interactions   *P. Drew* 21
3. Facework and control in multi-party talk: a pediatric case study   *K. Aronsson* 49
4. Suspect stories: on perspective-setting in an asymmetrical situation   *P. Linell and L. Jönsson* 75
5. Obstruction and dominance: uncooperative moves and their effect on the course of conversation   *M.-L. Käsermann* 101
6. Dialogue between expert and novice: on differences in knowledge and their reduction   *M. Wintermantel* 124
7. 'Teaching': conversational transmission of knowledge   *A. Keppler and T. Luckmann* 143
8. The taming of foes: the avoidance of asymmetry in informal discussions   *H. Knoblauch* 166
9. Dominance and asymmetries in *A Doll's House*   *R. Rommetveit* 195
10. Asymmetries in group conversations between a tutor and people with learning difficulties   *I. Marková* 221
11. Bodies and voices in dialogue   *R. Farr* 241
    Conclusion   *I. Marková and K. Foppa* 259

Preface

Volume 1 of this series, *The Dynamics of Dialogue,* explored some conceptual issues of a dialogical approach to the study of language and communication. In this second volume, *Asymmetries in Dialogue,* the focus is on empirical questions of the dialogical approach. This is to be followed by a third volume, *Mutualities in Dialogue,* now in preparation.

We are very grateful to the Werner Reimers Foundation for their continuing support of the work of our interdisciplinary Study Group, The Dynamics of Dialogue. We believe that an approach transcending the boundaries between the sciences and humanities is a most fruitful one in the pursuit of knowledge and understanding of language and communication. We would also like to thank Colin Wright for his very generous editorial help and to Harvester Wheatsheaf for their patience and efficiency in producing this volume.

1 | Asymmetries in dialogue: some conceptual preliminaries
Per Linell and Thomas Luckmann

The contributions to this volume deal with dialogue and spoken interaction, and especially with asymmetries in these kinds of discourse. The overall orientation implies that the authors have adopted a particular perspective; rather than studying, say, social power in society and culture, they seek their empirical basis in discourse data. The aim is to look for generalizations about asymmetries *in situ* in dialogue and discourse. This is, of course, the common point of departure for most analysts of conversation and discourse.

Another point, shared by many if not most dialogue-oriented scholars (Marková and Foppa, 1990; especially Marková, 1990), is that dialogue (discourse, texts) and contexts are mutually inalienable; a dialogue, or a contribution to it, is co-constituted by utterances and their relevant outsides. Yet there is considerable disagreement, at least in the scientific community at large, as regards how and to what extent analysts should bring contextual information to bear on the process of identification and interpretation of discourse patterns. Some researchers (e.g. Atkinson and Heritage, 1984; Schegloff, 1987) opt for an approach based more or less exclusively on discourse (or texts) as such. Others (e.g. Cicourel, 1980; Corsaro, 1982) strongly argue for the use of complementary sources of information: ethnography, data about individual actors and organizational frameworks; documents and instructions used by actors, especially professionals, as background and as inputs or outputs of institutionalized dialogues; and people's discourse *about* the discourse under study. The last mentioned point covers what people say they do in their respective social encounters; people's self-evaluations and self-interpretations of particular encounters as stated, e.g. in (post-)interviews and self-confrontations, as well as general statements and theories produced by individuals and organizations in, e.g. official rhetoric. While most of the contributors to this volume would insist on taking even historical and/or cultural contexts into consideration, at least in a more comprehensive analysis, they all retain an empirically based theoretical interest *in dialogue and discourse*. This volume focuses on the interactional environments and consequences of asymmetries.

Asymmetries in dialogue: the term and its extension

As is amply demonstrated in this volume, 'asymmetries in dialogue' can be taken to mean rather different things. The term does not stand for one well-defined notion. Rather, we prefer here to introduce it as a cover term for a wide spectrum of phenomena, each of which will need a more precise and refined analysis in various contexts.

Some neighbouring concepts in the semantic field

'Asymmetry' as an overall term can be used to describe several phenomena in and behind dialogue. (For a definition of 'dialogue', see Luckmann, 1990.) Sometimes other terms, like 'inequality' (or 'inequity'), 'dominance', and 'imbalance', are preferred in the literature. All these seem to be opposed to terms like 'symmetry' (in, e.g. participation), 'equality' or 'commonality' (of knowledge), 'mutuality' and 'reciprocity' (in, say, interaction and dialogue). In an attempt to establish some order in the semantic field, let us begin by briefly considering the last mentioned notions with respect to dialogue and its prerequisites (for a more thorough treatment see Graumann, forthcoming).

Commonality (or sharedness) of knowledge (or language, assumptions, etc.) refers simply to the knowledge (etc.) which is objectively shared by people who engage, or might engage, in communication with each other. *Mutuality* (of knowledge and assumptions), again with respect to dialogue, refers to the assumptions by each communicating individual that (s)he shares knowledge ('common ground') with the others, and that the others know or assume that each communicator makes this first mentioned assumption of common ground (Clark and Marshall, 1981). *Reciprocity*, finally, would be more directly tied to the dialogical activity itself, referring to the circumstance that, in the co-presence of others, any act by one actor is an act with respect to the other; more precisely, any act is done with the purpose or expectation that the other will do something in return, i.e. respond or, as we could also say, reciprocate the action. For example, if A greets B, he or she normally expects a greeting in return. Similarly, if A asks a question, he or she expects B to answer (or at least respond in some other way, e.g. by a counter-question), and if/when B responds, he or she, in turn, expects or anticipates a response or reaction from A. Reciprocity thus refers to the basic interdependence between interlocutors and between their dialogue contributions. Reciprocity inheres also in the smallest dialogue contribution, i.e. the utterance; such an elementary unit is dependent on the other's contribution(s), and it is codeterminant of the other's next contribution.

It can be argued that reciprocity in dialogue presupposes mutuality, i.e. mutually assumed common ground, and, of course, that mutuality entails commonality. If we take reciprocity as an abstract notion to be a defining feature of social interaction, of which dialogue is a special form (Luckmann, 1990), then it follows that dialogue must also involve some mutuality and sharedness of premises for communication, and of knowledge, presuppositions and interests. But this in no way means that the extent to which there is commonality, mutuality, and reciprocity, is total. On the contrary, we know that knowledge and opportunities to participate are only in part common and equally available, mutually assumed and symmetrically reciprocated. This means that asymmetries and inequalities of many kinds are compatible with mutuality and reciprocity. Also, mutualities and reciprocities vary; for example, some reciprocated actions as it were mirror each other mentally or socially (e.g. greetings), while others are of a complementary kind (e.g. question–answer); and the same applies at more global or aggregated levels (e.g. Linell, 1990, pp. 168–72). (It is important to be careful here; while reciprocity as an abstract notion (in the singular) is taken to be inherent in the nature of dialogue, reciprocities of different kinds (in the plural) are empirically present to different extents under varying social conditions.) In other words, asymmetries and inequalities are not only compatible with assumptions of mutuality and reciprocity, they are themselves essential properties of communication and dialogue. Indeed, if there were no asymmetries at all between people, i.e. if communicatively relevant inequalities of knowledge were non-existing, there would be little or no need for most kinds of communication!

We propose to use 'asymmetry' as a general term referring to various sorts of inequivalences in dialogue processes. Sometimes, the term 'inequalities' can be used almost coterminously, although we prefer to use that term for various background (e.g. social-structural) conditions for dialogue, such as (differences in the distribution of) knowledge and social positions (see Drew, Chapter 2; Keppler and Luckmann, Chapter 7; also p. 12-17 below).

'Asymmetry' as a comprehensive term can be used of both globally manifest patterns (e.g. what we call 'dominance' below) and local properties. Local asymmetries may be tied to single exchanges ('adjacency pairs') (a greeting and its reciprocation would be only mildly asymmetrical, while, e.g. a promise and its acceptance form a much more asymmetrical pair) or to single turns; there are basic asymmetries tied to the allocation of speaker versus listener roles. 'Dominance', on the other hand, should, as regards discourse, be taken as a less neutral and somewhat more precise term to be used of certain *global* properties, i.e. in principle quantifiable and aggregated patterns *emergent over sequences* (entire social encounters or dialogues, or parts or phases thereof), as will be further explained below[1] (on p. 8-9). Given such a usage, the term 'dominance' would not be productively applicable at the level of single turns; for example, to say that the speaker dominates over the listener in terms of amount of speaking or interactional control would be nothing but a trivial assertion. Farr (Chapter 11) points out that the asymmetries involved in the predicaments of speaker versus listener and actor versus observer can be symmetrically distributed, if we look at them over longer stretches of dialogue.

Following rather well-established usage, we take the term 'local' to refer to single utterances and turns, single exchanges (e.g. 'adjacency pairs'), and contributions in their relation to immediately preceding and anticipated next contributions (cf. Linell, 1990: 'local context'), while the term 'global' would apply to longer stretches of dialogue, or sequences treated at 'higher' levels, such as 'stories', 'topics', 'activities' or 'speech events' and 'phases' thereof; such global units are often anchored in socially or culturally sedimented genres. We can then say that 'reciprocity' inheres in the most local units as well as in the more global units, as Bakhtin (1986) points out. Asymmetries, too, are present at all levels. 'Symmetry', on the other hand, would be meaningfully employed, in the case of dialogue and discourse, only if applied to a sequence; it makes no sense at the level of the single dialogue contribution (utterance), since the asymmetries tied to the speaker versus listener roles are self-evident. In other words, we propose that the terms/concepts 'symmetry' and 'dominance' be used only globally, as referring to properties emergent over sequences, while 'reciprocity' and 'asymmetry' can be used both globally and locally.

Asymmetries of knowledge and of participant status

A dialogue is about something (the topic) and between people interacting (the participation framework). Using this simple dichotomy, we find that the chapters in this volume deal with asymmetries of different kinds.

Several of the chapters (Drew, Wintermantel, Knoblauch, Keppler and Luckmann, Linell and Jönsson) touch upon various aspects of *asymmetries* (or inequalities) of *knowledge*. As several of the authors note, asymmetries of knowledge are important only when they are made communicatively salient. For example, if A knows more than B about some topic T, this inequality is of no relevance until it becomes exploited and thematized, e.g. when occasioning A to launch an item of 'conversational teaching' (Keppler and Luckmann). Similarly, Drew (Chapter 2) emphasizes that, within dialogue studies, asymmetries are interesting only in as far as they become consequential for the talk in actual dialogue. This means that mere inequalities of cognitive states, for example A knowing things B does not know, and vice versa, are not in and by themselves of primary interest. Instead, we might look at inequivalences of knowledge with respect to the particular interactions and phases thereof under analysis. Such inequivalences may concern, among other things:

- Differences in rights (entitlements) to develop topics and exploit knowledge, and in the allocation of epistemic responsibility (Rommetveit).
- Varying access to and control of particular perspectives on topics (relevances), as in cases of professional-client or

expert–novice interaction (Linell and Jönsson, Wintermantel; see also Rommetveit).
- Differences among actors regarding their knowledge about each other (differences in possible partner orientations or recipient designs), and in authoritative access to knowledge (Drew).

Another focus in this book is on *asymmetries in participant status* among interactants: participation rights as well as actual patterns of participation (Aronsson, Rommetveit, Marková). Here we find:

- Asymmetries between speakers, addressees, side-participants, present observers (by-standers) and outside observers (e.g. researchers – see Farr).
- Asymmetries of interpersonal relations as displayed in dialogue (e.g. *Ich–du* versus *Ich–es* relations: Rommetveit, Marková).
- Relationships between participant status and entitlements or access to topics and topical perspectives (Rommetveit).

Of special concern are the dynamic aspects of the interactionally regulated participant roles, e.g. the role of intermediaries in multi-party settings, and the transformation of participants to third persons or even 'non-persons' in interaction (Aronsson, Marková).

It is important to realize that there is no necessary relationship between, say, interactional dominance and asymmetries of (interactionally relevant) knowledge. For example, a person who has no privileged access to authoritative knowledge may still manage to gain a good deal of interactional space (Drew). On the other hand, there are also plenty of instances in which the exploitation of asymmetries of knowledge leads to an asymmetry in participation, e.g. when one party is 'teaching' for a relatively extended turn (Keppler and Luckmann).

Asymmetries in dialogue: the theory

Having fixed some preliminary definitions, we will now proceed, bearing in mind dialogical principles of mind and language (Marková and Foppa, 1990), to discuss some general assumptions about the nature of asymmetries in dialogue.

Asymmetries are ubiquitous properties of dialogue

One may look upon social communication as directed towards making things 'common' to interlocutors, as based on efforts to equalize knowledge and mutual influence. Yet every new conversational move presupposes asymmetry of knowledge and, if it is a new initiative, it moves the interaction from a state of rest (silence) into a situation in which the speaker, by performing his or her communicative act, requires an additional move from the other, thus bringing about a disturbance in the equilibrium. At the same time, once a contribution has been jointly accepted and understood, a local topic has been settled. Dialogue thrives on this tension between exploiting asymmetries and returning to states of equilibrium.

We take asymmetry to be an *intrinsic feature of dialogue*. Basic asymmetries are also involved in the smallest units of dialogue. An utterance may be analysed in terms of its responsive and initiatory (retroactive and proactive) aspects; it is both dependent on prior context and defines the conditions for possible continuations. By responding to prior communicative events, by making his or her utterance 'conditionally relevant' in the local context, the utterer, at some level, complies with conditions already defined. On the other hand, by taking the discourse further, by initiating new topical aspects, he or she tries to govern the contributions to follow. Hence, there is a basic asymmetry involved in this dialectic between being controlled and being in control, which is part and parcel of the 'power' of basic dialogue mechanisms (Linell, 1990).

Similarly, there is an obvious asymmetry between speaker and listener. Even if the listener is 'present' in the speaker's utterance, both in its basic other-orientedness ('recipient design') and by the listener's co-authoring it (back channelling, filling in utterances, verbal duetting – see, e.g. Goodwin, 1979), the speaker is still its major author. However, there are cases where the responses are minimal simply because the speaker's contribution itself is minimal. In general, there are important differences between the predicaments of the speaker and the listener (Farr, Chapter 11).

In responding to prior talk as well as in taking topical and interactional initiatives, when speaking as well as when listening, actors in dialogue are profoundly dependent on each other. This interdependence, the crucial and mutual reliance on the other, is always present. Yet even if there are mutual interdependences, these are seldom symmetrically distributed; some interlocutors are characteristically more subordinated to their partners than others. It is particularly appropriate to recall that a child, in learning to speak and communicate, has no choice other than that of relying on its partner in getting to understand what its own words mean (Rommetveit, 1983). Therefore, learning to become a conversation partner presupposes asymmetries of various kinds.

Hence, we take it as a reasonable point of departure that *all* dialogues (and, of course, multi-party conversations) involve asymmetries (inequalities, inequivalences, etc.) at different levels. This can be stated as a general claim, *even if*, in some contexts, actors jointly orient to ideal norms of equal rights to speaking turns, equal rights and/or abilities to introduce and sustain topics, and symmetrical distribution of discourse participation (Habermas's notion of 'ideal dialogue' seems to be an attempt to characterize such a set of ideal norms),[2] *or if*, indeed, such properties are taken to be empirically true of some types of (weakly institutionalized) talk exchange, sometimes loosely referred to as 'informal' or 'ordinary' conversation. In other words, even relatively 'symmetrical' conversations involve asymmetries of various sorts.

This also means that 'asymmetries' must be taken as a concept that is neutral with respect to success or non-success in communication. Some asymmetries do lead to obstructions, problems and failures of communication (Käsermann, Chapter 5), but there is no logical relationship between asymmetries and problematic talk (Drew, Chapter 2). In fact, some asymmetries are arguably necessary for effective communication to develop (Wintermantel, Chapter 6; Linell and Jönsson, Chapter 4).

Asymmetries are multi-faceted and heterogeneous

Asymmetries can be further subcategorized along several dimensions, e.g. as regards domain (knowledge versus participant status) or scope (local versus global asymmetries). (See also below on source: exogenous versus endogenous types.) These, of course, are all in need of further analysis.

One family of asymmetries consists of those which can be seen as patterns of *dominance* emerging over sequences. In line with our introduction, we use the term 'dominance' of *manifest* properties of interaction, dialogue and discourse; of more or less 'objective' patterns which, once identified, may receive many different interpretations (e.g. with respect to social power, see below). Dominance in dialogue is clearly a multi-dimensional phenomenon. There are several ways to disentangle these dimensions. One categorization (Linell 1990) amounts to distinguishing between the following four types. *Quantitative* dominance concerns the relation between parties in terms of amount of talk, measured simply, e.g. in terms of number of words spoken. *Interactional* dominance has to do with the distribution of 'strong' versus 'weak' interactional moves (initiatives, responses). In talking about *semantic* dominance, one would characterize a person as dominant if he or she determined the topics sustained in a discourse, and imposed interpretive perspectives on things talked about. Finally, *strategic* dominance would involve contributing the strategically most important interventions. Interactional dominance, or, if you prefer, control, taken as 'a property of sequence management and turn design' (Drew, Chapter 2: p. 43) may be investigated in several ways, one of which would be the IR (initiative–response) analysis (Linell *et al.*, 1988) employed by, e.g. Rommetveit (Chapter 9) and Marková (Chapter 10). It should be pointed out that strategic dominance is not quite aligned with the other concepts; it comes closer to power (as defined below), it is more dependent on exogenous factors, and it involves evaluating retrospectively the outcomes of the whole interaction, including some more or less long-term effects.

Asymmetries are dependent on both individual and social factors

Dialogues are produced by individuals in social interaction, and patterns of asymmetry or dominance are generated in actual social intercourse. Some of these patterns may be dependent on properties of individuals (personality, biography, abilities and disabilities), and some on roles tied to professions, organizations, social strata, etc. It is important to emphasize that whatever asymmetries or symmetries are actually found, these are not merely expressions of individual intentions or motives. There are also social structures and traditions 'speaking through' actors. Accordingly, the speaker role is a complex one (Goffman, 1981). Some of these personal versus cultural identities in dialogue can be characterized in terms of 'voices' (Bakhtin, 1986; Wertsch, 1990; Aronsson, Chapter 3; Linell and

Jönsson, Chapter 4), which are heard with varying degrees of 'loudness' in different phases of dialogues.

Asymmetries in discourse are contextualized; dependence on and co-constitutive of endogenous and exogenous conditions

Another way to distinguish among asymmetries, especially patterns of dominance, is to attribute them to different sources: either they can be imposed or imported from outside ('extrinsic' or 'exogenous', derived from social power or authority and pre-established as constraints on interaction), or they are dialogue produced ('intrinsic' or 'endogenous', derived from asymmetries between dialogue initiatives and responses as basic mechanisms of interaction). (A distinction similar to the one just suggested would amount to distinguishing between setting-, status- or role-produced dominance and actor-produced dominance.) Of course, exogenous and endogenous asymmetries are not two independent sets of factors. Rather, the same manifest pattern usually exhibits both. Asymmetries dependent on extrinsic sources must be occasioned, reconstructed, sustained or confirmed in actual discourse, thus re-established *in situ*, and, conversely, dialogue-generated asymmetries are constrained by predetermined conditions (social structures existing prior to the interaction).

In the next section we will shift perspectives and look upon asymmetries in dialogue from the viewpoint of background social structures. However, let us emphasize here and now that dominance in dialogue and interaction, on the one hand, and social power, on the other, must never be confused. Yet, this is easily done since terms like 'power' and 'dominance' often go together, both having to do with someone's having direct or indirect access to, or possession of, resources (e.g. economic means or, in communication, e.g. discourse space), normally at someone else's expense (e.g. at the expense of one's interlocutors). It seems reasonable to define (by stipulation, but in line with existing tendencies in actual usage) 'power' as having to do with latent resources or potentialities, while dominance concerns manifest action properties or actualities, or, if you will, some sort of resources put to actual use (see above).

If 'power' is conceived of as latent potentialities, it seems convenient to discuss microphenomena in dialogue in relation to social power. Thus, social power is supposed to represent something relatively stable: socio-economically determined, culturally embedded and institutionally congealed.[3] A clear distinction between (social) power and (manifest) dominance roughly along these lines will allow us to capture some important features of discoursal practices. For example, a person who possesses power need not be, or at least not always be, dominant in interaction. In fact, there is ample evidence that, in many situations, power must be used strategically, not overused, in order for the actor to be efficient. Dominant dialogue behaviour, along one or other of the dimensions mentioned above, may sometimes indeed be a sign of relative powerlessness on the part of a given actor. Therefore, the analyst must always keep the distinction in mind; it is one thing to identify dominant actions, another thing to determine what they mean or what they are signs of.

Asymmetries are socially (re)constructed

Some aspects of asymmetries are clearly correlated with, even predefined by, positions in social hierarchies. For example, experts and professionals talking with clients and lay persons in various sorts of institutional contexts (Agar, 1985), such as court trials, police interrogations, doctor consultations, classroom interactions, occupy a position of power, authority and expertise. These, together with routinized ways of carrying out the interaction, will have a clear impact on the manner in which the discourse unfolds. Some classical positions in the sociology of power (Parsons, 1951) involve the assumption that patterns of interaction are predictable from the predefined power relationships; actors would just step into stable roles of interaction (Heritage, 1984). Without denying that social interaction may largely be institutionally congealed, many researchers who have *actually studied institutional discourse* have found that there is active and dynamic interactive work going on. As Goodwin and Heritage (1990: p. 14) put it, the 'way in which . . . discourse identities intersect with a range of social arrangements involving entitlement to knowledge can lead to participation framework dynamics of considerable complexity.'

Parties accommodate mutually, and there is room for variation even in such highly routinized environments as courtrooms (e.g. Linell, 1991). Yet interactants regularly collaborate on the reconstitution of roles and positions. For example, even if legal professionals, i.e. judges and attorneys, provide ample opportunities for defendants to lay out their own versions, such chances are not always taken. If defendants are unwilling or feel incapable of volunteering expanded answers to questions, professionals will then be forced to fall back into habits of posing highly specific and constraining questions permitting the interviewees to respond only minimally. Thus, both parties in court or in a police interrogation collaborate on reconstructing question–answer sequences of certain types (Linell, 1991; Linell and Jönsson, Chapter 4). Similarly, Heath (forthcoming) and Maynard (forthcoming) demonstrate, using data from medical interviews, that patients regularly refrain from voicing their own perspectives, particularly when the doctor delivers the most important information, the diagnosis, and that this is true even if the doctor's proposed diagnosis is strongly at variance with the patient's expectation. Patients strongly tend to adopt the clinical perspective. Yet, Maynard, in his paper on asymmetries in doctor–patient discourse, argues in the following vein (Maynard, forthcoming).

> Previous research, including language-based studies, say or imply that this asymmetry represents the imposition of physician's power and authority, which reproduces the society's overall, external, institutional structure. The argument here is that, within institutional discourse, more is going on than this. To be sure, patients and parents seek expertise in regard to their lifeworld difficulties and receive avowedly official reports and technical versions of these difficulties in ways that promote or reproduce the institution of medicine. However, if such reports and versions are bad news, their delivery will be predictably difficult in a purely local, embodied, interactional sense. Therefore, clinicians as ordinary members of society can be expected to have devices for handling these interactional difficulties. Exploring such a possibility requires comparative analyses of institutional discourse and everyday conversation, which shows that co-implicating a recipient's perspective in a bad news delivery allows for at least the appearance of understanding and mutuality in this highly-charged situation. In short, the asymmetry of discourse in medical settings may have an institutional mooring, but it also has an interactional bedrock, and the latter needs sociological appreciation as much as the former. Finally, if medical discourse has such a bedrock, no doubt various institutional discourses – in legal, educational, and other settings – do as well.

Asymmetries in dialogue: the contexts
Contexts in and contexts behind the text

One may surely assume that human beings from entirely different backgrounds, even alien cultures, would be able to interact when thrown together and thus build up patterns of practical sense which were not pre-existent as a background resource. It is an elementary philosophical–anthropological assumption that such patterns of action-orienting meaning are originally built up in the actions of human beings, somehow, somewhere, sometime. Yet it is also obvious that the majority of us most of the time do not start from scratch in social encounters but draw upon resources of a social reality which are *not* indigenous to the situation. We do not invent language anew in every dialogue nor even create patterns of the use of language. But (somehow) human systems of communications are the results of human interaction, and their maintenance and modification is a matter of concrete communicative processes. Similarly, we do not create systems of obligations, injunctions, sanctions – in short, the institutions of a social structure – again and again in each social encounter, although we maintain, modify and, on rare occasions, even overthrow social structures of various kinds in concrete social interaction.

The orderliness of practical sense in dialogue and, more generally, in social interaction is accomplished by human beings as actors – rather than as puppets controlled by instincts, social structures or other forces. Although it is produced in the here and now of social encounters, the producers draw both upon the immediate situational resources and upon the resources built up in the long chain of past accomplishments of their predecessors. In other words, the 'accomplishments' of the actors in a social encounter are always also 're-accomplishments'. The same, the closely or remotely similar interactional and communicative problems which they face have been encountered by others before them. 'Solutions' to the problems have been sedimented in the institutions of a social structure, the traditions of a language and of language use as, e.g. in communicative genres (Luckmann, 1989), and in a social stock of knowledge, which, of course, includes knowledge of institutions and communicative codes and genres.

All these realities are 'external' social facts in the Durkheimian sense, not subject to change by individual fancy. They are both resources to draw upon in social interaction and constraints upon individual action. The social structure, regulating among other things the distribution of power, the communicative media and the social stock of knowledge, are 'asymmetrical'. They are characterized by varying degrees of inequality in their distribution within a society. From the point of view of the empirical analysis of dialogue and social encounters, the social stock of knowledge is particularly important because both social structure and communicative media and genres are 'reflected' in it. As resources these 'external' social realities become relevant to actors inasmuch as they are 'represented' in their subjective stocks of knowledge. The point is obvious in the analysis of asymmetries of *knowledge* in dialogue, but it is also valid more generally for other asymmetries, e.g. those connected with power and dominance. Some general observations on the social distribution of knowledge are therefore in order.

Individual and social stocks of knowledge

Individual stocks of knowledge are formed in biographically unique sedimentations of the experience of individuals.[4] The necessary condition for their being built up is a substructure of cognitive operations, an elementary structure of consciousness. But it is not a sufficient condition, and it explains very little of the concrete systems of orientation of individual actors. No more than a small portion of knowledge in any individual stock is constructed in autonomous problem-solving activities. The larger portion is derived from a social stock of knowledge, i.e. a *socially* objectified and *socially* distributed reservoir of meanings which is capable of functioning as an *individual* system of orientation for individual action. Human beings do not acquire knowledge by starting from scratch. They are born into a world in which other people already know a good deal. Sometimes, indeed they must solve problems themselves; more often they only need to learn the solution found long ago by others. There is not only a division of labour in the functioning of society, there is also something akin to a division of labour over generations in the history of culture.

The processes by which elements of a social stock of knowledge are transmitted to individual stocks of knowledge are determined by a historical social structure. The social structure is a network of institutions and a set of inequalities; to this extent it restricts the distribution of elements of the social stock of knowledge to typical individual members of the society. The social structure thus also contains typical transmission processes, regulations of access to knowledge, and strategies and rhetorics of legitimation for the inclusions and exclusions of potential recipients of knowledge.

The social distribution of knowledge

A completely equal distribution of knowledge is impossible except under highly unrealistic conditions (Schutz and Luckmann, 1974: Chapter 4). One such condition is that the biological differentiation of human beings should be without any social consequences. Another condition is that the biographically unique sequence in which knowledge is acquired should play no role. Furthermore, the concrete intersubjective, face to face conditions for the communication of knowledge, one of the essential presuppositions for the development of any social stock of knowledge, would have to be eliminated and the accumulation of knowledge would have to be stopped at a given level. But granted that these are highly unrealistic assumptions, what would be an *almost* equal social distribution of knowledge?

A simple social distribution of knowledge concerns elements that are universally relevant and are, accordingly, routinely transmitted to everyone. The processes of transmission are phased temporally. At every given point of time, all 'normal adults' therefore possess all those elements of the social stock of knowledge that are socially defined as relevant for 'everyone'. But there are also elements which, e.g. are relevant only for men or only for women, according to how men, women and relevance are defined in a given society. Some knowledge will be routinely transferred only to men, some only to women.

Though we have used obvious and, empirically, the most important concrete examples of factors contributing to the social distribution of knowledge in 'simple' societies, it must be stressed that a generally valid *material* determination of the kinds of knowledge involved is not possible. The structural factors on which rest simple social distributions of knowledge generally determine the distinction between 'general knowledge' and 'special knowledge'. But what belongs to special knowledge in a society can be general knowledge in another and vice versa.

General knowledge is routinely transmitted to everyone, special knowledge only to certain kinds of people, although in principle all knowledge would seem to be accessible to everyone. However, there is no compelling motive for everyone to acquire special knowledge, and occasionally institutional barriers oppose such an acquisition. But everyone knows more or less who is in possession of which forms of special knowledge. The social distribution of special knowledge is an element of general knowledge.

Complex social distributions of knowledge, on the other hand, are characterized, first of all, by a certain 'inequality' in the distribution of general knowledge. This at first seems paradoxical if, as the term implies, general knowledge consists of the socially objectified solutions to such problems as are relevant for 'everyone'. But what does 'everyone' mean here?

In societies with an extremely simple division of labour and without established social strata, the problems that are imposed on 'everyone' may also be assumed to be presented to everyone in essentially similar perspectives. As soon as the division of labour becomes more complicated, and as soon as well-defined social strata – castes, feudal estates, classes – emerge, few problems, even those that are basically the same, are seen in the same way. Similar 'biographies' develop, for obvious structural reasons, in the course of the progressive division of labour. These similarities in 'biographies' are responsible for the emergence of similar ways of looking at the world. The transmission or, at least, the reception of elements of general knowledge is modified accordingly. Language offers an obvious, but by no means the only, example. As a component of the general knowledge of every society, the core elements of language can and must be distributed in a relatively equal fashion. Given a certain complexity in the social structure, and the emergence of different types of biographies that are ultimately linked to the division of labour, however, a common language containing only idiosyncratic variations is converted into socially conditioned, socially established, and socially transmitted 'versions', such as dialects, sociolects etc. In this restricted sense one can speak of an 'inequality' in the social distribution of general knowledge. It is this 'inequality' which is one characteristic of complex social distributions of knowledge.

Another important characteristic consists of further developments and subdivisions of special knowledge. Through progressive subdivisions and internal developments, e.g. 'theoretization' and 'professionalization', special knowledge gains a certain limited autonomy. Special knowledge becomes institutionally separated from general knowledge. The distance between 'laymen' and 'experts' becomes greater. Involved, often tedious, sometimes painful presuppositions (learning sequences, tests, initiations) precede the acquisition of special knowledge. Even the *transmission* of special knowledge becomes a job for specialists in the teaching of specialities. The subdivisions of knowledge are specialized as meaning-systems and the transmission of knowledge is itself institutionally specialized.

Given a complex social distribution of knowledge, special

knowledge in its totality is, of course, no longer accessible to everyone. But there is an interactionally, and communicatively, perhaps, even more important consequence of the increasing specialization of knowledge in modern societies. Information about specialized knowledge, where and when it is to be found, is no longer a part of the supply of 'equally' distributed general knowledge. Therefore, uncertainties about the degree to which knowledge is shared by participants in interaction who do not know each other well will be found more often in such societies and, therefore, the problems of recipient designs are likely to be more acute.

Asymmetries *in* dialogue: some methodological remarks

If one is interested in the analysis of empirically occurring dialogue, it is safest to start out from phenomena which are *demonstrably there*. Drew (Chapter 2: p. 44) underscores the aim of identifying asymmetries which 'are demonstrably relevant to the participants themselves, and so have consequences for, and are manifest in the details of talk'. Similarly, Goodwin and Heritage (1990: p. 16) identify one of the salient aspects of the contribution of conversation analysis (CA) as 'its insistence that the categories used to describe participants, action and context be warranted by demonstrating that the participants themselves are demonstrably oriented to the distinctions embodied in the categories in the course of their activities'. In other words, we would deal with 'distinctions' which are relevant for actors as they produce and make sense of talk: differences which are occasioned and dealt with in discourse, confirmed, negotiated or reconstructed in interaction, regulating it or being regulated in it. Yet we may not always agree on what is 'demonstrably there'. Despite Drew's (Chapter 2) recommendations to stick to what is 'brought to the interactional surface', some of us will occasionally be interested in less transparent phenomena: deeper asymmetries, hidden meanings, silent misunderstandings, etc. Given this, it may be appropriate to end this introduction with some *methodological* remarks on 'external' realities as the context of dialogue (cf. the previous section).

It is an important analytical principle to search for explanations of social interaction in the concrete encounter itself. There is no doubt that the 'orderliness' of the interaction, its practical sense, is an accomplishment of the actors. Nor can there be serious doubt that actors draw upon situational and external resources in accomplishing practical sense. Social realities 'external' to social encounters and dialogue are the 'context' first for the actors on the social scene who produce their 'texts' in mutual awareness of that 'context' (Schegloff and Sacks, 1973), and second, therefore, necessarily also for the observer who wants to understand the scene.

So if the analyst, too, must draw upon the context for an understanding of the discourse, why should he or she obey the methodological principle of staying with the text, with what is concretely 'there' in a social encounter? One reason is fairly obvious. General knowledge about social structure, language and culture is in considerable danger of being distorted for dogmatic and ideological reasons. And even if it is reasonably free from distortion, it tends to guide the analysis from the specific to the general too soon. The principle thus does not deny the importance of 'external' context, nor is it anti-theoretical – but it does direct attention to the details of concrete evidence *first*.

Furthermore, although it may be assumed that 'external' social realities, relevant as context to the actors, will manifest themselves more or less obviously in their actions, the 'more or less' points to a serious methodological problem. In the case of the 'more' it will be relatively easy to link a dialogical asymmetry, e.g. of knowledge, to an external structural asymmetry in the social distribution of knowledge. The evidence will be in the text. But what about the 'less'? The actors may reciprocally take so much for granted about the context that they will not *show* the relevance of a particular external factor in talk. Here the analyst should resist the temptation to speculate prematurely. An even more intricate problem is presented by another situation. The actors may be ignorant of a particular external factor which thus does not contribute to their accomplishment of practical sense in interaction. But the all-knowing observer who has done careful ethnographic background work may be convinced that the factor determines the conditions for the interaction and for what is accomplished within it. It is therefore a thorny methodological issue how, and under what conditions, analysts can identify 'silent' features in empirical data. Yet although this issue cannot be resolved here, many prefer to remain with what is *there* in the dialogue as long as possible.

Notes

1. There is, in other words, a need for a cover term for the phenomena just mentioned, and 'dominance' seems to be a reasonable candidate. However, we should be careful not to confuse this use of the term with other uses which are more or less established in various disciplines. For example, we are not taking 'dominance' in the senses developed within the psychology of personality (where it refers to certain personality traits) or within primatology (where dominance refers to certain (overt) primate behaviours). And, above all, dominance must not be confused with (social) power (see p. 10 above).
2. Assumptions of symmetry and equality are clearly also part of folk theories of what a 'true dialogue' is. Also, in conversation analysis (e.g. Atkinson and Heritage, 1984), equal rights to participation and topics are stated as characteristic of 'ordinary conversation'.
3. Linell, however, in his paper 'The power of dialogue dynamics' (Linell, 1990), uses the term in two senses: somewhat metaphorically, as potentialities inherent in dialogicality (thus related to 'intrinsic' properties); and as the deployment of this power, and the potentialities derived from it, in exercising social power (cf. the 'extrinsic' aspects).
4. This paragraph is based on considerations presented in Luckmann (1982).

References

Agar, M. (1985), 'Institutional discourse', *Text*, 5, 147–68.
Atkinson, M. and Heritage, J. (1984), (eds), *Structures of Social Action*, Cambridge University Press: Cambridge.
Bakhtin, M. M. (1986), *Speech Genres and Other Late Essays*, translated by V. McGee, edited by C. Emerson and M. Holquist, University of Texas Press: Austin, Texas.
Cicourel, A. (1980), 'Three models of discourse analysis: the role of social structure', *Discourse Processes*, 3, 101–32.
Clark, H. H. and Marshall, C. R. (1981), 'Definite reference and mutual knowledge', in A. K. Joshi, I. A. Sag and B. L. Webber (eds), *Elements of Discourse Understanding*, Cambridge University Press: Cambridge.
Corsaro, W. (1982), 'Something old and something new: the importance of prior ethnography in the collection and analysis of audiovisual data', *Sociological Methods and Research*, 11, 145–66.
Goffman, E. (1981), *Forms of Talk*, Blackwell: Oxford.
Goodwin, C. (1979), 'The interactive construction of a sentence in natural conversation', in G. Psathas (ed.), *Everyday Language: Studies in ethnomethodology*, Irvington: New York.
Goodwin, C. and Heritage, J. (1990), 'Conversation analysis', *Annual Review of Anthropology*, 19, 283–307.
Graumann, C. F. (forthcoming), 'Commonality, mutuality, reciprocity', in C. F. Graumann, K. Foppa and I. Marková (eds), *Mutualities in Dialogue*, Harvester Wheatsheaf: Hemel Hempstead.
Heath, C. (forthcoming), 'The delivery and reception of diagnosis in

general practice consultation', forthcoming in P. Drew and J. Heritage (eds), *Talk at Work: Social interaction in institutional settings*, Cambridge University Press: Cambridge.

Heritage, J. (1984), *Garfinkel and Ethnomethodology*. Polity Press: Oxford.

Linell, P. (1990), 'The power of dialogue dynamics', in I. Marková and K. Foppa (eds), *The Dynamics of Dialogue*, Harvester Wheatsheaf: Hemel Hempstead.

Linell, P. (1991), 'Accommodation on trial: processes of communicative accommodation in courtroom interaction', in H. Giles, N. Coupland and J. Coupland (eds), *Contexts of Accommodation*, Cambridge University Press: Cambridge.

Linell, P., Gustavsson, L. and Juvonen, P. (1988), 'Interactional dominance in dyadic communication: a presentation of initiative-response analysis', *Linguistics*, **26**, 415-42.

Luckmann, T. (1982), 'Individual action and social knowledge', in M. von Cranach and R. Harré (eds), *The Analysis of Action: Recent theoretical and empirical advances*, Cambridge University Press: Cambridge.

Luckmann, T. (1989), 'Prolegomena to a social theory of communicative genres', *Slovene Studies*, **11**, 159-66.

Luckmann, T. (1990), 'Social communication, dialogue, and conversation', in I. Marková and K. Foppa (eds), *The Dynamics of Dialogue*, Harvester Wheatsheaf: Hemel Hempstead.

Marková, I. (1990), 'Introduction', in I. Marková and K. Foppa (eds), *The Dynamics of Dialogue*, Harvester Wheatsheaf: Hemel Hempstead.

Marková, I. and Foppa, K. (1990), (eds), *The Dynamics of Dialogue*. Harvester Wheatsheaf: Hemel Hempstead.

Maynard, D. (forthcoming), 'On the interactional and institutional bases of asymmetry in clinical discourse', *American Journal of Sociology*.

Parsons, T. (1951), *The Social System*, The Free Press: New York.

Rommetveit, R. (1983), 'In search of a truly interdisciplinary semantics: a sermon of hopes of salvation from hereditary sins', *Journal of Semantics*, **2**, 1-28.

Schegloff, E. A. (1987), 'Between micro and macro: contexts and other connections', in J. Alexander, B. Giesen, R. Munch and N. Smelser (eds), *The Micro-Macro Link*. University of California Press: Los Angeles, CA.

Schegloff, E. A. and Sacks, H. (1973), 'Opening up closings', *Semiotica*, **8**, 289-327.

Schutz, A. and Luckmann, T. (1974), *The Structure of the Life-World I*, Heinemann: London.

Wertsch, J. V. (1990), 'Dialogue and dialogism in a socio-cultural approach to mind', in I. Marková and K. Foppa (eds) *The Dynamics of Dialogue* (1990), Harvester Wheatsheaf: Hemel Hempstead.

2 | Asymmetries of knowledge in conversational interactions

Paul Drew

In this chapter I shall focus on asymmetries of knowledge between participants in naturally occurring interactions, for the most part in ordinary conversations. Many of the ways we think about discourse rely on our treating conversations as some kind of standard of 'equal participation' between speakers. Discourse in other settings - especially in workplace or institutional contexts - seems characteristically to be a distortion of what is taken to be the symmetrical relationship between speakers in conversation. However, Linell and Luckmann (this volume, Chapter 1) caution us (as others have done) that such a dichotomy between symmetric conversation and asymmetric institutional discourse oversimplifies the nature of asymmetry, and disregards ways in which speakers' participation in conservation may on occasion be asymmetric. Linell points out that it would be 'counterproductive to believe in two mutually exclusive families of situations', if that were to result in our ignoring the ways in which 'mundane conversation' may from time to time be characterized by asymmetries between speakers (Linell, 1990). With that in mind I shall consider some episodes in conversation in which asymmetries of knowledge are manifestly relevant for the talk.

To begin with, I should explain why I choose to focus on asymmetries of *knowledge*. There are, of course, other dimensions of asymmetry, not the least of which concerns participation rights in talk. In conversation, turns are allocated equally between participants: more precisely, the rules or procedures for allocating turns (Sacks *et al.*, 1974) do not favour any particular participant or category of participant (except perhaps 'current speaker', who may get first shot at allocating a next turn). So, in principle at least, participants in conversation generally share equal rights of speakership, even if unequal distributions of turns are observed empirically in particular cases. By contrast, in institutional settings there may be quite striking inequalities in the distribution of communicative resources available to participants. For example, the specialized turn-taking systems which operate formally in such settings as courts, classrooms, and news interviews pre-allocate the order of speaking and differentially distribute access to types of turns between speakers (or more properly, speaker identities). Talk in such settings may therefore be restricted in terms of the verbal activities which speakers perform, as well as of how those relevant activities are designed or 'packaged' in the talk.[1]

But in the many other institutional or workplace settings in which interactions are not similarly subject, formally anyway, to specialized turn-taking systems, the kinds of ways in which asymmetries are manifest need to be more carefully specified in the details of the talk. Other chapters in this volume attempt to do just that. For example, focusing on such settings as doctor-patient consultations (Aronsson, Chapter 3); psychotherapeutic sessions (Käsermann, Chapter 5), and the instruction of novice garage mechanics (Wintermantel, Chapter 6), these studies show that even where the talk is not formally directed by specialized speech exchange systems, participants nevertheless do not make equal contributions to the interaction. In Käsermann's terms, impediments to equal participation in the talk may result from certain communicational moves, especially those moves associated with the position of one participant being regarded as an 'expert' relative to the other (e.g. the therapist, in relation to a client in psychotherapy: Käsermann, this volume, Chapter 5, p. 107ff). Wintermantel's study is especially explicit about the matter of how experts orient to novices' states of knowledge, e.g. the ways in which experts' corrections of novices' mistakes are designed differently according to the level of knowledge which the novice is assumed to have (Wintermantel, this volume, Chapter 6, p. 136: on this see also Drew, 1981).

Perhaps, then, unequal distributions of knowledge are a more general source of asymmetry in almost all institutional settings: and especially so in those settings in which members of the public or lay clients may not have access to the professional's specialized technical knowledge or knowledge about relevant organizational procedures. A simple example is Jefferson and Lee's (1981) observation that in calls to an emergency ambulance service difficulties arose quite recurrently because the caller telephoning on behalf of the stricken person assumed that the emergency service would want the name of the victim, whereas in fact the agency personnel wanted the name only of the caller, and did *not* want that information about the sick or injured person. This incorrect assumption resulted in callers, by volunteering the sufferer's name, frequently 'disrupting the orderly progression of the form-relevant questioning', as in this example (from Jefferson and Lee, 1981, p. 414):

> Extract 2.1 [For transcription convention key see Appendix, pp. 272-3.]
> Desk: I'll have them out there approximately at six then.
> Caller: O kay.
> Desk: ⌞.hhh and –
> Caller: And the employee's name is Randall.
> Desk: Uh no. May I have *your* name please.

This illustrates the kind of disruption which can be generated by an asymmetry between the expectations of a lay caller, and the specialized procedures operated by the emergency service as regards the collection of essential information.

Other chapters in this volume begin to document some of the ways in which asymmetries of knowledge may generate difficulties of various sorts, including misunderstandings and breakdowns in mutual comprehension between professional and client. Two further examples from the wider literature about discourse in institutional settings may help to illustrate this. In their study of small claims courts in the United States, O'Barr and Conley (1985) have documented the difficulties which litigants face in presenting their cases (unaided, as they are, by legal representation) in ways which are legally effective. Even though the procedures and evidentiary rules of such courts are relatively less formal than in other judicial settings, lay plaintiffs are usually unaware of the specifically legal standards of causal adequacy which the court will use to assess their complaints. Plaintiffs do not appreciate the difference between their ordinary commonsense notions of causality, and what it takes to demonstrate or prove the legal responsibility and culpability of the defendants against whom they are bringing an action. Hence their story narratives, although perhaps suited to the standards of ordinary conversation, fail to address appropriate legal criteria of blame, responsibility and agency. Accordingly it appears that litigants' chances of success in claiming reparation are jeopardized, not because their cases are intrinsically weak, but because they are unaware of the relevant standards of legal adequacy in constructing their narratives (O'Barr and Conley, 1985, especially pp. 684-90).

A second illustration is taken from one of the many studies documenting asymmetries of knowledge in medical consultations. In their study of a pediatric clinic, Tannen and Wallat (1986) consider how differences arise between a pediatrician's and a mother's assessments of the seriousness of a child's condition – an issue which is similarly considered by Aronsson (this volume, Chapter 3). It appears that doctor and parent may attribute different 'meanings' to the same term describing a particular symptom, with the result that the parent's version of what is wrong with a child does not accord with the doctor's. In one case, for instance,

> [t]he doctor's reassurance focussed on the mother's misuse of the term 'wheezing', which the mother used as a general term to describe noisy breathing but, for the doctor, is a technical term describing a constriction of the air passages. While crucial for the physician, this distinction is of no significance to the mother. Her experience of hearing noises that sound to her as if her child is gasping for air is far stronger and more enduring than the doctor's reassurance.
>
> (Tannen and Wallat, 1986, p. 309)

In this case the persistence of the mother's concern about her child's breathing, and her contradiction of the doctor's assessment, arose from the incongruence between the knowledge schemas within which each interpreted evidence. The mother did not share the medicalized version of the symptom of wheezing, and therefore could not concur with the pediatrician's assessment of its (medical) unimportance. (Similar cases of the difficulties engendered by the incongruence between medical and lay schemas of knowledge about symptoms are discussed by Silverman, 1987, e.g. p. 56).

These examples illustrate the sorts of asymmetries with respect to specialized bodies of knowledge which have been identified through analyses of the discourse between professionals and clients in institutional settings. I would like to highlight some of the principal features of such accounts of asymmetry as these. I do so partly because, whereas Linell has categorized certain types of asymmetries in terms of important conceptual distinctions (e.g. the domain, source and scope of asymmetry), I shall focus more on a consideration of the distinguishing or characteristic features of asymmetries of knowledge. In doing so, I shall be questioning how far the kinds of features underlying such accounts of asymmetries in talk-in-institutional-interactions are equally applicable to asymmetries of knowledge in conversation.

So initially it may be worth drawing attention to four features of the kinds of accounts of asymmetry outlined above. First, one party, the client (litigant or parent) is treated as not having access to some technical knowledge possessed by the professional (the court adjudicator and doctor respectively). Asymmetry is characterized by one party lacking knowledge possessed by the other. Second, states of relative knowledge are attributed to role identities. Thus asymmetry of knowledge is taken to be the product of factors which are exogenous to a given occasion. Third, lack of access to a body of knowledge is associated with putting one of the participants at a disadvantage. And fourth, asymmetry is associated in such analyses with communicative difficulties of one sort or another – misunderstandings, mutual incomprehension or one party failing to understand and respond to the full significance of what the other has said. Whatever misunderstandings or troubles may have been identified by the analyst, there is not necessarily evidence that participants themselves recognized such difficulties. The 'incoherence' in the talk between doctor and patient may be apparent only to the researcher who, on reviewing transcripts, can see that they were really talking past one another, or that one of them had failed to properly interpret what the other had really meant (analyses along these lines are offered also by Paget, 1983, and Cicourel, 1983). That is, there may be no indication that either participant recognized an ambiguity or misunderstanding as they were talking during the consultation.

In summary, then, the analytical dimensions associated with asymmetry of knowledge in institutional settings appear to be that by virtue of exogenous factors, participants do not share access to the same body of knowledge; and because that knowledge is consequential for some decision or outcome, this works to the disadvantage of the one who does not have access to it. And the communicative effects of such asymmetries are detected by the analyst locating instances of the participants' mutual incomprehension, even though they may have been unaware at the time of such breakdowns.

While one may have reservations about the empirical substantiation of some of these dimensions in some studies,[2] they are in principle matters of real importance in analysing the often unequal resources and incongruity in perspectives between participants in institutional settings (and of real importance, too, in research aimed at improving the effectiveness of communication in such settings). My purpose in drawing attention to them is not, therefore, to demur at their relevance in the context of institutional discourse. It is, rather, to highlight how asymmetries of knowledge in ordinary conversation may be differently manifest. Specifically, the data considered below suggest that participants' knowledge asymmetries in conversation are not necessarily associated with one party not knowing something, or with one being at any disadvantage relative to the other. Where, however, one is put at some disadvantage by the other, that is achieved interactionally. Furthermore, the ways in which knowledge asymmetries are consequential for conversational interaction arise from speakers' orientations to such asymmetry. Thus we are looking for ways in which asymmetries of knowledge are demonstrably relevant to the participants in the design of their talk.

It may be useful briefly to highlight this precept of showing that phenomena in talk-in-interaction are demonstrably relevant for the participants engaged in the talk. In the kinds of analyses to which I have referred above, misunderstanding and mutual incomprehension are generally identified by the analyst, sometimes even by contrasting what was said on one occasion with what was said on another (Cicourel, 1983, employs this method). Communicative difficulties detected in this way do not depend on their having been experienced as such by the participants as they were talking. They may have believed that they understood one another: the analyst can show that they did not really do so, fully. As Schegloff has commented, 'problems in understanding' thus identified may be theoretical, rather than empirical or real for the participants involved (Schegloff, 1984, p. 37). By contrast, in his analysis of the source of misunderstanding in conversation, Schegloff works through instances in which 'the parties themselves address the talk as revealing a misunderstanding in need of repair' (Schegloff, 1987, p. 204).

Two of our objectives in conversation analysis are, first, to show how, in the sequential organization and the construction/design of turns at talk, participants manage to achieve coherence of talk – including how they identify and repair troubles in their talk. And second, to show how participants orient to the procedures or organizations of conversation as normative matters. As the chapter is written from the point of view of conversation analysis, it is important to show that such phenomena as devices, procedures, organization are evident in the details of the talk, and so in the details of how it is managed by the participants. This constraint - that of showing that asymmetries of knowledge identified in the talk are demonstrably relevant for the participants in the talk - may be considered inappropriate for some perspectives in discourse analysis. In my view the constraint is necessary if we are to document the intersubjective reality and interactional consequences of asymmetries of knowledge.

Authoritative access to knowledge

There are, of course, very many differences in the states of knowledge between participants in conversation. There are things which one speaker may ask the other about, or tell a story about to the other, or may deliver news about, which he or she is able to do by virtue of what he or she knows and the other does not. Our knowledge about other people's lives is not, after all, as good as their own knowledge about their own activities and experiences. And this is one respect in which there are inequalities in the distribution of states of knowledge between speakers.[3] But it would perhaps be jejune to treat all such unequal distributions of knowledge as asymmetrical. Any question in which one asks for information which the other has ('How was your day?', 'Can you tell me the times of the trains this morning from York to London?', 'When did you get back?') would fall within the compass of asymmetry. So, too, would all linguistic realizations of deixis (Levinson, 1988). While questioning and deixis are tied up with a systematic or structural basis for a difference in perspective - the dichotomy between self and other - some account needs to be given of the types of knowledge whose distribution is normatively organized by that dichotomy (about which some points are made later). In considering asymmetry as an interactional phenomenon, we need to do more than plot unequal states of knowledge arising from the difference in perspective between self and other.

A suggestion of what more might be involved is illustrated in the following extract from a telephone conversation between Cloe and Dave. They are discussing the troubled nature of Dave's marriage, including the problem which arises from his going out with other women from time to time, even though he still lives with his wife.

Extract 2.2
Cloe: *De*finitely fo:r the: *fif*teen years I:ve known you, (0.3)

yihknow you've *really bo*:th *basic*'ly *h*onestly gone yer own ways.
(0.8)

Dave: *E*ssentially:: except we've had a good relationship at home *yih*know

Cloe: Ye:s but I mean it's a relationship whe:re uh: *yih*know *pa*:ss the butter dear, .hh
(0.5)

Cloe: Yihkno ⌈w make a piece of toa:st dear *this*
Dave: ⌊*N* o *n*ot really
Cloe: type of thing.
Dave: *We*'ve actually had a real health- I think we've had a very healthy relationship y'know. =

Cloe: =.hhh *Why*: becuz you haven't knocked each other's *t*ee:th ou:t?
(0.7)

Dave: Tha:*t*, *a*:nd we've had a good communica:*tion* and uh: *t*he whole- *yih*know *I* think it's been healthy, =

Cloe: =.hhhhh Yah but it's lacked a *lo*:t Dave I mean be honest with your*se*:lf

Plainly they are not just discussing but arguing about the state of Dave's marriage. They do, of course, have different perspectives on that, Dave's being an insider's perspective and Cloe's being an outsider's. But the fact that they are arguing gives a particular relevance to their different states of knowledge: to the extent that Dave has first-hand knowledge of his marriage, he is an *authoritative source* of knowledge about his relationship with his wife, while Cloe is in an asymmetrical position with regard to the knowledge resources which she can employ in the argument. This connects very much with Linell's observation that asymmetry might be a sequential property, that is a property of the action structures of sequences. Here Cloe's participation in the type of sequence it is – an argument – is constrained, if you like, by the asymmetry of her (outsider's) knowledge with respect to his authoritative knowledge.

Nevertheless this does not prevent her from participating in the argument (and now one can begin to notice the difference between being constrained and being prevented, a distinction which is disregarded in much of this literature). The kind of constraint imposed by her asymmetrical position as regards knowledge about Dave's marriage is, perhaps, evident in the design of her turns. For example, in his first turn in this extract Dave disagrees with Cloe that he and his wife have 'gone their own ways', and asserts instead that 'we've had a good relationship at home'. Now the relationship between two people 'at home' together is something only they know about at first hand: inevitably the presence of another person can be claimed as (is accountable as) making a difference to how they 'really' are (i.e. when alone together). On the basis of what else one knows about a couple, one can speculate about their relationship when they are alone. But that is always inferential knowledge, and cannot be authoritative. In the present example this puts Cloe in an asymmetrical position, because to substantiate his side in the argument Dave has used evidence about matters to which Cloe does not have the same first-hand access. Whether or not this is a self-conscious move on Dave's part, it puts Cloe in a 'weak' position: to pursue the argument, she has to manage the interactional difficulty of challenging evidence about which Dave is the authoritative source.

The solution she has to this interactional problem is to use a formulaic or stereotyped image of a bankrupt marriage. She characterizes their relationship as being one in which the communication between partners is of the kind 'Pass the butter dear, make a piece of toast dear' – that is, as nothing better or more intimate than the superficial talk over the breakfast table. (Note in this respect that the supposed reported speech is the giving of an order: and that the address term is, conventionally, an almost neutral endearment term.) The imagery employed in her language is a clichéd depiction of a marriage reduced to communication about only the most mundane matters. It thus challenges Dave's version of their having a 'good relationship'. The significance of Cloe's selection of a formulaic clichéd expression with which to describe their relationship is that it is 'anyone's knowledge'. Formulaic expressions such as idioms and proverbs can be used to describe some circumstances without reference to (and hence without needing access to) their empirical details. Cloe's version does not rely on claiming such first-hand knowledge as Dave has: it is instead an outsider's version of a likely scene between Dave and his wife when alone together.

Using a cliché or an idiom may then be a solution to the interactional problem confronting a speaker who does not have first-hand access to knowledge, when challenging the version of a co-participant who is in certain respects an authoritative source. This is because idioms and other formulaic expressions are glosses for evidentiary details: they stand on behalf of, but do not describe, the details of what is being spoken about. In being metaphorical, they do not claim literal truth (Drew and Holt, 1988): they may therefore be employed, as here, by a speaker who does not have direct access to knowledge about the events, etc., being described.[4]

Of course, the status of one speaker's account as an authoritative version is not to say that that version is necessarily believed: the speaker may be thought to be dissembling, lying or engaged in self-deception (hence, perhaps, Cloe's adding in her last turn 'be honest with yourself'). Nevertheless the use of a version employing one speaker's authoritative access to knowledge puts the other in an asymmetric position if he or she is to challenge what has been said. Cloe finds a solution to this problem by formulating a description in terms of knowledge to which 'anyone' has access. Idioms, proverbs and the like are one such solution to managing the asymmetry occasioned by the authoritative and hence privileged access to knowledge claimed in the other's version.

So the asymmetry between Cloe's and Dave's states of knowledge does not arise simply from their 'having' different knowledge, e.g. by virtue of their different experiences. The asymmetry is occasioned by the interactional work in which they are engaged, in challenging each other's versions. In that sequential environment, Cloe's unequal access to knowledge puts her at a disadvantage insofar as there is a body of detail/evidence about Dave's relationship with his wife which is not available to her for her to employ on behalf of her position in the argument. This asymmetry does not immobilize her because, as with any interactional difficulty with which a speaker may be faced, she may employ any of a variety of strategic interactional solutions.

The relevance of exogenous identities: putting the other at a disadvantage

I want to develop further this sense of one speaker's authoritative access to knowledge putting the other at a disadvantage. In this case asymmetry is generated out of interactional moves, and is not simply the 'natural' or 'necessary' product of differential distributions of knowledge. I want to do so by comparing two extracts, from the greetings or initial exchanges in a telephone call, in the first extract, and when visitors arrive at someone's home, in the second. Linell and Luckmann (this volume, Chapter 1) have pointed out that 'Local asymmetries are then tied to single exchanges ("adjacency pairs") (a greeting and its reciprocation would be only mildly asymmetrical)'. Here they seem to be suggesting, quite correctly, that in greetings or introduction exchanges which go according to form (on which see Schegloff, 1986), while at one stage the caller might have the advantage of knowing to whom he/she is speaking without the other being in a reciprocally informed position, that temporary asymmetry is fairly quickly resolved, probably in the next turn, when the caller self-identifies, either through a voice sample, or by giving his or her name. Furthermore, that temporary asymmetry has no subsequent interactional consequences for the participants. But in the following extract that asymmetry is not resolved right away; and moreover, it is put to use by one of the participants in a way which is bitter-sweet.

Extract 2.3
(Marge is caller)
Sam: Hello.
Marge: Yeah. Hi : : :. How are you boyfriend?
Sam: I'm good. How are you.
Marge: ha ha ha You don't know which one of these girls you eh that's talking to you.
Sam: Huh?
Marge: You do not know which one of your girlfriends is talking to you.
Sam: Yes I do.
Marge: You do.
Sam: Yeah.
Marge: And so who.
Sam: Is this Mary?
Marge: Ahh haa! I knew it, see:, I knew I wasn't the only girl you had on your string.
(1.0)
Marge: This is Marge.
Sam: *Marge* ⌈How are ya honey.
Marge: ⌊ha ha
Marge: Oh I'm fine. How are you. Listen . . .

It should be clear enough that in her first turn, Marge initiates an elaborate tease which trades off the fact that while she knows to whom she is speaking, he does not recognize her. Her advantage as caller is sustained through until she identifies herself ('This is Marge'). There is evidence in her first turn that she anticipated that he might not recognize her voice, and thereby sets up the tease. In that turn she does not provide a self-identification (e.g. 'Hi, this is Marge'): and furthermore she addresses him with a form ('boyfriend') which conveys the kind of intimacy which would usually be associated with the ability to instantly recognize one another's voices over the telephone. From these 'clues', Sam can detect that he is being expected to recognize who is calling – an expectation to which he orients in his return greeting ('I'm good. How are you?'): by not asking who is calling or checking that it is who he thinks it might be, he thereby claims to recognize the caller. However, Marge manages the talk so as to expose that he is bluffing.

In terms of our consideration of asymmetry, Marge's first turn is perhaps the key to a participant's strategic use of his or her differential access to knowledge. By not self-identifying, and through using the recognitional relevant 'boyfriend', she misleads Sam into believing that he ought to recognize her. As the caller, she has an advantage over the other, the recipient of the call. But the asymmetry in their access to knowledge about whom they are speaking to is not resolved in the manner in which Linell and Luckmann (this volume, Chapter 1) suggest it usually is. The caller does not self-identify: instead she playfully encourages the recipient to search for the caller's identity in the wrong collection, among the special intimates of 'girlfriends'.[5] The tease which plays off that asymmetry continues for some while. When Marge correctly analyses the equivocality of his return greeting ('I'm good. How are you?') as indicating that he does not recognize her voice, she proceeds to 'string him along', playfully testing and then exposing his lack of knowledge. This has a kind of double edge; through her testing/pursuit of the matter, he is exposed not only as having failed to recognize the voice of a (possible) 'girlfriend', but also as having falsely claimed to have recognized her, i.e. as having tried to cover up his not recognizing her. This example illustrates that an unequal distribution of knowledge between participants may be used as a strategic device by the 'knowing' party to do something interactionally, to play games with the other. Thus 'unequal access' is turned into an interactional asymmetry.

A further point about this case: two sets of exogenous identities or categories are occasioned by the strategic playfulness in which Marge engages. These are the caller/called set, and the intimate/stranger set. These sets of relative identities are, of course, always applicable to persons speaking on the telephone. This is not to say that they are always applied in some interactionally relevant way. While any speakers on the the telephone might be described as caller and called, those identities may not be relevant for any stretch of talk: their relevance may be occasioned for local interactional purposes. So in (Extract 2.3) one participant 'uses' these exogenous categories of speakership to sustain an interactional asymmetry. We can begin to see how exogenous structural categories can come to matter for the endogenous or local production of talk. Again, this is alluded to by Linell and Luckmann (this volume, Chapter 1) when they say that 'extrinsic conditions must somehow be reproduced by the actors in the actual interaction': I would only substitute 'occasioned' for 'reproduced', to capture the way that participants may, but need not, orient to the relevance of their relative exogenous categories in doing some interactional work (see also Schegloff, 1987, pp. 201-3; and Drew, 1987, for an analysis of how identities which speakers 'possess' can be occasioned to do teasing).

The data with which I would like to compare Extract 2.3 is the following extract from a video recording of some visitors arriving at the apartment in which Ivy and her student-aged daughter Betty live. The occasion of the visit is Ivy's birthday. The visitors are relatives – Ivy's sister Grace, Grace's husband Jim, their two children, Paula and Rob, and an elderly male relative, Victor, who is visiting them from Germany. I will be focusing on what occurs between Betty and Victor later in the extract.[6] However, to get a sense of how the greeting between Betty and Victor differs significantly from Betty's greetings with her other relatives, the transcript – here simplified – begins at the point when, having heard the doorbell, Betty opens the door.

Extract 2.4
```
 1 Rob:     Good mor ning,
 2 Betty:           [H i :
 3 Jim:      [We didn't know whether
 4 Rob:      [Did we get you out of bed, =
 5 Betty:    N:o:
 6 Rob:     [How are you Betty hh
 7 Betty:   u:nh [:
 8 Ivy:          [Not quite. Come on in. =
 9 Rob:     Hi girl.
10          (0.6)
11          ((Betty and Rob kiss))
12 Rob:     How are you,
13          ((Rob moves in towards Ivy))
14 Grace:   Hi Betty,
15 Betty:   Hi
16          ((Betty and Grace kiss))
17          ((Grace moves in towards Ivy))
18 Paula:   Hello::.
19 Betty:   (  )
20          ((Paula and Betty kiss))
21          ((Paula moves in towards Ivy))
22 Betty:   Hi:.
23 Victor:  That's Betty.
24          ((Victor and Betty shake hands))
25 Victor:  *Kennst du mich noch?* = Do - do you know me:?
26 Ivy:     See hehe [hh
27 Victor:           [Huh? Do you *know* me?
```

```
28            (1.9)
29  Betty:    Unh (0.4) I don't know (h) (h) ⎡(whether I)
30  Jim:                                     ⎣Uh lets go =
31  Betty:    remember ⎡(you)
32  Jim:               ⎣= inside 'n close the door.
33  Ivy:               ⎣remember
34            ((Victor moves in towards Ivy))
35            (1.0)
36  Jim:      How are you Betty
37  Betty:    (uhn ((Betty and Jim kiss)) fine.
38            (1.7)
39  Jim:      Let's - let's see how ta:ll you got.
```

In lines 22–24 it is evident that the greeting between Betty and Victor is less intimate than the previous greetings; for instance, they shake hands. Following that greeting, at line 25, Victor asks Betty if she knows who he is. After some evident difficulty, Betty admits that she does not know whether she remembers him (lines 29 and 31). As it happens, there are good grounds, ethnographically, for supposing that Betty does know who he is, and that he is her relative, Victor. These relatives are expected to visit them to celebrate Ivy's birthday (that they are expected is plain from an inspection of the first few lines), and Betty knows that their relative from Germany will be with them. Although they have not seen one another for many years, since Victor last visited America, it should be straightforward enough for Betty to pick him out as the one who is Victor. He is the only 'outsider' in the family group, and in terms of age and gender he fits the identity of the relative whom she is expecting: moreover, he does the first version of his enquiry in German ('*Kennst du mich noch?*'), which should further help to identify him. A kind of puzzle, then, is why Betty has such evident difficulty in answering his question; why does she not answer 'Yes, you're Uncle Victor'?

In Extract 2.3 Marge detected from the equivocality of Sam's return greeting that he did not recognize her voice. Betty's greeting to Victor in line 22 is similarly equivocal: it is the kind of greeting which may conventionally make a claim to know the addressee and to be known by him (Schegloff, 1986, p. 127). At the same time, she does not – as Sam also did not in 2.3 – accompany that with some identification of the other: she does not greet him with something like 'Hi Uncle Victor', which would have displayed that she knew who he was.[7]

In both 2.3 and 2.4, then, the equivocality of a greeting as regards the speaker's recognition of the other's identity generates a *test* of recognition. The interactional activity of testing already occasions an asymmetry between the participants. The one who does the testing has the advantage of knowing the identity of the other (notice that in line 23 Victor specifically identifies Betty by naming her), in circumstances in which it appears from the equivocality of the other's greetings that he or she may not recognize the tester. So by testing whether Betty knows who he is, Victor is choosing to pursue this asymmetry.

That is to say – and this is most important for the way in which the asymmetry is being *managed* interactionally, and is not simply being driven by the participants' different states of knowledge – Victor does not need to pursue the matter of Betty's suspected non-recognition. He has the option of letting the matter be handled *en passant*, as the interaction develops. Instead he chooses to make an issue of Betty's apparent failure to recognize him, rather than leaving that failure buried in the interaction. As it is, by asking, and repeating, 'Do you know me?' (lines 25 and 27) Victor brings the asymmetry to the interactional surface: his testing/pursuit makes an asymmetry in their knowledge an interactionally relevant feature of the context.

But more needs to be said about their asymmetrical states of knowledge because, as I have pointed out, Betty does have a way of knowing who this elderly man is. She can easily infer that he is Victor, visiting from Germany, whom she has been expecting to accompany her aunt and uncle and cousins. Notice that in her response in lines 29–31, Betty specifically treats the matter of whether she 'knows' Victor (lines 25 and 27) as whether she 'remembers' him. Thus she treats 'knowing' him as a matter of whether she recognizes him – and therefore not simply as a matter of whether she can *identify* him as Victor. And this difference between 'knowing' and 'remembering' introduces another aspect of the asymmetry in their states of knowledge.

Victor last visited his relatives in the United States when Betty was a very young child, a toddler. Now, were Betty to claim to be able to remember him, she would have to retrieve a picture of him from her memory of the time they last met. However, in *not* laying claim to recognizing him, she is not claiming to recall a picture of him in her memory.[8] She thereby orients to a conventional attribution to the category 'children'; that is, that they do not possess the ability to 'know', and hence to remember, something or someone in the way adults do. Children may not be credited with the same kind of experience – and hence ability to picture and recall experience – as adults. The state of cognizance necessary to picture some person in the mind, which can be claimed and displayed by adults, is not a competence ordinarily attributed to children.[9] Thus Betty's dilemma can be characterized as follows. Although she is an adult now, and although she can quite easily know/guess/infer who he is, insofar as she treats Victor's enquiry as a test of whether she remembers him, if she were to identify (name) him it might appear that she was claiming to *recognize* him. And that in turn would then be to lay claim to just that state of cognizance of him at the time she was a child which children are not 'permitted' to have. In this way, an interactional dilemma or difficulty is related to conventional attributions to exogenous social categories.

A final point about the symmetry which is achieved interactionally through Victor's *testing* Betty. One can notice that he does not assist her when her difficulty in not being able to respond to his initial enquiry becomes evident. Victor might have engaged in the kind of remedial actions which both analyse and deal with the difficulties which it can be inferred the other (i.e. Betty) is having in answering.[10] Most straightforwardly, he might have simply introduced himself in line 27 (as in 'I'm your Uncle Victor'). Alternatively, he might have provided an account, on her behalf, for her difficulty in recognizing him. He could have offered something like 'It's been a long time since we last met'; or he might have noted changes in his appearance which might account for her difficulty in recognizing him now. This is a regular way in which a speaker who has gone unrecognized by the other deals with, and accounts for, the other's non-recognition; as with, 'My hair is longer/I've grown a moustache', etc. - often a fiction which nevertheless re-establishes contiguity between the unrecognized and the one who failed to recognize. In not assisting her in any of these ways, but instead repeating 'Huh? Do you *kn*ow me?' in line 27, and then waiting through the pause in line 28, Victor pursues his testing until Betty is 'forced' into her admission that she does not know whether she remembers him.[11] Thus the absence of remedial work by Victor on Betty's behalf is a further way in which the asymmetry is sequentially and interactionally managed in the talk.[12]

What Extracts 2.3 and 2.4 have in common, then, is that local differences between speakers' states of knowledge are discovered in the talk. Thereafter, those differences become interactionally salient by virtue of the sequential work of one participant 'testing' the other. 'Testing' has the sequential consequence of managing to expose something about the recipient's state of knowledge which was suspected by the speaker 'all along', i.e. from an equivocal utterance by the recipient. In both cases, the matter is pursued in a way that brings the other's lack of knowledge to the interactional surface, and thereby makes the asymmetry interactionally relevant for a spate of talk.

These cases also have it in common that the asymmetries occasion the relevance in the interaction of exogenous categories or speaker identities. In 2.3 those were the categories of caller/ called, and boyfriend/girlfriend (i.e. intimate). In 2.4 the categories most relevant for Betty's dilemma in answering Victor's test question are child/adult. Even though she is a (young) adult now, she orients to permissible states of knowledge for the child she was when she last saw him. But asymmetries in distributions of knowledge do not arise 'naturally' from the mere fact that it is possible to categorize participants in these ways. The relevance of those categories is occasioned by the sequential/ interactional work engaged in by speakers. In Extract 2.2 that was the work of pursuing a disagreement, or arguing; in 2.3 and 2.4 it is 'testing'. Thus asymmetries are generated in the talk through occasioning the interactional relevance of those exogenous or structural categories. And it is this which makes asymmetry a phenomenon which is different from merely 'different states of knowledge'.

Normative entitlements to knowledge

The dilemma which Betty faced in answering Victor's enquiry arose from her orienting to a self-identifying category – 'child' – for which certain states of knowledge are not, conventionally, appropriate. Such a category of person is not an authoritative source of some kinds of knowledge. A corollary of this is that she is not 'entitled' to the knowledge which would enable her to answer that she remembers him.

This is to point to a property of those categories which may be applied to persons. Entitlements to knowledge are attached to, or belong to, categories – and not to persons (a phenomenon similar to that described by Sharrock as 'ownership of knowledge': Sharrock, 1974). This has the consequence that a speaker may possess some knowledge, but nevertheless have an asymmetrical position with respect to that knowledge. The connection between categories or speaker identities and normative entitlements to knowledge begins to separate the notion of asymmetry from actual states of knowledge and ignorance. The interactional consequences of this show up in cases where speakers use some piece of knowledge, but simultaneously display their asymmetrical position of non-entitlement to – or of not being an authoritative source of – that knowledge.

Rather clear examples of this phenomenon are found in medical consultations, when patients use medical terminology. This connects back to the asymmetry which I discussed at the beginning of this paper, between doctors and patients with respect to bodies of technical medical knowledge. Despite their asymmetrical position with regard to such knowledge, patients may from time to time perfectly well know what medical terms apply to their symptoms or illnesses, and they may refer to these in talking with doctors. However, in doing so, they may simultaneously display that they are not authoritative sources of such knowledge about their medical condition. Here are two such cases.

>   *Extract 2.5*
>   Pt: B't th*i*s time I have a little pr*o*blem.
>   (0.9)
>   Pt: I s*ee*m to have
>   (0.8) ((during which thumping sound, as
>   though thumping hand on desk))
>   Dr: nY*e* ⌈:s.
>   Pt: ⌊what is it – c*o*ntracted
>   (0.4)
>   Dr: khn ⌈Y*e*:s.
>   Pt: ⌊tendon:.
>   Dr: That's r*i*ght. H*o*w long have you been: in developing th*i*:s.

>   *Extract 2.6 (from Cicourel, 1983, p. 224)*
>   Dr: What can I do for you?
>   Pt: Well, uh, I was concerned about, uh . . . last summer, I guess, I
>   – I was having a problem in the uh . . . uh, I guess w–what you
>   call the bulk of the outer uh part of the organ. There's like
>   paper thin uh cuts . . .

In each of these extracts from medical consultations, a patient uses what is recognizably medical terminology in reporting to the doctor a diagnosis, in 2.5 ('contracted tendon'), and in 2.6 a symptom (a problem in 'the bulk of the outer part of the organ'). However, they do not come right out with these terms/phrases: their uses are in certain respects mitigated. Not only is there evidence of hesitancy (notably, pausing and self-repair) associated with the production of the medical terms; these are also prefaced with 'attributive' phrases – that is, phrases which attribute authority on such terminology to the other. In 2.5 'what is it . . .', and in 2.6 'I guess w-what you call', defer to the doctor as the proper authority as to what the malady is, or what it is called.[13] So the patients are simultaneously using a medical term, but deferring to the doctors as authoritative sources of such terminology.

Such cases rather dramatically illustrate that an asymmetry of knowledge is not equivalent to 'not knowing'. Here the patients know what is wrong with themselves, and know the medically appropriate name for their condition. But in the mitigated use of these names they treat such terminology as normatively 'belonging' to the other, and hence orient to their asymmetry with respect to medical knowledge.[14]

Now we can discern such orientations to speakers' non-authoritative (and hence asymmetrical) use of medical knowledge showing through in ordinary conversation. The evidence here is less dramatic or stark: it is associated with the fact that their co-participants are not medical experts, so that they are in an asymmetrical position not with respect to their recipients, but in relation to medical knowledge in general. While their co-participants are, like themselves, lay persons, nevertheless when they refer to information derived from medical sources, they display that in the design of their talk. Two such cases follow. In 2.7 Carol is reporting on the illness of her daughter; evidently it was feared that she was suffering from glandular fever, but '[t]hey discovered it was her wisdom teeth in the e:nd,'.

> *Extract 2.7*
> Carol: Apparently they came through on Friday ni:ght, .hh a:n:d burst through the surface 'n were infected. 'n that was that was causing the abcesses in her mou:th.
> Leslie: Oh:: dea:r.
> Carol: So she's now whispering, you can hear what she says no:w

And in 2.8, Emma is telling Nancy about an operation she has just had to remove an infected toe-nail.

> *Extract 2.8*
> Emma: . . . then my other toe's got it it's something you get'n he says one in a: thousand get it and I: got it.
> Nancy: Wul wuddiiyih get it fro⌈:m
> Emma: ⌊.hh.hh God he doesn't kno:w,
> (0.2) He can't tell yuh they don't know a thing yihknow I've had it in my fingernails . . .

The medical circumstances which Carol and Emma describe do

not at all involve technical medical terminology: indeed in 2.8 part of Emma's report is quite colloquial ('one in a thousand get it'). However, the authority for thus describing the circumstances is *attributed to a third party*. In 2.7 Carol prefaces her report of her daughter's condition with 'apparently', and thereby 'cites a source' for her report of these details (Pomerantz, 1984b); although this source is not specified, it is recognizably medical, i.e. from a doctor. And when in 2.8 Emma reports how many people suffer from her medical complaint, but that the cause is not known, she similarly attributes these items of knowledge to a third party, 'he', quite readily identifiable as a doctor. So she does not treat herself as the authoritative source of that knowledge.

In these examples, speakers *mitigate* their reports of certain medical information, and thus orient to a contrast between technical information whose source is a medical authority, and their ordinary access to the signs or symptoms of medical states which they can know about at first hand. Mitigated forms of reporting display speakers' orientation to their asymmetry with respect to a body of technical knowledge (note, not with respect to the knowledge of their co-participant). They may know something about their (or their daughter's) medical condition. But they display the fact that their warrant for knowing is that they were told it, and therefore they are not entitled to treat that knowledge as if it were their own.

This phenomenon has a quite general relevance for conversation, one which goes beyond access to bodies of technical or expert knowledge. It is similarly the case that there are kinds of knowledge, not particularly specialized knowledge about oneself or events in the world, to which speakers have an asymmetrical position *vis-à-vis* others. This relates to a point Sacks (in his unpublished lecture in 1971) made concerning an interchange between a child and his mother. The child came home from school and reported 'I'm bright'; to which his mother responded, 'Who told you that?'. Sacks points out that the mother thereby treats such knowledge as that one is bright as the kind of thing which, properly, is said about oneself by another. For competent speakers (the child not yet being one), certain kinds of knowledge about oneself are non-equivalent. There is a normative, socially organized distribution between those kinds of knowledge for which one is entitled to claim to possess a first-hand warrant, i.e. of which one is an authoritative source (one's own name, first-hand experiences, etc.) and those things which are conventionally 'mediated knowledge', known about only by virtue of what others say about us, and for which therefore they are the authoritative source.

These issues connect very much with the discussion above about Betty's position in Extract 2.4. We need to distinguish between, on the one hand, speakers' actual states of knowledge and, on the other hand, their orientations to the normative distributions of rights and entitlements to certain kinds of knowledge. Certainly some of these involve bodies of specialized technical knowledge: thus there may be asymmetries between lay or novice participants, and experts (see, e.g. Wintermantel, this volume, Chapter 6). But other kinds of quite non-specialized knowledge also have organized distributions, whereby, for instance, there are matters which speakers cannot claim to possess on their own behalf. 'Demurring to say on one's own behalf' and 'citing another as the source' (i.e. reporting something as having been said by another) are, perhaps, quite general devices in conversation by which speakers orient to their asymmetrical rights or entitlements concerning socially distributed knowledge.

Asymmetry is not equivalent to control

Before concluding, it may be worth drawing attention to an implication from the analyses of the extracts above: namely, that 'control' or 'domination' are not conterminous with 'asymmetry'. There are some respects in which, at least in Extracts 2.3 and 2.4, one participant manages to put his or her co-participant at a disadvantage; and insofar as the speakers press their advantage for a short sequence, they exercise that much 'control' over the sequence and their co-participant's involvement in it. But the other examples serve to illustrate that a speaker may have an asymmetrical position *vis-à-vis* some organized distribution of knowledge, but is not thereby necessarily controlled by his or her co-participant. For instance, in 2.5 the patient was not prevented from offering the doctor a technical diagnosis of his own ailment – although in the details of the design of the turn in which the patient offers that diagnosis, he orients to the doctor as having authority over such knowledge.

The possibility that 'control' and 'asymmetry' may be empirically independent is more explicitly illustrated in this next extract, taken from the first visit to the home of a newly born child by a health visitor.[15]

Extract 2.9 (HV = health visitor, M = mother)
```
HV: Lovely. = Will you be going back to the hospital for you:r (.)
    post-natal.
M:  Yes. (.) I wi:ll. =
HV: = Oh you won't forget to go will you.
M:  No:. hheh (              )
HV:                         ⌊I think that's very - very important.
M:  Ye:h.
HV: Uh:: :m to make sure everything is - is back together in its
    rightful place.
M:  You don't have to go to them then.
    (0.7)
M:  Y'know I - I thought you had to go:
    (1.5)
HV: Well none 'v- nothing: I mean n: - nothings compulsory, it's
    obviously very sensible
M:                         ⌊Oh I- I am going.
HV: Ye:s
M:  Yea:h
    (.)
M:  Yeah but I thought it was a thing you had to go to:,
HV: We:ll ⌈it it's highly recom- yes I th⌈i- I think you
M:        ⌊You kno:w                     ⌊Yea:h
HV: shou:ld I think - I think it's *very* important.
```

The health visitor advises mothers about the procedures for registering with a doctor and health clinic, about how often they should attend, about the relevant forms which need to be completed, about the procedures for making developmental and growth checks, about immunization programmes, about registering childminders and all the rest.[16] Some of these procedures are statutory requirements: others, while being recommended, are matters of parental discretion. Mothers may not always be clear whether the procedure about which a health visitor is advising them is one which they are (legally) required to follow, or alternatively is only recommended, and hence a matter of choice.

This distinction between legally required and recommended procedures comes to the interactional surface in Extract 2.9. When the mother says 'You don't have to go to them then. (0.7) Y'know I- I thought you had to go:.', it is apparent that she has discovered that what she took to be a statutory, compulsory procedure is in fact a matter of her choice. She has detected that just from the way in which the health visitor phrased her enquiry about whether the mother would be going to hospital for a post-natal check up. The equivocality of that phrasing (as between being compulsory or recommended) by the health visitor is what enables the mother to learn something about the status of the procedures which the health visitor is advising her about. Subsequently the health visitor is then in the position of having to 'admit' (note the structural similarity with Alan's admission in 2.3 and Betty's in 2.4) that such a check up is not compulsory; which causes her some, perhaps unwanted, difficulty in persuading the mother that nevertheless a check up is 'highly recommended' and that she should have one.

The mother's discovery in the health visitor's talk of the discretionary status of the procedure (i.e. the check up) does not, of course, alter the asymmetry in their relative access to technical knowledge about post-natal care procedures. In this extract the mother continues to orient to the health visitor as the authoritative source of knowledge about those procedures. But at the same time, the mother's asymmetrical position does not mean that she is 'controlled' by the health visitor. The mother has resources, from the emerging talk of the other and the unfolding sequence, for gaining a certain kind of access to knowledge about the matters on which she is being advised. This illustrates why 'control' and asymmetry should be treated as analytically independent of one another, the possible intersections between them being an empirical matter. Interactional control is a property of sequence management and turn design and may, on occasion, be generated out of an advantage one speaker has by virtue of participants' asymmetries of knowledge; but that advantage does not guarantee interactional control. 'Control' and asymmetry of knowledge are not conceptually conterminous; their connections should instead be matters of empirical investigation.

Conclusion

A common strategy for identifying asymmetries of knowledge between participants, especially in institutional environments, is to show that because of their different socio-cultural knowledge or perspectives, participants attribute different meanings or make different inferences from events in the interaction, and therefore 'talk past one another' (see, e.g. Gumperz, 1982; Erickson and Shultz, 1982). But the lack of congruity between meanings in the talk is not necessarily visible to the participants in the surface of the talk. Indeed, the very invisibility of such inferential differences may sometimes be treated by an analyst of the discourse as an indication of how thoroughly asymmetrical their talk is. So that the conversational or interactional consequences of their not sharing some common body of socio-cultural knowledge or expectations may, it is claimed, remain hidden to the participants in the course of the interaction.

A different strategy has been adopted here. The aim has been to identify ways in which asymmetries of knowledge are demonstrably relevant to the participants themselves, and so have consequences for, and are manifest in, the details of talk. In some instances those details concern the sequential development of the talk, albeit only for brief sequences; in other instances they concern the design of the turn in which reference is made to some body of knowledge to which the speaker does not have access as an authoritative user. Where interactional troubles or 'incongruities' do arise, as in Extracts 2.3 and 2.4, they are oriented to as such by participants. But some of the cases which have been discussed illustrate that asymmetries of knowledge by no means necessarily generate interactional troubles, or failures on the part of co-conversationalists to understand one another. Indeed, even in 2.3 and 2.4 the interactional difficulties which arise are not created by failures of understanding. The participants happen sufficiently to share some fundamental conversational procedures for production and interpretation of behaviour (Heritage, 1984, p. 241) to comprehend fully what is being managed in the talk – even if they are put in a position where they cannot respond adequately or appropriately. The essential point is, then, that speakers' orientations to asymmetries of knowledge need not always be manifest in interactional incongruities or troubles. And even when such conversational troubles do arise, they may not stem from any lack of understanding by one or other of the participants.

In a sense, also, I am trying to rescue the notion of asymmetry from any cognitive associations it may have. I have tried to emphasize the difference between actual states of knowledge, and asymmetries of knowledge. States of 'not knowing' something are not, in many of these examples, the consequence of asymmetries of knowledge. And it is also, perhaps, misleading to refer to any situation in which one speaker knows something which the other does not as involving asymmetrical states of knowledge. The result of doing so would be to treat a whole bunch of questions (all those in which one speaker asks the recipient about things which the speaker does not know but supposes that the recipient does), in story telling, news delivery and the like, as asymmetrical interactions. To be sure, such activities *may* involve asymmetries – but not simply by virtue of the fact that one knows what the other does not. When speakers orient to their asymmetrical position as regards some knowledge, they orient to the normatively organized social distributions of authoritative access to bodies or types of knowledge.

The phrase 'social distribution of authoritative access' pulls together two fundamental components of asymmetry of knowledge. First, 'social distribution' indexes the exogenous or social structural identities by which participants may relevantly be categorized, and thus to which they can be shown to orient in sequences of talk. The instances of asymmetry discussed above tend to involve a speaker orienting to his or her identity from one of a set of paired relational categories – caller/called, adult/child, patient/doctor, self/other, etc. Second, 'authoritative access' refers to the conventional ascription of warrantable rights or entitlements over the possession and use of certain kinds of knowledge. Such entitlements are ascribed to members who may be categorized by one of those paired identities (e.g. other or adult), but not to those categorized by the other paired identity (self or child). Thus a speaker's asymmetrical position *vis-à-vis* some knowledge has to do with socially organized distributions of knowledge, and not – or not necessarily – with the cognitive state of knowing or not knowing what the other knows. And only in some cases, as in 2.3, are such asymmetries the product of some strategic moves by one of the participants. Strategic manoeuvres through which interactional asymmetries are generated have largely been beyond the scope of this chapter.

Notes

1. The literature on the ways in which specialized turn-taking systems in institutional settings create asymmetries in such things as the distribution of turns, participations rights, topic management and the like is too vast to be cited here. However, for a notable example see Clayman's analysis of the asymmetrical rights which interviewers have to bring news interviews to a close (Clayman, 1989).
2. Very briefly, I think it can be shown that many such studies are too ready to attribute communicational difficulties to differences in speakers' relative socio-cultural identities: where it can turn out that there are more proximate sources of interactional troubles, which do not at all involve incongruent meaning systems and the like. And as I go on to argue in this paper, asymmetries need not be coterminous with interactional breakdown or miscommunication.
3. There is some research documenting the ways speakers orient to

such inequalities, for example in telling stories (Sacks, 1971), in eliciting information about the other (Pomerantz, 1980), and in the recipient design of talk (Goodwin, 1981, Chapter 5; 1986).
4. Although this will not be developed here, it is noticeable that each of Cloe's turns in the argument in this extract employs an idiom, such as 'gone your own ways', 'knocked each other's teeth out'.
5. In being playful or teasing the person she has called, she relies on the recipient orienting to the routine features of the organization of telephone call openings, including the structural slots for self-identifying and displaying recognition which the organization provides. The (intersubjective) assumption by the called that the caller is similarly oriented to, and conducting herself according to, that organization is what enables the caller to play games with the called. For a description of the routine organization of telephone openings see Schegloff, (1986).
6. The discussion here is based on a fuller analysis in Drew, 1989: but in addressing the theme of asymmetry, some of the points from that version have been revised and developed.
7. And whereas her recognition, at sight, of her other relatives can be taken for granted, Betty's recognition of Victor cannot be a similarly routine, unnoticeable matter. So what she says in that slot, in line 22, may be inspected for its recognitional import.
8. And it is possible that she did not greet him by saying 'Hi Uncle Victor' specifically in order to avoid the implication that she might be trying to claim that she 'remembered' him.
9. It should be emphasized that this refers to conventional attributions of cognitive states to a class of members (here, children), and *not* to actual cognitive states of particular members (i.e. a particular child).
10. For an account of the remedial actions whereby speakers may try to deal with recipients' evident difficulties in responding, see Pomerantz, (1984a).
11. Notice the precise way in which her turn is designed: when she says 'I don't know whether I remember you' - rather than 'I don't remember you' - she is avoiding, or not asserting that she does not know him.
12. Parenthetically, I think there is a very real connection between this explication of Betty's dilemma here, and the kind of analysis Käsermann offers of 'uncooperativeness' in her psychotherapeutic data. Käsermann is pointing to instances in which a client is prevented from reacting to moves by the therapist, as manifest in the client remaining silent on certain points (see Käsermann, this volume, Chapter 5, e.g. p. 117). This might resemble Betty's 'remaining silent' between lines 26 and 29, and then 'withholding' answering that she 'knows' Victor.
13. For further cases, see Silverman, (1987), for example case 1, p. 48.
14. Meehan's analysis of how doctors and patients use medical terms during consultations identifies some closely related issues. In particular, he examines how doctors tailor their explanations, especially when patients have displayed some difficulty with medical terms, to take into account or to anticipate the likely extent of patients' medical knowledge. In this way doctors design their

answers to patients' enquiries in ways which orient to asymmetries of knowledge (see Meehan, 1981).
15. I am grateful to John Heritage for permission to use these data.
16. For a fuller discussion of the interactional management of 'advice giving' by health visitors, see Heritage and Sefi, forthcoming.

References

Cicourel, A. V. (1983), 'Language and the structure of belief in medical communication', in S. Fisher and A. Dundas Todd (eds), *The Social Organization of Doctor-Patient Communication*, Centre for Applied Linguistics: Washington, DC.

Clayman, S. E. (1989), 'The production of punctuality: social interaction, temporal organization and social structure', *American Journal of Sociology*, **95**, 659-91.

Drew, P. (1981), 'Adults' corrections of children's mistakes', in P. French and M. MacLure (eds), *Adult-Child Conversation: Studies in structure and process*, Croom Helm: London.

Drew, P. (1987), 'Po-faced receipts of teases', *Linguistics*, **25**, 219-53.

Drew, P. (1989), 'Recalling someone from the past', in D. Roger and P. Bull (eds), *Conversation: An interdisciplinary perspective*, Multilingual Matters: Clevedon PA.

Drew, P. and Holt, E. (1988), 'Complainable matters: the use of idiomatic expressions in making complaints', *Social Problems*, **35**, 398-417.

Erickson, F. and Shultz, J. (1982), *The Counsellor as Gatekeeper: Social interaction in interviews*, Academic Press: New York.

Goodwin, C. (1981), *Conversational Organization: Interaction between speakers and hearers*, Academic Press: New York.

Goodwin, C. (1986), 'Audience diversity, participation and interpretation', *Text*, **6**, 283-316.

Gumperz, J. (1982), *Discourse Strategies*, Cambridge University Press: Cambridge.

Heritage, J. (1984), *Garfinkel and Ethnomethodology*, Polity Press: Cambridge.

Heritage, J. and Sefi, S. (forthcoming), 'Just a chat: dilemmas of advice giving in interactions between Health Visitors and first time mothers', in P. Drew and J. Heritage (eds), *Talk at Work*, Cambridge University Press: Cambridge.

Jefferson, G. and Lee, J. (1981), 'The rejection of advice: managing the problematic convergence of a "troubles telling" and a "service encounter".' *Journal of Pragmatics*, **5**, 399-422 (to be reprinted in P. Drew and J. Heritage (eds), *Talk at Work*, Cambridge University Press: Cambridge.

Levinson, S. (1988), 'Putting linguistics on a proper footing: explorations in Goffman's concepts of participation', in P. Drew and A. Wootton (eds), *Erving Goffman: Exploring the interaction order*, Polity Press: Cambridge.

Linell, P. (1990), 'The power of dialogue dynamics', in I. Marková and K. Foppa (eds), *The Dynamics of Dialogue*, Harvester Wheatsheaf: Hemel Hempstead.

Meehan, A. J. (1981), 'Some conversational features of the use of medical terms by doctors and patients', in P. Atkinson and C. Heath (eds), *Medical Work: Realities and routines*, Gower: Farnborough.

O'Barr, W. and Conley, J. M. (1985), 'Litigant satisfaction versus legal adequacy in small claims court narratives', *Law and Society Review*, **19**, 661-701.

Paget, M. A. (1983), 'On the work of talk: studies in misunderstandings', in S. Fisher and A. Dundas Todd (eds), *The Social Organization of Doctor-Patient Communication*, Centre for Applied Linguistics: Washington, DC.

Pomerantz, A. (1980), 'Telling my side: "limited access" as a "fishing" device', *Sociological Inquiry*, **50**, 186-98.

Pomerantz, A. (1984a), 'Pursuing a response', in J. M. Atkinson and J. Heritage (eds), *Structures of Social Actions: Studies in conversation analysis*, Cambridge University Press: Cambridge.

Pomerantz, A. (1984b), 'Giving a source or a basis: the practice in conversation of telling "how I know",' *Journal of Pragmatics*, **8**, 607-25.

Sacks, H. (1971), Unpublished lecture 4, 19 October (edited by G. Jefferson as 'The interaction of couples in the telling of stories').

Sacks, H., Schegloff, E. A. and Jefferson, G. (1974), 'A simplest systematics for the organisation of turn-taking for conversation', *Language*, **50**, 696-735.

Schegloff, E. A. (1984), 'On some questions and ambiguities in conversation', in J. M. Atkinson and J. Heritage (eds), *Structures of Social Action: Studies in conversation analysis*, Cambridge University Press: Cambridge.

Schegloff, E. A. (1986), 'The routine as achievement', *Human Studies*, **9**, 111-51.

Schegloff, E. A. (1987), 'Some sources of misunderstanding in conversation', *Linguistics*, **25**, 201-18.

Sharrock, W. (1974), 'On owning knowledge', in R. Turner (ed), *Ethnomethodology*, Penguin: London.

Silverman, D. (1987), *Communication and Medical Practice: Social relations in the clinic*, Sage: London.

Tannen, D. and Wallat, C. (1986), 'Medical professionals and parents: a linguistic analysis of communication across contexts', *Language in Society*, **15**, 295-311.

3 | Facework and control in multi-party talk: a paediatric case study

Karin Aronsson

In his final publication, Goffman (1983) forcefully argued against simplified notions of 'recipient design'. Talk is more than speaker–hearer engineering. Talk-in-interaction often draws on social factors beyond simplistic speaker intentions. Co-participants partly shape utterances – through their verbal or non-verbal collaboration in orchestrating talk – and they are, to some extent, the co-producers of meaning (Rommetveit, 1989; forthcoming). Similarly, third parties in talk are, at times, quite important in forming what will be said (and not said). Many studies of conversation are flawed by a dyadic bias on the one hand (leaving out multi-party talk), and by a unilateral speaker/hearer bias on the other hand, ignoring collaborative aspects of the interaction order. Recently, others have sided with Goffman in his critique of the dyadic bias. In a scholarly discussion of cross-linguistic data related to speaker roles (e.g. pronouns, evidentials, etc.), Levinson (1988) shows how language as such often bears testimony to some of the complexities pertaining to speaker roles.

Obviously, multi-party talk is one of the primary contexts for revealing speaker role equivocalities, and much of Levinson's discussion draws on multi-party talk. Yet he primarily analyses different realizations of address, etc., in different languages, and his investigation is not focused on language as revealed through coherent descriptions of, say, institutional talk.

Levinson advocates more work on multi-party talk in institutional settings. Moreover, he points to the importance of investigating adult–child discourse, where one party has quite restricted participation rights (which at times results in so-called 'out-louds' and other attention-getting devices).

Obviously, the presence of children highlights the difference between participant roles in that children are quite often non-ratified participants (over-hearers) rather than primary addressees.

I will subsequently analyse multi-party facework and control in adult–child discourse. Adult–child interaction is asymmetrical in that the adult party is often the party in control. In pediatric settings the adult–child relation is even more asymmetrical in that the expert (the doctor) is the one who has access to privileged information about medication, etc. The analysis to follow will be grounded in a case-study account of a pediatric consultation with conflicting alliances (doctor–parent; doctor–child; parent–child) as manifested in consultation talk, on the one hand, and post-consultation interviews on the other. Facework phenomena tend to stand out more clearly in situations of greater conflict (and greater face threat). The present encounter is chosen from a large set of thirty-two consultations (Aronsson and Rundström, 1988; 1989) because of its latent conflicts (between doctors' permissiveness and parental protectiveness concerning the child patient's physical activities; between medication and non-medication).

Pediatric allergy consultations, with children suffering from asthma or food or animal allergies, etc., entail a variety of facework strategies in that doctors' recommendations often intrude into the everyday management of family life (physical exercise, pet-keeping, etc.), which means that medical authority may threaten or challenge parental authority. Parental authority may also be challenged from within, in that children may disagree with parental decisions in areas that concern their everyday lives in an immediate and intimate sense.

Aronsson and Rundström (1989) have drawn on Brown and Levinson's linguistic anthropological model of facework (1987). The model discusses politeness in terms of respect behaviour (negative politeness) on the one hand, and familiar and affiliative, attentive behaviour (positive politeness) on the other. Both types are seen as mitigating discourse strategies, which soften face-threatening actions (such as criticism, requests, threats) by embedding them in a joking or familiar mode (positive politeness) or making them more indirect. The indirectness of negative politeness is associated with greater face threats and greater social distance between speaker and hearer. Similarly, a relatively powerless position is linked to indirectness, whereas greater relative power is more likely to co-occur with directness and clarity. The model may be read as a facework hierarchy in order of decreasing directness as the face threat becomes greater: bald on record (lesser threat), positive politeness, negative politeness, off record and no action (greater threat to face).

In the larger set of pediatric consultations (Aronsson and Rundström, 1989), it was shown that the doctors sometimes formed something of a joking relationship with the children (positive politeness culture, in the Brown and Levinson terminology), displaying playful exaggerations or dares, inappropriately respectful forms of address, such as 'sir', 'm'lady', etc., and jokes and teasing behaviour. In so doing, doctors may alleviate tension. More importantly – for our present purposes – they could also be said to bracket the doctor–child alliance as something that is not quite serious and which need not threaten the doctor–parent or parent–child alliance. In fact, the doctor–parent alliance may appear more real, more serious in that it is not set apart.

Relatedly, it was also shown how the doctors would, at times, exploit the presence of a third party (the child) when criticizing the parent – talking to the parent through the child. Normally the doctors would address the parents rather indirectly when presenting critical or sensitive questions. In contrast, they would address the children quite bluntly – 'No, no! No such foolishness!' – or 'and don't start smoking or something crazy like that!' (Aronsson and Rundström, 1989). In several cases in the investigation it was also documented how parents would, in fact, ratify the doctor's blunt directives to the child. For instance, if the doctor said to the child, 'You have to cut your finger-nails!', the mother would immediately latch on with 'he must do that!', followed by the child, 'I must do that' (Aronsson and Rundström, 1989; see Extract 3.7). At times, the parent would come out more baldly than the doctor. If the doctor told the child that smoking is 'not exactly great', the parent would, for instance, upgrade his comment into 'exactly down-right crazy' (Aronsson and Rundström, 1989, see Extract 3.12). Parents would thus ratify or disambiguate doctors' directives. In so doing, they also strengthened the present obliqueness interpretation (that part of doctor's talk to children would primarily serve to convey face-threatening information to parents – concerning children's hygiene, etc.).

In its present form, the Brown and Levinson model (1978; 1987) does not explicitly address the role of third-party contributions. Hence, it does not rank the present phenomenon ('talking to the parent through the child') within the politeness hierarchy.

This 'indirect directness' can, of course, be interpreted as an off-the-record or indirect move (from a parent addressee perspective) or as a positive politeness move (from a child addressee perspective). From a truly interactional philosophy of language point of view (Rommetveit, 1985; 1989; forthcoming; Rorty, 1979), language is basically open ended and incomplete in that meaning partly resides in ongoing dialogue work. Yet triadic discourse renders language equivocal in a new and different way in that the participants may at times have to decide whether or not to participate in a dialogue (or whether to listen to one).

As pointed out by Brown and Levinson in their critical assessment of their model (1987), family life highlights issues concerning conflict and aggravation, rather than politeness and mitigation. For that very reason conflict talk may be of interest in that it can illuminate the application range of the politeness model in multi-party contexts. In the following, I will present an authentic pediatric consultation in order to discuss in what ways multi-party conflicts and alliances may be explained in terms of the Brown and Levinson model (1987), and whether children's limited participation rights lead to specific types of multi-party control.

Some multi-party strategies for facework and control have previously been documented within the larger set of pediatric consultations (Aronsson and Rundström, 1988; 1989). Yet these strategies have not been situated within a coherent and sequential framework, which means that the interconnections between different types of multi-party strategies have not been analysed. Nor have different types of multi-party strategies been detailed or schematized. I will therefore try below to outline a model of control in multi-party talk.

Method

In a series of pediatric consultations (in an allergy out-patient clinic), entire consultations were audio-taped and half the consultations were followed up by post-consultation interviews with the child (patient) and his or her parent(s). In the present study, the post-consultation interviews were employed as a means for identifying unvoiced parent or child disagreements that can be related to consultation topics. The case of eleven-year old Valentin was chosen for case-study presentation as it contained conflicts between the boy and his mother, on the one hand, and the mother and the doctor, on the other. At the same time, the conflicts are routine, in that similar conflicts can be found in many other pediatric encounters. Ultimately, many conflicts pertain to issues where experts (doctors) and laymen (parents) hold opposing views on the same issue.

Valentin is a boy who suffers from a type of asthma which requires rather heavy medication. He uses several different types of prophylactic medicines, as well as medicine for acute problems. Medication is dependent on the boy's physical condition, which means that dosages may need to be increased or decreased in relation to his level of physical exercise. The case of Valentin was drawn from a larger set of thirty-two pediatric consultations, described in detail in Aronsson and Rundström (1988). In the aggregated descriptions of Aronsson and Rundström, two groups of parents were identified; high-control and low-control parents (above or below a median of 48 per cent parent appropriations of doctors' child-allocated turns). As can be seen (Table 3.1), Valentin's mother belongs to the high-control group (48-100 per cent appropriations), even though her 61 per cent control is relatively moderate within this group. As can be seen, the doctor dominates the pediatric encounter in terms of his quantitative control of the discourse space, that is the total quantity of talk. Yet the parent is the one who ultimately seems to determine whether the child will be more or

Table 3.1 Parental control in doctor–parent–child encounters, and the case of Valentin

Groups	Distribution of discourse space: mean percentage words			Parental appropriations: mean percentage parental appropriations of the doctor's child-directed turns
	Doctor	Parent	Child	
Low-control ($N = 16$)	60	30	10	37
High-control ($N = 16$)	55	38	6	67
Valentin	54	44	2	61

Note: Figures for Valentin are drawn from Aronsson and Rundström (1988); patient age range in the low-and high-control groups was 5-15.

less severely cut off from the ongoing discourse. In the high-control group, the children have about half as much discourse space as the low-control children, and there is also a significant difference between the high- and low-control parents, but not between the doctors in the two groups (Aronsson and Rundström, 1988).

Transcription

The consultations were transcribed *in extenso*, according to a simplified modification of the transcription system developed over time by Gail Jefferson and other ethno-methodologists (see Schenkein, 1978).

:	indicates prolonged syllable
----	demarcates overlapping utterances
/ /	encloses description of how talk is delivered
( )	encloses description of non-audible talk
(.)	denotes audible pause
(pause)	denotes marked pause
CAPITALS	indicate relatively high amplitude (e.g. 'Yeah: BUT we eat vegetarian food')
x	indicates inaudible word
-	is a self-editing marker
...	is a deleted fragment of talk

All names have been fictionalized to protect patients' and parents' anonymity.

Translation

The number of overlaps, pauses, hesitation, hedges, self-editings, etc., are kept constant, as is their location in relation to turn junctures. The translation from Swedish has been kept as literal as possible, except where minor modifications have been necessary in order to preserve conversational style.

Regulation of the child's participant status

Obviously, multi-party talk will raise quite complex problems if there are conflicts – and different potential alliances – between the different participants. The present case has been chosen for closer examination precisely because there is an underlying conflict. It could be seen in the post-consultation interviews with the child and his mother that this boy had had a long-standing dream of playing football, whereas his mother had opposed any physical exercise which would have entailed more medication or more parental supervision. In the consultation, the doctor's and the child's goals (permissiveness) thus converged, whereas the parent pursued an opposing line of argumentation (protectiveness). This paper will analyse the consultation discourse, seen as a case of conflict talk in ongoing interaction in depth. We will see in what ways conflicting goals may shape adult discourse control, and whether multi-party talk requires complementary or different types of strategies, comparing our results with those of Brown and Levinson's (1978; 1987) facework strategy studies.

Valentin's mother controlled his moves in different ways and for different purposes. At times it was possible to identify quite rational time budget considerations, as in the following exchange (Extract 3.1).

Extract 3.1 Parental repair work (reframing) and regulation of the child's participant status

59 Dr: Yes, well you take medicine before PE, don't you?
Child: Yes

Dr: You always take it, what do you take?
Child: Neb–Lomu–Lomudal.
Mother: No, you use Ventoline spray

Dr: He does, <u>yes</u>
Child: <u>Mhm</u>

Dr: How long before PE do you see it?
Mother: About ten minutes beforehand.

In this sequence, the mother performed some repair work on her son's response. Yet, his response ('Neb–Lomu–Lomudal') was correct in as far as he did not take Lomudal before PE at school. He had taken this medicine earlier on in the day. In general, there is an asymmetry in knowledge between the child patients and their parents. Valentin's mother - who was more familiar with medical framings of events - knew that the doctor was trying to find out what type of medicine Valentin took immediately before PE. The mother's repair thus involved a reframing of the doctor's question. In accordance with Brown and Levinson's predictions on facework and directness (1987), elaborate facework is not required in the case of parental criticism of children. Consequently, it can be seen how the mother came out bluntly in her repair 'No, you use Ventoline spray'. This dependency relationship between directness and relative power fits the Brown and Levinson model. In the same repair sequence it is possible to identify some multi-party phenomena that can be less directly predicted from the Brown and Levinson model. It can be seen how the parent regulates the child's participant status, alter-casting the child as a side-participant. The child's participant status is gradually transformed from a dialogue partner (second person) into a third person, which can ultimately be seen in the mother's last turn (where, without any prelude, she responded in her son's place).

Besides her medical reframing (correction of Valentin's answer), the mother thus also accomplished a redirection of the participation role structure in the consultation conversation, casting the child as a more distant 'he' rather than the more intimate 'you'. The parent's contribution thus served to regulate social distance. As pointed out by Aronsson and Sätterlund-Larsson (1987), social distance is not merely a background variable in discourse. Social distance is embedded in ongoing discourse and it is regulated by the different participants.

In other parts of the dialogue, it can be seen how Valentin's mother took over in ways that were less obviously dictated by repair-work concerns (Extract 3.2).

Extract 3.2 Parental elaboration (and regulation of child's participant status)
216 Dr: Open wide! Stick out your tongue! (pause) but it's worst at this time of the year isn't it?
    Child: Yeah.

220 Dr: You think so.
    Mother: /laughs/ the worst of it is when he wants to go out but knows that he can't.

The physical proximity of the medical examination tends to elicit face-to-face communication between the doctor and the child. Yet in the present investigation, the child's turns during the physical communication were generally appropriated by the high-control parents (Aronsson and Rundström, 1988). The case of Valentin was no exception. The boy was granted but one turn before the parent (laughingly) interfered. In this sequence there was no need for reframing on the part of the parent. Yet, she apparently wanted to elaborate on the topic 'this time of the year'. Her son's response was, admittedly, not an exhaustive one. Yet if we leave the rationality of elaborations aside, the parent simultaneously transformed her child into a non-person in that he was cast as a third person ('he') rather than a second person addressee. In a discussion on dyadic discourse, Linell (1990) has discussed how controlling versus inhibiting moves may be analysed in terms of parents' regulations of children's participant status, whereas controlling moves may be analysed in terms of parental embeddings of children's contributions. In the present discussion such embeddings may take the form of repairs, reframings and elaborations (see Extracts 3.1 and 3.2 above), as well as ratifications (Extracts 3.4 and 3.5 below).

Medical framing and adult–child talk

As was shown in Extract 3.1, parental repair work at times concerns the medical framing of what constitutes appropriate responses to doctor's questions. There is a knowledge asymmetry between doctors and parents on the one hand, and parents and children on the other. Quite often, children are not aware of central presuppositions that have a bearing on anamnestic questioning and consequentially on response relevances. Yet the allergic child is the one who has the most intimate experience of medication, in that he/she alone has first-hand experiences of what medication does to his/her body. This first-hand experience must be balanced against the adult person's (parent's) greater background knowledge of medical framings, etc.

Many allergic child patients (including Valentin) consume several different medicines and the prescriptions are at times quite complex. In the present corpus of thirty-two consultations, doctors therefore generally addressed parents when they inquired about medication. This was also the case in the Valentin consultation. Initially, the doctor started out with a series of questions to the mother, which eventually led to some uncertainty on her part (Extract 3.3).

> Extract 3.3 Anamnestic talk on medication (addressed to mother)
> 236 Dr: Which type of Lomudal did he get? Does he use this one?
> Mother: Naa
>
> Dr: Does he use the old type?
> Mother: M:
>
> Dr: This one?
> Mother: Naa.

> Dr: He's got the spray
> Mother: Yeah
>
> Dr: Uhm, we've got one right here
> Mother: Uhm
>
> Dr: The <u>common</u>
> Mother: <u>Yes</u>
>
> Dr: spray?
> 249 Mother: Yes, it's probably that one. I- I (don't know know x give up)

In the above sequence, the mother provided but minimal responses. As discussed in Aronsson and Sätterlund-Larsson (1987), a minimal response is ambiguous in that it may signify agreement ('I agree') or merely reception ('I hear you'). The mother did not spontaneously retrieve the specific name of the medicine. Moreover, she was able neither to explicitly disconfirm nor to confirm the doctor's suggestion about the 'one right here' (line 244), which probably prompted the ensuing explication on the doctor's part (line 246, 248 'the common spray?'). In this situation of unresolved uncertainty, the doctor ultimately chose to address the child as well (Extract 3.4).

> *Extract 3.4 Anamnestic talk on medication (addressed to child)*
> 250 Dr: This one contains common spray, that's the one you've got, isn't it?
>   Child: Mm, mm
>   Mother: M:

Valentin responded in a brief manner. Yet, he repeated his 'M', which rendered his response somewhat more emphatic, and his mother immediately ratified it.

Collaboratively, they had now established that Valentin indeed consumed the 'common spray'. In this specific case, the doctor elicited Valentin's response (and the mother ratified it). On other occasions, the mother herself addressed Valentin (Extract 3.5).

> *Extract 3.5 Medical prescriptions and parental ratifications of child contributions*
> 297 Dr: Theo-dur?
>   Mother: I'm uncertain about whether we've got - (.) we did get eyedrops (.) and we got (.) uhm, but we didn't get Lomudal nose spray, did we (.) <u>that's what I think</u>
>   Child: M: yes it's finished! (.) <u>One:</u>
> 300 Mother: <u>Yes, yes</u> that's what we would need, I'd guess

Again, it can be seen how the child may provide the response. Yet it is the mother who ultimately ratifies what is said. Moreover, there are cases where the high-control parents degrade the children or their responses (Aronsson and Rundström, 1989). Valentin's mother complained about the boy's hygiene at some point of the consultation, and on yet another occasion she complained about the boy's carelessness (Extract 3.6)

> Extract 3.6 Parental regulation of child's participant status
> 301 Dr: Did you bring his stamp?
> Mother: No.
>
> Dr: His card, I mean.
> Mother: 'E did 'ave, I thought 'e was big enough to look after himself but then 'e just lost his wallet and everything /laughs/
>
> Dr: Well, Valentin, how do things go! (pause) er, Lomudal Nasal Spray (pause) Did you find that worked? /to Valentin/
> Mother: Yeah, we thought so.
> Child: I don't know
> 308 Mother: (xx) although others don't seem to him so but (xx)

What are the potential facework benefits for the parent in degrading the child or in increasing the doctor–child distance? Any such gains must evidently be understood within the participant role structure of the social multi-party matrix of pediatric encounters. The social distance between doctor and child seems to be of immediate concern to the parent in a conflict situation. First, doctor–child alliances threaten the parent–child relationship in cases where the parent and the child hold opposing interests. Second, any potential challenge of parental authority on the child's part can probably be more easily bracketed if the child is cast as careless or unreliable. In a social situation such as the pediatric one where one participant (the parent) is in control of another one (the child), it is necessary to analyse the social distances of both doctor–parent and doctor–child alliances if we are to understand the inner dynamics of ongoing facework. As can be inferred from Extract 3.6, the parent may try to soften her delivery of criticisms through laughing. The doctor continued within a joking mode, mitigating the mother's critique through re-establishing an alliance with Valentin, turning to him in a somewhat playful way 'Well, Valentin, how do things go!' Immediately, it can then be seen how the parent directs the doctor away from the child in that she appropriates his response turn, recasting the child as a third person, 'Yeah, <u>we</u> thought so'.

The parent's restructuring of the participant role structure (increasing doctor–child distance, and recasting the child as a side-participant) can be seen as a type of self-oriented facework on the parent's part, who may wish to align with the doctor, thus increasing her positive face (which may partly be accomplished by distancing Valentin from the doctor). Recently, some researchers (Coupland, Grainger and Coupland, 1988; Craig, Tracy and Spisak, 1986; Penman, 1990) have criticized the Brown and Levinson model for neglecting self-oriented facework. One argument for greater focus on self-oriented facework is that there is a certain interdependence between self-oriented and other-oriented facework. For instance, self-oriented facework may at times save co-participants the need for the other-oriented type. In the present case, the mother's regulation of the participant role structure apparently entailed such two-level facework (both on the mother's self-oriented level, and on the doctor's other-oriented level). In controlling Valentin's contributions, she may have avoided open conflicts that would have required complex facework on the part of the doctor as well.

Doctor–parent negotiations and family alliances

In the case of Valentin there was an underlying tension between protectiveness and permissiveness. The doctor, as well as the boy himself, would have preferred more physical exercise in the child's life (more football in particular). The mother was against medication, though, which means that she was also sceptical about physical exercise in that more exercise would have entailed medication and, more specifically, more preventive medicine of a cortisone type. In the following extracts (Extracts 3.7–3.13) I will try to demonstrate how conflicts can be traced in routine-type discourse about physical exercise and medication, and how the multi-party structure can be exploited for displaying different alliances (doctor–parent, parent–child, doctor–child).

In an opening series of questions on sports, the doctor tried to discover whether Valentin participated in any sports (Extract 3.7).

> *Extract 3.7 The doctor's questioning about physical exercise*
> 315 Dr: Does Valentin participate in any sports except at school?

Mother: No.

Dr: Nothing at all?
Mother: No.

Dr: You live where there's perhaps nothing nearby
Mother: Well, there's a football- (.) field only a few hundred metres away

Dr: Yeah.
322 Mother: And he's crazy about that but he (.) doesn't quite measure up to it (I think) and then it-

Somewhat reluctantly, the mother revealed that there was indeed a football field a few hundred metres away (line 320). The doctor then went on to propose that they should perhaps almost overmedicate the child so that he could participate in sports (Extract 3.8).

Extract 3.8 Parent-child alliance on football? (parent talking through child)
324 Dr: Well, one could perhaps, the question is perhaps - whether one shouldn't for a while, if one should'n. (.) perhaps almost overmedicate him so that he is able to participate
Mother: WELL, THERE YOU ARE! /to Valentin/

Dr: I mean it - it's completely obvious that er, we- we cannot accept that he should not participate in football and (xx)
Mother: He sure is crazy about sports

Dr: Yes.
329 Mother: All sports.

On a superficial level, the mother seemed to go along with the doctor's advice. Yet, she did not agree with the doctor directly. Instead, she talked to her son as if matters had been settled (325 - Well, there you are!). Thereby, she indirectly told the doctor that she had agreed to his prescriptions on medication and physical exercise. Probably, it was the doctor who was the target addressee (see Levinson, 1988). She thus talked to the doctor through the child. The child was but an intermediary addressee. In this manner, she came off as the child's ally and as someone who was in favour of football. Yet, she had not said as much. Quite soon she also revealed that the matter was not completely closed (Extract 3.9).

Extract 3.9 Doctor, parent and anticipated other parties (here, football coaches)

333 Dr: But he - can run for a while before he gets the asthma attack?
Mother: A while, yeah
Child: (x)
Mother: But it's what the football coaches think because it's such 'ard training

Dr: Oh yes, the training
Mother: Because they only let in the best and that's it
Dr: Well of course - it's a dilemma er: the coaches can think what they like, er: he's still only ten and er it's not a case of any elite sport is it? (and that is x)
Mother: No (pause) but usually they they almost sort of are

Dr: Yes, which clubs have you got where you live?
Mother: Well, there's Lunden Sports Club

Dr: Well, it's important that they understand that it's still a social activity for the kids (xx)
344 Mother: Mm:

As can be seen, the mother revealed some misgivings about the football coaches and the training. She apparently felt that the doctor was talking about a world of ideals rather than the world as lived (340 'No (pause) but usually they almost sort of are'). Yet, she did not really voice her opposition. Her final minimal response 'mm' can be read as a sign of silent opposition, though, and later on her post-consultation interview confirmed this reading (as will be shown in Extract 3.14 below). The doctor did not openly address the mother's concern. His last turn can be read as an indirect criticism though (if 'they' is substituted with 'you' . . .). Medication was also a sensitive issue. Again, the mother would often respond in a series of minimal and ambiguous responses (Extract 3.10).

Extract 3.10 Doctor-parent alliance on medication?
345 Dr: But what I think you should do during the period when he's troubled like this
Mother: Mm:

Dr: And while he has got his asthma then what would happen is that he gets cortisone-er-spray to use, right?
Mother: Mm:

Dr: What he should do then is to use the Ventoline spray first.
Mother: Yeah

Dr: He uses it when he needs it, right?
Mother: Mm:

Dr:	He uses the Lomudal spray in the morning and in the evening and he also gets Becotide which is a cortisone spray to clear the bronchial tubes and reduce the swelling, so we can see (pause) if this helps at all.
Mother:	Mm:
Dr:	As he's so (x) now, right
Mother:	Mm.: mm
Dr:	So I think it could be worth giving him a prescription for that as well.
Mother:	I'm glad to hear that it's gonna do some good as well/laughs/this time.
Dr:	Of course.
360 Mother:	There's been such a fuss about it when we've tried to supplement it in another way but it's rather 'ard

Ultimately, the mother seemed to give her consent to medication. 'I'm glad to hear that it's gonna do some good as well'. In this reply, she had possibly incorporated Valentin's voice and his protest against protectiveness, his 'fuss about it'. The multi-voicedness or multi-perspectivity of the pediatric situation probably also provided part of the explanation of her misconstruals of the consultation. The mother did not register that the doctor was in fact talking about cortisone (see above). Second, she misconstrued his prescriptions. (Extract 3.11).

Extract 3.11 Miscommunication and the doctor's repair work
363 Dr:	Twice a day.
Mother:	Oh yeah, should 'e take it every day all the time or sort of only when 'e' going to something like that?
Dr:	NO:, no, no no! It's not a preventive medicine in that way, but
366 Mother:	Naa?

At this point, the doctor realized that he had perhaps been somewhat vague or unclear in his relatively indirect recommendations (see Extract 3.10, for 'could', 'perhaps' and other negative politeness substrategies). He then clarified his directive in a bald on record way, but softened by an exaggerated playful delivery 'NO:, no, no no!' In the whole sequence on medication (see Extracts 3.10 and 3.11), the mother was probably quite torn between different loyalties in that she had to take into account her alliance with Valentin, on the one hand, and her own opposing interests on the other. Moreover, she had to maintain some type of working alliance with the doctor (even though she did not fully accept or understand his reasoning).

An inspection of sequences that concern football reveals a typical pattern of uncommitted 'mm' replies from the mother. This pattern can also be seen in the concluding sequence (Extract 3.12).

Extract 3.12 Football and the doctor-child alliance

389 Dr: Well, then you can get in touch with the football team, and we'll see how things go/to the child/the important matter is <u>also</u>/to mother/
Mother: /laughs/<u>yes</u>

Dr: What is important that is that he should also warm up before playing football, <u>properly</u> (xx)
Mother: <u>Mm mm</u>
Child: (x)

Dr: He must not just inhale his sprays and get going.
Mother: No: no:

Dr: Instead he should take his sprays and then he could start warming up and he will have to do a warming up programme of his own before the others.
Mother: <u>Mm;, yes</u>

Dr: And <u>I</u> would like to say, one does not need to play outside right, one can play full back, and, possibly even be a <u>goalkeeper, right</u>

Child: <u>Mm</u>: /with enthusiasm/
400 Mother: /laughs/There you are then

The mother's minimal responses are open ended in that they can only be resolved through further dialogical work. In this specific sequence, she ultimately seemed to produce an implicit consent. 'There you are then', which was simultaneously a ratification of her son's enthusiastic 'Mm:'. From an outsider perspective it could be thought that the doctor had indeed influenced her views on football in that she, finally, appeared to go along with the doctor's advice. Yet she did not directly tell the doctor that she would indeed get in touch with the football club or encourage her son to do so. Instead, she could again be seen to talk to the doctor through the child as it were. She had not committed herself directly. Yet she seemed to agree on the desired course of action (football and medication). Interpreted as a multi-party strategy, her contribution was clever in that she came out as constructive (and helpful) without really committing herself. Also, her response probably appeared as less evasive (and thus less offensive) than alternative avoidance type strategies (hints, no action, etc.).

Second, her implicit consent 'There you are, then!' can be interpreted as a way of restoring the parent–child alliance which had probably been somewhat threatened during the preceeding discussion. She was well aware that her son wished to play football, and that a strong doctor–child alliance would threaten her parental authority. Apparently, she felt that she might lose solidarity with her son if she protested openly or too rigidly. Her implicit 'consent' appeared in the closing phase of the consultation, and it probably contributed to a relatively pleasant parting. In this context, the doctor chose to address Valentin in a joking format, offering him a piece of final advice (Extract 3.13).

> Extract 3.13 The doctor's farewell to the child (joking mode)
> 405 Dr: So keep going! Harder, harder!/to Valentin/
> Mother: Well, well. Okay. Let's say so
>
> Dr: Bye, then
> 408 Mother: Well, thank you very much.

Symptomatically, it was the mother and not her son, who responded to the doctor's playful directive (line 405 'so keep going! harder, harder!') Valentin left without saying goodbye (he may have nodded, but this was, of course, not registered in our audio-tapes). Yet his low key goodbye did, of course, fit in with his somewhat restricted participant status. In contrast (in the present corpus of thirty-two consultations), the children with low-control parents in most cases took part verbally in the closing phase of 'goodbyes'.[2]

Vagueness and voices of the future

Multi-voicedness generally refers to past voices that are incorporated into ongoing discourse (see Wertsch, 1991). In a pediatric consultation, medical recommendations may reach far into family life. Decisions about pet-keeping, food regimens, etc. often concern several family members, and one person may not feel able to make far reaching decisions on his or her own without consulting the other family members. At least, the family representative probably feels accountable to the others. In this particular case, this accountability may also be one of the determinants of the mother's uncommitted minimal responses. In the ongoing pediatric dialogues, it could hence be deduced that the mother might have been quite influenced by anticipated dialogues, that is by voices of the future, by what different persons would say about it. More particularly, in the present case, there were specific other voices who were also important in the present case, in deciding on Valentin's future activities, notably her husband, the football coaches and, of course, Valentin himself.

The present consultation should be understood against a background of discontent. During the medical interview, the mother was quite guarded and uncommitted in her responses to the doctor's recommendations about more physical exercise (football) in combination with more heavy medication. Yet she did not voice her discontent, which can, of course, partly be explained in terms of the power asymmetry. In the post-consultation interview she did reveal her misgivings more directly when talking to a non-authority person (Extract 3.14).

> Extract 3.14 Parental reflections on the doctor's football recommendations (post-consultation interview with mother)
> Mother: Oh well: I know that–(pause) but I thought it was stupid when he said he/Valentin/was going to the football ground, I thought that was stupid in some way, you know (pause)

Moreover, she listed several reasons why the doctor's recommendations about football were 'stupid'; the coaches would be busy with other matters, new coaches would not be informed about Valentin's asthma, some coaches employed teenaged co-coaches (who would not feel responsibility), no one would really notice if Valentin became overworked. In all, she was quite convinced that football was not a realistic alternative for Valentin. Most importantly, she felt that it was not likely that the coaches would genuinely accept her advice (about not overtaxing Valentin, about reacting to early signs of exhaustion, etc.). She did not feel that they would really listen to her. This means that part of her opposition may have resided in misgivings about future social negotiations (talk with the coaches).

Moreover, she was also accountable to Valentin. In her discussion with the doctor, she repeatedly returned to the fact that 'he loves it' when talking about football and sports. It apparently worried her that she was not able to comply with Valentin's wishes. After the consultation she had been discussing matters with her husband, and evidently he had not taken a strong stand in either direction (mother's protectiveness or doctor's permissiveness). Yet, in collaboration with her husband, she had thought of a solution that might satisfy the opposing interests (Extract 3.15).

> *Extract 3.15 Husband as ally* (post-consultation interview)
> Mother: and I said to Tore/husband/then, if we shouldn't take 'im down to the football ground, an 'e could go five or six times, and that perhaps 'e'd realise that it wouldn't work, then it ain't only me (pause) we've both said no, right. Then maybe it's (pause) then 'e'll really get the idea that 'this can't (pause) I can't do it', then it's not like we're are stopping 'im (pause) or forbidding it, right. If it were obvious like, I thought. But we ain't done nothing yet, because it's all been such a mess 'ere and we've been poorly an' all (pause), we've not been able to talk about it.

During the consultation talk, the mother had been on her own, as it were. After the consultation, she had talked again with her husband, a woman friend, and with Valentin, and she evidently planned to see the football coaches. The woman friend, who was known to be against medication, had warned her about cortisone. Valentin's mother reported that she had told her friend that the new medicine probably did not contain cortisone but that she would call the doctor to check before administering the new medicine to Valentin (yet, it can be seen in Extract 3.10 that the doctor talked about cortisone twice). All these persons seem to have formed different potential alliances for or against medication, for or against football and an active boyhood lifestyle. The core conflict was an old one, and the different voices for or against permissiveness had blended in different contexts and for different purposes.

This also meant that the mother was not completely on her own during the consultation talk. Analytically, it could be said that she also voiced her ideas about what would come out of anticipated future dialogues (and more particularly), talk with the coaches and her husband. This would place future multi-perspective accounts within the context of ongoing dialogues. In this broader sense, interactional embeddedness would also include future-oriented projections.

In this ongoing conflict between permissiveness (doctor, child) versus protectiveness (mother), the mother evidently felt that she had been challenged in her parental authority. Yet she managed to stay in control. At least, this is the way Valentin, her son, had experienced the consultation talk (Extract 3.16).

> *Extract 3.16 Valentin's reflections on football and the doctor-parent alliance* (post-consultation interview with Valentin)
> Int: Was there anything that you wondered about?

V: Naa, I just wondered a bit about the football.

Int: Yes. Did you talk enough about the football? With the doctor do you think?
V: Naa, I couldn't *I* didn't find out that much.

Int: Well, why not, do you think?
V: Well Mum kn(ows), I don't know if Mum wants me to go there 'cause of (pause)

Int: Mm: but Mum did talk to the doctor about football?
V: Yeah.

Int: Do you remember that?
V: Mm:

Evidently, Valentin did not feel that he had been able to talk to the doctor about football. Also, he perhaps wished to say that it did not really matter what was said as long as Mum does not really 'want' him to play. Dialogue is not really possible if one powerful side-participant (parent) has already determined what can be said or not said.

Face threats and third parties

Much facework in the present pediatric case can be traced to two-party control and to underlying power structures along Brown and Levinson (1987) type predictions. For instance, there are more examples of directness when the two adults confront the child than when they criticize each other (Table 3.2). As can be seen, bald on record communication is typically reserved for adult to child talk. The doctor at times softened his delivery through a joking (positive politeness) mode, though. In other pediatric cases, we have demonstrated how parents, in contrast, at times overstate the doctor's directives to the child; in the parental reformulations doctor's 'no' can be transformed into 'No, that's silly' etc. (Aronsson and Rundström, 1989). This is in line with Brown and Levinson's recent statement about family life as rich in aggravations (rather than politeness moves).

In the case of Valentin, some aggravations can be interpreted in terms of multi-party versus two-party social contexts. That is, the degree or size of a face threat can be linked to the participant role structure. The 'same' face threat may take on quite different values if produced in a two-party dialogue or in a multi-party context. This can, for instance, be deduced by the fact that the child (Valentin) did not voice his opposition (to his mother's protectiveness) during the consultation talk. He had voiced it

Table 3.2 Type of authority, facework strategies and directness in a pediatric case

Locus of threat	Multi-party strategies (capitals) and traditional Brown and Levinson facework strategies	Brown and Levinson predictions	
		Danger to face	Clarity
		Least	Most
Child's autonomy	P → C: bald on record critique (3.1) Dr → C: BRACKETING DR-CHILD ALLIANCE Joking directive (positive politeness, 3.12, 3.13)	↑	↑
Parental authority	Dr → P: playfully exaggerated correction (positive politeness, 3.11) Dr → P: indirect critique (negative politeness, 3.8, 3.9) Dr → P: THIRD PARTY OFF THE RECORD DIRECTIVES ('TALKING TO THE PARENT THROUGH THE CHILD') (3.13)		
Doctor's authority	P → Dr: indirect protest (negative politeness, 3.9) protest (3.9) P → Dr: THIRD PARTY OFF RECORD PROTEST ('TALKING TO THE DOCTOR THROUGH THE CHILD', 3.8, 3.12)	↓ Most	↓ Least

Note P = parent, C = child. Numbers refer to extracts. 'Off the record' is taken in the broad sense of the present text.

many times before (in dialogues with his mother), to which she gave witness when referring to all the 'fuss' he had made about sports and football. Similarly, he voiced some indirect opposition in the post-consultation interview (Extract 3.16). Yet, he remained silent during the consultation as such (a 'no action' strategy in the Brown and Levinson terminology). His behaviour illustrates the difference between saying something in a dialogue and saying the 'same' thing within an institutional setting in the presence of a powerful authority. Obviously, his nagging or 'fuss' could be seen as an innocuous type of critique

Table 3.3 Face threats in two-party and multi-party contexts

Two-party versus multi-party context		Proposition	Potential face threat for parent (M)	
C →M;	two-party dialogue	'I should play football'	Innocuous nagging	Least
C →M;	pediatric multi-party setting	'I should play football'	Intrusion into parental authority	
C →M;	pediatric multi-party setting when there are conflicting alliances	'I should play football'	Challenge of parental authority. Aggravated challenge	Most
Dr →M;	two-party dialogue	'I should play football'	Intrusion into parental authority	Least
Dr →M;	pediatric setting, in the presence of C	'I should play football'	Challenge of parental authority	
Dr →M;	pediatric setting, in the presence of C when there are conflicting alliances	'I should play football'	Aggravated challenge	Most

Note C = child, M = mother.

within the home setting, but would take on other connotations in the presence of a third-party authority person (Table 3.3). If the boy had criticized his mother in the present consultation, this criticism would have been particularly face-threatening in that he would have sided with the doctor, that is the opposing party (pro-permissiveness), rather than with his mother. It can thus be seen how the different contextualizations (two-party versus multi-party contexts) entail different sets of social roles and potential alliances.

Interactional embeddedness and multi-party talk

The child's participant status can become visible in two related ways. First – and most obviously – the parent may filter the child's talk in various ways, ratifying, repairing, reframing or elaborating on what is said. In so doing, he or she indicates that it is ultimately the parent who may legitimize family talk. In this manner, child talk is bracketed, in that it only counts if embedded in parental discourse. In high-control families where the child's talk is generally more or less embedded in adult completions, corrections, validations, etc., child talk is thus set apart. On a meta-level, a high relative frequency of parental embeddings can be said to signal that the child's contributions do not really count (or phrased differently, it is the doctor–*parent* alliance, and not the doctor–child alliance that counts). This latter reading is particularly relevant in the case of parent–child conflicts, as in the present case. Second, the child himself may become invisible in that the parent regulates his participant status into that of a non-person, which means that the child as a person is bracketed. He, himself, is set apart and not only what he says (Table 3.4). Both types of bracketing can be discussed as a type of large-scale alter-casting where child talk or where the child himself is cast as off record. That is, many of the child's contributions will be treated as off record contributions, and the two adult parties may strategically choose when to understand or when not to understand what is said.

Marková (1989) has discussed how language is *incomplete*. First, language evolves and changes in the course of social history and changing human practices and perspectives. Second, language is dependent on its social and linguistic contexts. In the present case study consultation talk is incomplete in two different, but related, ways. On the one hand, consultation talk is embedded in other dialogues, including future dialogues not yet lived. This more global embeddedness can be linked to language as such, as a linguistic system viable to diachronic change (Wertsch, 1991). In a more local sense, language is incomplete in that it can only exist in ongoing discourse between different participants with different perspectives, which means that language is basically indeterminate.

Table 3.4 Parental control in multi-party talk

Type of negotiation	Parental control moves	Excerpt or table in the present text
Negotiation of meaning	*Topic control*: Repair work (corrections) Reframings Elaborations Ratifications	Extract 3.1 Extract 3.1 Extract 3.2 Extract 3.4, 3.5
Negotiation of personhood/ non-personhood	*Regulation of child's participant status*: Quantitative control Recasts C as third person Talks to the doctor through the child Discredits the child as a competent participant	Table 3.1 Extracts 3.1, 3.2, 3.3 (3.4, 3.5) Extract 3.8, 3.12 Extract 3.6

Vagueness and other imperfections can be temporarily disambiguated, but one problem resolved will but give way to new vague or fussy exchanges. Ambiguity is partly built into the human condition, if we accept a dialogical conception of cognition and communication (Rommetveit, 1989; forthcoming; Rorty, 1979).

Such ambiguity in language is very evident in pediatric discourse with conflicting alliances. This can be seen, first, in the way in which 'same' face threats take on quite different meanings if produced in a two-party dialogue or in a multi-party context. Second, the influential facework model of Brown and Levinson (1978; 1987) can be applied to such multi-party discourse, but probably only if we interpret off record strategies in an extended sense, covering different types of adult bracketings of third-party (child) contributions. The most prototypical off record strategy is the substrategy of ambiguity. In pediatric asymmetrical discourse, the role of the weaker party (the child) is ambiguous in that he or she can be exploited for different facework strategies. At times, the child is addressed directly and without any underlying other-oriented messages. At other times, he or she is alter-casted as a side-participant or non-participant by the parent, or is exploited as the doctor's medium for conveying potentially face-threatening information to the parent in a clear, yet non-direct way. The child's participant status is hence ambiguous in that, at times, he or she is treated as a person and at other times as a non-person. Negotiations in multi-party talk do not only concern meanings but, directly or indirectly, also concern *personhood/non-personhood*. The role status of the child is, thus, often open to negotiation, and language will take on different meanings depending on whether the child is seen as a participant or non-participant.

Notes

1. This study was financed by a grant awarded to Karin Aronsson and Per Linell by the bank of Sweden Tercentenary Foundation (RJ 83/137). The project as a whole is concerned with discourse and control in institutional settings. Bengt Rundström worked as a research assistant with the pediatric consultations. Thanks are extended to the participating families and to the doctors and staff at the hospital clinic for their generous assistance in this study.
2. Children with low-control parents would say goodbye ('bye', 'thank you', etc.) in about two-thirds of all cases, whereas the high-control group children would only participate in the parting sequence in a third of all cases. The parting sequence could be heard in twenty out of the thirty-two consultations. In the other twelve cases, the child was sent off with a nurse for further tests, etc., which meant that he or she could not participate for reasons that had to do with administrative routines rather than with factors pertaining to the interaction order.

References

Aronsson, K. and Rundström, B. (1988), 'Child discourse and parental control in pediatric consultations', *Text*, **8**, 159–89.
Aronsson, K. and Rundström, B. (1989), 'Cats, dogs, and sweets in the clinical negotiation of reality: on politeness and coherence in pediatric discourse', *Language in Society*, **18**, 483–504.
Aronsson, K. and Sätterlund-Larsson, U. (1987), 'Politeness strategies and doctor–patient communication: on the social choreography of collaborative thinking', *Journal of Language and Social Psychology*, **6**, 1–27.
Brown, P. and Levinson, S. (1978), 'Universals in language usage: politeness phenomena', in E. Goody (ed.), *Questions and Politeness: Strategies in social interaction*, Cambridge University Press: Cambridge.
Brown, P. and Levinson, S. (1987), *Politeness: Some universals in language usage*, Cambridge University Press: Cambridge.
Coupland, N. Grainger, K. and Coupland, J. (1988), 'Politeness in context: intergenerational issues', *Language in Society*, **17**, 253–62.

Craig, R. T., Tracy, K. and Spisak, F. (1986), 'The discourse of requests: assessment of a politeness approach', *Human Communication Research*, **12**, 437-68.

Goffman, E. (1983), 'Felicity's condition', *American Journal of Sociology*, **89**, 1-53.

Levinson, S. C. (1988), 'Putting linguistics on a proper footing: explorations in Goffman's concepts of participation', in P. Drew and A. Wootton (eds), *Erving Goffman: Exploring the interaction order*, Polity Press: Oxford.

Linell, P. (1990), 'The power of dialogue dynamics', in I. Marková and K. Foppa (eds), *The Dynamics of Dialogue*, Harvester Wheatsheaf: Hemel Hempstead.

Marková, I. (1989), 'Incompleteness of speech and coping with emotions in therapist-patient dialogues', *Studies in Communication 28*, University of Linköping Studies in Communication.

Penman, R. (1990), 'Facework and politeness: multiple goals in courtroom discourse', *Journal of Language and Social Psychology*, **9**, 15-38.

Rommetveit, R. (1985), 'Language acquisition as increasing linguistic structuring of experience and symbolic behavior/control', in J. V. Wertsch (ed), *Culture, Communication and Cognition: Vygotskian perspectives*, Cambridge University Press: Cambridge.

Rommetveit, R. (1989), 'Psycholinguistics, hermeneutics and cognitive science', in J. Björgen (ed.), *Basic Issues in Psychology: A Scandinavian contribution*, Sigma: London.

Rommetveit, R. (forthcoming), 'Outlines of a dialogically based social-cognitive approach to human cognition and communication', in A. Heen Wold (ed.), *Festschrift for Ragnar Rommetveit*.

Rorty, R. (1979), *Philosophy and the Mirror of Nature*. Princeton University Press: Princeton, NJ.

Schenkein, J. (ed.), (1978), *Studies in the Organization of Conversational Interaction*, Academic Press: New York.

Wertsch, J. V. (1991), *Voices of the Mind*: Harvester Wheatsheaf: Hemel Hempstead, and Harvard University Press: Boston, MA.

4 | Suspect stories: perspective-setting in an asymmetrical situation[1]

Per Linell and Linda Jönsson

Human cognition and communication are always perspectivized and contextualized (Rommetveit, forthcoming); topics are always treated under some specific aspects. At the same time, communication is often understood as establishing common ground (Clark and Schaefer, 1989) or as achieving shared understanding of things talked about. Yet in many situations of real life, the mutuality of perspectives is only partial or superficial, and actors entertain different visions and versions of their world (Goodman, 1978). Our data from authentic interrogations will illustrate some cases in point.

We will discuss our data in terms of *perspectives* in discourse. The notion of perspective has been applied to human cognition and communication in many scholarly traditions, e.g. Husserl's phenomenology, Mead's social psychology and narrative theory (for an excellent overview, see Graumann, 1989). Basically, we conceive of a perspective as an orientation adopted by one of the dialogue participants or by both (all) of them jointly; it is typically partly implicit and involves starting from some abstract vantage point, building upon (usually taken for granted) background knowledge and developing the discourse topics in a certain direction, e.g. focusing on some aspects of things talked about, and trying to get certain points communicated and possibly also accepted. Though culturally infiltrated, perspectives are dependent on goals and purposes, concerns and commitments that actors entertain, whether consciously or not.

Perspectivization in dialogue and discourse involves both perspective-setting and perspective-taking (Graumann, 1989; 1990). Yet, in the literature, this process has often been discussed primarily in terms of actors' mutual taking of each other's perspectives; one often seems to presuppose some situation in which actors have more or less equal opportunities, abilities and willingness to take each other's perspectives. Furthermore, empirical studies of perspectives have been mostly studied in the contexts of experiments on comprehension and memory of texts (Graumann, 1989), and more on perspective-taking (as opposed to setting). By contrast, we will, in this study, attempt to look at perspective-setting (and taking) in authentic, i.e. non-experimental, discourse. We are dealing with an *asymmetrical* situation in which the parties arguably have quite different opportunities to set perspectives and varying obligations and abilities to take the other party's perspective. Furthermore, we might expect the perspectives surfacing in a police interrogation to be rooted in rather different worlds, namely, the everyday-life world of the suspect, on the one hand, and the legal, professional or semi-professional,[2] framework of the police, on the other.

The policeman's interview of the suspect is designed to shed light on some supposedly or possibly criminal acts in which the suspect has allegedly taken part; the suspect is supposed to account for this, preferably to 'tell his story'. However, since the whole situation is dialogical, and the institutionalized task of the police is to produce a judicially relevant report, the stage is set for a potential clash between attempts to organize the substance of the story in different ways. In our analysis of this dynamic situation, we will draw upon theories of oral storytelling. Narration will be seen as a communicative event; stories must be studied as told and apprehended in the particular context in which they are told (Goodwin, 1982). Furthermore, we will assume that the *same story* (sequence of events) can be told in different ways, yielding *different narratives*, which organize the substance of the story so as to focus on different points and thus regard different aspects as important and relevant. In our analysis, perspectives will be identified not so much in the structure of micro-units such as individual sentences (Rommetveit, this volume, Chapter 10), but rather in the global patterns of narrative macro-structure, e.g. in the allocation of space to different aspects of contents. These, partially different, narratives can be said to voice different kinds of background knowledge and different interests and concerns.

Stories, and more generally discourses, are indeed often analysed in terms of the *voices* entering them. However, the recent, somewhat excessive use of the term 'voice' has pointed to several different (metaphorical) exploitations of its meaning potential. Apart from the various uses in grammar and narratology, Silverman and Torode (1980) have applied the term 'voice' to the philosophies and theories of scholars as different as Husserl, Wittgenstein, Sacks and Bernstein. Bakhtin (1986; see also Wertsch, 1991), with whom the term has recently been coupled, demonstrates how the same speaker (and listener) may assume, or move between, several identities in producing (and interpreting) discourse. In a somewhat different vein, Mishler (1984) (who builds upon Silverman and Torode) has analysed doctor–patient encounters in terms of two voices, those of the everyday-life world and the medical profession. In relation to Bakhtin's 'voices', these would be generalized voices articulating perspectives and concerns that are prototypical of different traditions of thought and discourse in modern society. Characteristic of the voice of the life world would be the grounding of one's problems, such as those of ill health or economic problems, in a wider range of life circumstances and socio-economic or psycho-social conditions than is usually referred to in various professionals' attempts at coming to grips with their patients' and clients' problems, these attempts then often being subject to specialized relevance criteria. The two speaking subjects, in our case the police officer and the suspect, tend to express attitudes and identities which are socially and culturally constituted, thus transcending the speakers as individuals. The Mishlerian notion of voice is therefore more or less equivalent to a prototypical *perspective*, or point of view, of a person who occupies a certain position, or role, in a given activity type, such as the police interrogation. We therefore prefer to speak about perspectives voiced (set) and adopted (taken) by the police and the suspects. Note, incidentally, that Silverman and Torode trace 'voice' back to the 'perspective' of Husserl's phenomenology (see also Graumann, 1989).[3] Since perspectives are different modes of speaking about approximately the same subject matters, we also come close to Wertsch's (1991) notion of *social language*.

Stories told by delinquents in trials, probation interviews, police interrogations and other legal settings have received some, but still relatively little, attention in earlier discourse studies. A classical study is Cicourel (1968), which follows the construction of legal cases through the various stages (see also Soeffner, 1984, on German data). Cicourel could not, however, tape-record all the encounters involved and therefore was not able to micro-study the relation of dialogue to report. This, on the other hand, has been done by Spencer (1984; 1988) on probation interviews, and, to some extent, by Caesar-Wolf (1984) on judges' summaries of witness testimonies in a civic court trial.

Some aspects of story-telling, including the authorization of accounts, in police interrogations (in murder cases) have been touched upon by Watson (forthcoming). Stories told in everyday life as well as in institutional settings typically involve *accounts*, i.e. 'statements made to explain untoward behavior and bridge the gap between actions and expectations' (Scott and Lyman, 1968, p. 46). Accounts are either justifications, in which the speaker accepts responsibility for the act in question, but tries to argue that it was the right thing to do, or excuses, in which the person admits that the act in question was bad, wrong or inappropriate, but provides mitigating circumstances, thus denying full responsibility. This dichotomy (from Scott and Lyman) has been developed by, among others, Schonbach (1980) and Cody and McLaughlin (1988). As regards stories and arguments typically brought up by delinquents, and their defence attorneys, probation officers and others, we find empirical studies by, e.g. Spencer (1984), Cody and McLaughlin (1988) (justifications, excuses, etc., in court) and O'Barr and Conley (1985) (litigants' stories in small claims courts). Caesar-Wolf (1984), in her study of accounts in a West German civil court hearing, has noted that witnesses sometimes 'organize their testimonies around factors different from those which are judicially relevant in the context of a lawsuit' (p. 207). Likewise, in their paper on Swedish courtroom interaction, Adelswärd *et al.* (1988) have identified some features of defendants' framing of the criminal court trial and their construction of legal meaning.

The data

Our data comprise thirty police interrogations with persons suspected of having committed some minor economic offence such as fraud, larceny and shop-lifting. The age span of the suspects was 16-73 years. Twenty-one were men, nine women. Seven police officers, all male, volunteered to participate. The interviewees' consent was also secured; no one declined. The interrogations took place in a small office with only the police inspector and the suspect present. The interactional style of these 'mild' interrogations was quite informal and sometimes colloquial. In most cases, the interactions gave the impression of two parties cooperating on a joint task. In spite of this, there were clear differences in perspectives and understandings between police and suspects. The interrogations were tape-recorded, and after each interrogation the suspect was interviewed by one of the authors. The official police reports from the interrogations involved were provided by the police some time after the interrogations. (For a full description of the data corpus see Jönsson, 1988).

Police interrogations are highly institutionalized. Barring some minor variations, we could identify the following phase structure in the interrogations (optional phases within brackets):

Greetings
(Introductory small talk)
Identification/filling in a form with personal data
Presentation of the case/charge, etc.
Interrogation proper   (1. Preparatory interrogation)
                                        2. Report-oriented interrogation
                                        (3. Supplementary interrogation)
(Reading and approval of report)
(Concluding small talk)
Farewells

The central part of the whole encounter is the *interrogation proper*, in which the suspect is interviewed on the subject matter of the case, anything concerning the alleged offence or associated with it by at least one of the parties. In practice, this is brought up almost exclusively within one or several of the phases of the interrogation proper, and we will, in this paper, deal only with this (plus, to some extent, the written report).

The interrogation proper is typically organized in three subphases, two of which are not obligatory. The first phase is a preparatory interrogation, in which the suspect is typically asked to tell his or her own story and does so rather freely without too many interventions from the police officer. However, this phase sometimes does not materialize, either because the policeman starts asking specific questions right at the outset, or because the suspect is not able or willing to provide a coherent account of his or her own. (In our corpus, twenty out of thirty interrogations contained at least some lengthy, narrative turns by the suspect.) The obligatory report-oriented phase is the main activity in the whole encounter. The major objective of the policeman is to provide a written report, which is supposed to sum up the relevant and important aspects of the criminal actions and their background. Toward this end the policeman will ask a number of more or less specific questions, and produce the report as he goes along, recording (and perhaps rephrasing) some of the things said and omitting others. Some officers take notes with pen and paper, others record sentence by sentence on a tape-recorder.

In some cases the report-oriented phase is followed by a supplementary phase, where the policeman usually goes through what he has written down, or spoken on the tape, and asks for supplementary information and clarification here and there. The suspect can, of course, make corrections and additions too, although very few of our suspects made use of this opportunity.

The final report is then typed on a form consisting of two parts, one with very narrow slots where personal and administrative data are entered, and then a large space where a lengthy text can be written under the rubric of 'story' (Swedish *berättelse*). What is actually entered there is clearly a joint accomplishment by suspect and police officer. A quantitative measurement, in which the primary sources for the various pieces of information (each roughly corresponding to a sentence) in the report texts were traced (Jönsson, 1988), gave the following results: 36 per cent originated in suspects' lengthy narrative turns, 18 per cent were given by suspects as answers to open but specific (wh- word) questions from the police, 29 per cent were simply confirmations (yes/no answers to closed-ended questions) and, finally, 17 per cent were statements with no basis in the interrogation (usually taken from documents available to the police).

Police interrogations are part of a more comprehensive judicial process. Though this must be taken into account in the discussion, it is important to remember that this study is concerned only with discourse in police interrogations and police reports. As such, however, these seem to provide a nearly ideal locus for studying different perspectives in story-telling, since the 'same story' is usually told several times, i.e. in the preparatory interrogation, in the report-oriented interrogation, and then, in written form, in the report itself, and all this takes place in a process in which a good many contextual factors remain constant.

Opportunities for perspective-setting

If we think of the boundary conditions of a police interrogation of the kind investigated here, we might say that the suspect is supposed to provide information about actions he has been involved in, and that the police officer's responsibility is to sift through this information and to assign legal significance to some points and to leave other data aside. In the simplest case, one would then expect the suspect to contribute the story substance, while the policeman adds the perspective to the resulting narrative. In practice, this comes rather close to the truth in some cases, but there are clearly other possibilities, as we will soon see.

First of all, it is quite clear that the police perspective is always present, and usually quite dominant, in the written reports. On the other hand, when it comes to the dialogical interaction in the interrogation, things are more complicated. True enough, the interviewee enters the interaction labelled as a 'suspect', something which in itself logically presupposes the priority of the perspective of the legal system. Furthermore, we find a strong institutional dominance in the identification phase, which usually occurs right at the beginning of the encounter. Here the police officer goes through the first part of the preprinted form, entering information from the suspect into the appropriate slots. The form thus functions as an *external filter* on the oral exchange of information. The questions are systematically narrow and designed to evoke a yes/no answer (to be ticked off in the blank) or a specific piece of information (name, profession, income, etc.). In Extract 4.1 we see part of the identification phase of an interrogation, in which the suspect, a recidivist who denies guilt of shop-lifting, tries to supply unsolicited information rather systematically (cf. the fragments italicized):

Extract 4.1 [4]
(P = police officer, S = suspect)
(. . .)
P: Profession, title, what do you usually call yourself?
S: Well I ah – am listed as a brick-layer
P: I see
S: *It's a long time since I built, of course* (P:Yes) but . . .
P: Now, let's see, what shall we write as address of residence now?
S: Well, you see, *I am waiting for an apartment*, you see
P: Mm, but until then?
(. . .)
P: Nine years of ah primary school, right?
S: No, I only went seven, *my mum died in connection with that so I broke off*
P: Employment at the moment?
S: Well, *I ah had to get emergency public work now*

P: Mm, but earlier employments, where have you been working lately if we go back a few years?
S: Well, I worked with my ah sister's former boyfriend, with signboard work, Signs Limited (P: I see) *you know such things that hang over shops*
P: How long did you have that job?
S: Well, I had it for a rather long time, you know, it was – *it was seasonal work*, you know (P: Mm) *so he worked down in the Helsingborg this year when it was winter, half a year*. (.) Then ah I have . . . the last job I had now we can take (P: Mm) it was at Lights Limited with the Ekbergs (P: I see), *then I had both my hands in plaster, after an accident*
P: Mm, we can leave that, I will just write what you have said
S: Yes
P: Ah healthy and fit for work we usually write, you know. You have no illnesses?
S: Noo, I hope not . . . No, illnesses, *I have had a cold since last autumn* but ah ah (P: Mm) (p) well, *that counts as an illness*, I guess
P: Well, this is, they're referring to more serious illnesses

As shown by the italics, the suspect continuously sneaks in extra information, modifying categorical statements, mentioning relevant background explanations, etc., and hence we get some fragments of the suspect's biography. But the identification procedure is not designed for this purpose, and its questioning format does not allow the suspect to provide a coherent narrative. The fragments will not be assembled as a story; instead, the extra information provided is routinely ignored in the dialogue (no feedback is given), and it will not find its way into the report.

It is in the interrogation proper that the suspect is supposed to tell his story. But there is much variation in the data. In some cases, the police perspective takes precedence immediately and dominates completely in the interrogation; the policeman is interactionally quite dominant (Linell, 1990) by asking closed questions, suggesting formulations of answers and in general defining the conditions for answering very narrowly. Consider Extract 4.2, which shows the very beginning of the interrogation proper with a young woman suspect who has, knowingly, overdrawn her bank account (this being a crime in Sweden):

Extract 4.2
P: (---) this attempt, you admit it, you say?
S: (whispered) Yes
P: Ah (into tape-recorder) 'Mrs Nilsson admits (p) attempted fraud in this case. Full stop.' Alright, how did it happen, you went out there to Nystad to (p) get some money from that

account which you (p) knew that there was no cover for, huh? You were, was it perfectly clear to you?
S: Yes
P: Because that's what's decisive you see (S: yes) here. (p) And there were no (p) messengers or anything like that.
S: Mm.
P: Maybe you had a paper here. (puts on tape-recorder) (---) 'Ah she was made aware of the notification and the eh payment order from ah which was sent in from the post office. Full stop.' This is your signature which is written here?
S: Mm.
P: (speaks into tape-recorder) 'She eh indicates that she herself wrote the signature (p) on (p) this sheet and wrote the amount on it herself. Full stop. (p) She knew very well at the time that her account was eh overdrawn (p) Full stop. Eh she admits therefore (p) the offence. Full stop.' There isn't very much to say about that. Do you have anything to add about that?
S: No.

In cases like this there is no preparatory interrogation, and the police officer sets the perspective all the time, on an utterance-to-utterance basis, in almost every question and its answer. The police officer suggests what might have happened by asking closed questions, and the suspect just provides confirmatory responses; the police officer produces a report on-line by speaking into the tape recorder. In this case, and in other similar cases, the suspect never articulates a personal perspective. Yet, in the post-interview, this suspect did disclose another interest and perspective; she had wanted to talk about a wider set of circumstances surrounding the offence. This is quite typical of a majority of the interrogations in fraud cases; the police officer takes the written reports that have been given in to the police as his point of departure, and what then materializes is a series of quite specific questions, in which the only opportunities offered to the suspect are those of confirming or denying information already available. The existence of a structured file thus strongly determines the interview, something which seems quite typical of bureaucratic organizations.

The other extreme consists of cases in which two perspectives are indeed voiced. The suspect is both given and takes the chance of telling his or her own version of the story, and then the policeman takes the lead in a report-oriented interrogation. Of course, the report itself will be organized according to the police perspective; thus, the suspect perspective so clearly voiced in the dialogue is only sparsely represented there. It turned out that most of the suspects, who provided lengthy narratives of their own, belonged to the category of middle-aged first-time offenders accused of shop-lifting. It is on these cases that most of our attention will be focused.

The suspect voice and the police voice in dialogue: two perspectives in interaction

The preparatory and report-oriented phases are quite different in dialogue participation structure. In the former, the suspect typically contributes long monological turns, while the police officer sticks to back-channel items, minimal responses, some second assessments, etc., and asks a few specific questions which, if avoided by the suspect, are rarely followed up. In the report-oriented phase, the interaction format and the distribution of discourse space (amount of speech) are quite different. The police officer typically asks specific questions, which are often closed in format and organized coherently, serving specific goals, thus arguably subject to a consistent professional perspective. The suspect is then expected to give short answers. If he or she should indulge in expanded responses, these are sometimes interrupted or just not followed up if they should digress too far from the judicially relevant aspects of the subject matter. Hence, it seems safe to say that while the suspect tells his or her version of the story in the preparatory phase, in the report-oriented phase the whole thing is recycled with the police officer in strict control. The professionally perspectivized narrative then comes out still more unequivocally in the written report, although, in our data, the final reports are almost identical to what the police officer formulated in the later phases of the interrogation. Very little editing seems to be done afterwards.

To provide some illustration of the differences in dialogue form between phases, consider extracts 4.3 and 4.4 taken from an interrogation involving an elderly man accused of having taken some goods from a food store. Extract 4.3 is drawn from the beginning of the preparatory phase. The suspect has already told the police officer about his illnesses and how he gave himself the wrong kind of injection, and the police officer now comes to the 23rd of the month, the day of the shop-lifting.

Extract 4.3
P: OK, it happened .. it happened then on the 23rd, so it was . . .
S: And the consequence was that I woke up with this (P: Yes) and that I went down to the doctor in Forsby, because all along the edge of my jaw here, and my tooth hurt here, y'know (P: Yes),

and it swelled up, and they became agitated because I've had abnormal cells in my body (P: mm). And that day was okay (P: mm) anyway, but it hurt something terrible, and then I took a pain killer next morning, and then I took one at noon, 'cause it hurt so that (P: mm) I couldn't eat a berry cause it hurt, the whole gum down here (P: Yeah) it hurt like a tooth-ache (P: Yeah), so what happened was that I took a pain killer in the morning and then at lunch-time (P: Yeah), and then I went, then I drove to the doctor and then I got a referral to the hospital, and then it was maybe, yeah it was four or five days afterwards it got worse. So I came to the hospital and they went into the saliva gland here and they've taken four or five tests, and then they went in here y'know (suspect points to chin) (P: Yeah) and that got me into trouble so I wasn't a human being all that week (P: yeah, no, right) and I don't think it was such a good idea with that salubrine 'cause otherwise this wouldn't have happened. I hope that's got shot of it now and there are not any abnormal cells because they did it, they said, they did.
P: You injected something wrong of course, then it was clear that that could bring about of course . . .
S: (new monological turn)

In this phase the suspect is allowed to talk at length, and he remains firmly in his life-world perspective most of the time. The police officer accepts this temporarily, and he does not contribute any substance to the talk; apart from some abortive attempts at cutting off and getting to the legally relevant matters, his interventions are mainly politely supporting utterances. Then, in the report-oriented phase, the police officer starts to ask fairly specific questions on how the actual shop-lifting was carried out. Here, the suspect has comparatively little to contribute, often limiting himself to quite short answers. Extract 4.4 deals with what happened when the suspect was stopped after having passed the check out counter without having paid for some articles:

Extract 4.4
(From report-oriented phase)
P: (. . .) An' then it was then that they saw that, that is, that you had (S: Yes) the goods on you?
S: Yes exactly (inaudible)
P: She went up there then?
S: Yes, right into the office.
P: 'And then he picked out some articles that he had in his pockets', right? Is that correct?
S: Yes, that's correct.
P: He paid for these articles afterwards at the check out counter. Right? (S: Yes) And it was these articles that it was all about, in other words it was two packages of bacon, one package of

lard, one package of hot dogs, one package of lunch sausages, one smoked ham and a package of wheat flour.
S: But it, but it, but it was included, 'cause it doesn't matter, 'cause it..
P: Regarding the wheat flour it was a small bag
S: The wheat flour?
P: Yes, it must have been a small bag, right?
S: Yes, it was a two.. two, two kilo or what is there in those ...
(continued)

While the police officer is asking these specific questions, he is also making notes and suggesting formulations for the reports, which explains the statements in the third person ('he picked out', 'he paid', etc.). The suspect's answers are typically short and uncertain, almost as if he is trying to avoid the topic.

One story – two narratives

There are quantitative indications that preparatory and report-oriented phases are quite separate activities, differing in terms of, among other things, distribution of discourse space and initiative-response structure. However, to show that the discourses also exhibit different perspectives, it is necessary to show that they are different in terms of content. We shall analyse these discourses further to show that we are faced with two narrative versions of the same story.

Modern narrative theory (Toolan, 1988) makes a distinction between *story* and *narrative*, where 'story' stands for the sequence of events forming the substantial basis of what is told, and 'narrative'[5] refers to how (when, by whom) the story is told in a specific discourse situation; a narrative, then, would be a structured story. It is well-known that stories tend to be geared structurally to a certain overall pattern or schema. Labov and Waletzky (1967) have provided a model for (oral) narratives which we have reproduced and slightly modified in Figure 4.1. Simplifying matters a little (Figure 4.1, right-hand column), narratives have a Background, in which the teller introduces the actors and explains the circumstances that form the starting point for the complications to come. Then comes the Central Event (or Action) Sequence, a train of events leading to some critical incident, the climax, which is then somehow resolved, with a return to normal discourse. A third part, sometimes given at the end but sometimes inserted somewhere else or dispersed over the entire story, contains the Resulting Evaluation, which describes the teller's or protagonist's reactions or attitudes to

Perspective-setting in an asymmetrical situation   87

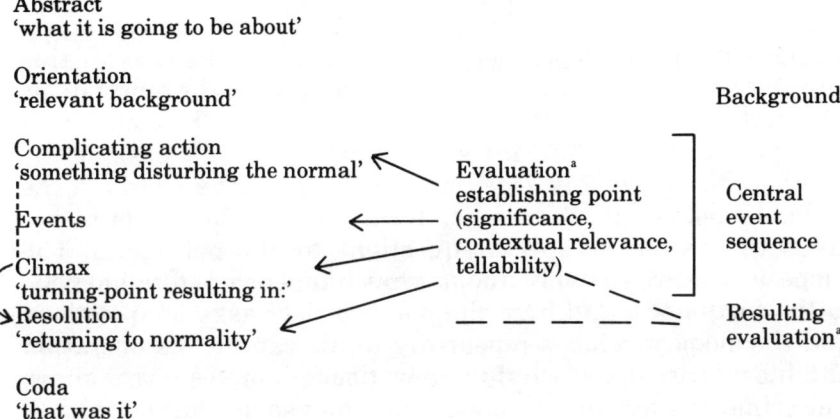

[a]May occur at several places in the narration, but is often not appreciated until later.

Figure 4.1. The structure of oral narratives (modified after Labov, 1972:ch IX)

what happened. This last part tries to establish the significance of the story told (or the point in telling it). At the same time, it provides an opportunity for explicating the return to normality.

Now, if we accept this account, we could imagine the same story given in different narratives, or, if you will, the same information structured, perspectivized and biased in divergent ways. For different tellers, or in different contexts, the same story would have, e.g. different climaxes and varying significances, and we might conjecture that these narratives would be different in terms of their respective perspectives. What parts of the story are displayed as important and relevant? What are the central, critical actions, what is the climax of the story, why is it told at all, what is the point, how is it to be evaluated? We will now subject suspects' stories to these questions.

In order to get a rough overview of the differences between the suspect's narrative, which the suspect tells orally, and the police narrative, the version most unambiguously given in the written report, we had a look at the discourse space allocated to three major topics, i.e. 1) background (including the suspect's biography); 2) technical aspects of the criminal acts; and 3) attitudes towards the offence expressed by the suspect. These would roughly correspond to the general categories of Background, Central Event Sequence, and Resulting Evaluation respectively (Figure 4.1). It turns out that these occupy very different portions of the two narratives. In Extract 4.3 more than 50 per cent of the suspect's version is devoted to his illness story, whereas the police report uses 18 per cent of the space for this topical domain. On the other hand, 38 per cent of the report deals with technical aspects of the crime – details about how packages were put in pockets, how the suspect behaved while passing the cashier, etc. while only 7 per cent of the suspect's words in the dialogue belong to this topic. Furthermore, these words are given in answers to specific questions by the policeman. The suspect talks extensively about what happened *before* he came to the food store, and here the police officer asks no questions and the suspect returns repeatedly to his cancer, his operation and his worries about what the new tissue samples might show. The crime as such, in his version, becomes somewhat peripheral and accidental, except that he expresses at length his repentance and contrition; 21 per cent of his words deal with the third major topic, attitudes to the offence, while the police officer devotes no less than 44 per cent to this. So when the suspect comes to the offence as such, thus approaching the police officer's perspective, the focal point centres on his exculpation, his explanations and excuses, not on how the shop-lifting was technically accomplished.

What is the point of the story as told by the suspect and the police? What are their narratives about? We have seen that, in allotting rather varying amounts of space to different aspects of the story, the two parties assign different degrees of significance to them. The suspect's own story is about complications he had had with his health, his mistake with the injection, the pain in his throat, the medication (taking pills to decrease the pain), all ending up in a state of confusion. All this is embedded in a more comprehensive illness history, where his worries about a new appearance of cancer are overwhelming. At the same time, of course, this provides the ground for excuses and 'explanations' of the shop-lifting incident. The latter event is, however, treated by the suspect as a minor side-effect of the above-mentioned unfortunate train of events, and the suspect has nothing to say about its technical details. He is, however, very much ashamed of having done what he did. For the police officer all this is backgrounded (except that he does include a substantial part about the suspect's attitudes in his report), while the aspects magnified and emphasized are the technical details. It appears that, although the story substance is much the same, there are different narratives with different perspectives, climaxes, resolutions and major points.

Table 4.1 Discourse and text space allotted to different topics in three shop-lifting interrogations (percentages of all words devoted to the subject matter, i.e. the crime and its related circumstances, cf. text)

	Dialogue		Report
	Suspect	Police	(Police)
Elderly woman (see Extract 4.7)			
Background	64	12	40
Technical aspects	9	9	43
Reactions and attitudes	6	0.0	17
	79 +	21 = 100	100
Depressed elderly widow (see Extract 4.6)			
Background	38	4	18
Technical aspects	18	35	77
Reactions and attitudes	5	0.0	5
	61 +	39 = 100	100
111 elderly man (see Extracts 4.3, 4.4, 4.5)			
Background	53	4	18
Technical aspects	7	9	38
Reactions and attitudes	21	6	44
	81 +	19 = 100	100
Totals			
Background	56	8	30
Technical aspects	10	13	48
Reactions and attitudes	11	2	22
	77 +	23 = 100	100

Note The percentages relate to the whole interrogations, not just the extracts quoted in the text.

This is far from an isolated case. As examples, we will briefly refer to a couple of partly similar stories (Table 4.1 gives some quantified data on the cases reviewed here).[6] One suspect is an elderly woman, a widow for three years, who tells a story about illness (stomach pains, suspicion of cancer), depression and loneliness: a life situation which, in her version, lies behind her petty thefts. She tells the police that she has not been able to sleep for some time, and she is anxious that her children should not get to know about her shop-lifting. Thus, she conveys the impression of someone who is out of balance and needs to restore her self-respect, which cannot be done unless the offences are cleared up. These aspects, treated at length in the suspect's narrative, are given three sentences in the police officer's report (these sentences primarily dealing with the question of intent). Again, the police officer assigns importance to rather different story components. He asks and reports about some down to earth technical matters of the shop-lifting. What did the suspect's bag look like? When exactly were the goods transferred from the foodstore carrier to her own bag? Did the suspect still keep the carrier as she passed through the check-out counter? Were the goods visible in the suspect's bag? (See Extract 4.6).

The case of another elderly woman accused of shop-lifting is fairly similar. From an outsider's point of view, the offence as such is certainly banal; the suspect was stopped by the main exit of a department store with a jar of Nescafé, a packet of hard bread, and two cans of shrimp salad and crayfish tails in dill under the waistband of her trousers. But the suspect tells a very elaborate story about morals and values, her brooding over what is right and wrong in society and over lonely people's misery, and her idea that if she performed a crime, some shop-lifting, she would both experience how it felt and she would in the end free herself of thoughts about guilt and punishment (see Extract 4.7 below). This story of her shop-lifting case is a story about anguish, suffering and relief, the latter partly brought about by talking with the policeman. In the police report a substantial amount of the suspect's story is, indeed, left, although as usual the report (and the underlying report-oriented interrogation phase) focuses on technical details about the shop-lifting as such, a topic to which the suspect contributes very little.

Local reflections of perspectivity conflicts

The everyday perspective and the police perspective sometimes invoke different meanings of one and the same expression. The term 'suspect' itself is a nice illustration. For the police, this is a technical legal term implying, among other things, that the person so designated has been informed that he or she is accused of having committed a certain crime and might therefore have to appear as defendant in a criminal case (which involves certain responsibilities and certain rights, e.g. right to a defence lawyer). For the layman, 'suspect' means that someone believes that the person involved has done something (untoward or maybe criminal). Belief, which implies at least some degree of uncertainty, is then an important ingredient, and if this component has been weakened or eliminated, e.g. by the person's admitting the crime, the term 'suspect' seems inadequate in the lay perspective. Thus, we have here a point of frequent misunderstanding as can be seen in this further extract from the interrogation of the elderly man worrying about cancer.

> *Extract 4.5*
> P: That is, according to this you are suspected of shop-lifting, that is, stealing some goods.
> S: Well, I'm not suspect 'cause you know I <u>was</u> a shop-lifter (P: yes), the way I behaved.
> P: Yes, yes, but that's what it's called, you know (S: That's it) that it's called shop-li. . .(S: Yes, I know) that you are suspected of shop-lifting, see (S: Yes) 'cause you are suspected until until the circumstances have have, what are we to call it, been dealt with by a prosecutor (. . .)

In general, however, the two perspectives tend to surface in different phases of the story formulation process, and they do not always clash locally. In those cases where there is a marked transformation or alteration of perspective from the suspect's story-telling to the policeman's report, any clash can be removed simply by deleting entire segments of the suspect's narrative, often those which deal with biographical information, or by summarizing them in one or two sentences. However, to some extent the corpus allows us to observe the transformation of utterances to text units (sentences) on a unit to unit basis. We shall therefore turn to a micro-analysis of a few suspect's contributions and policemen's reformulation and reperspectivation of them.

The transfer from dialogue to report will, of course, involve some changes in linguistic style: from conversational language to police written prose, the latter representing a hybrid linguistic style featuring colloquialisms as well as bureaucratic and legal language. However, the transformation from dialogue to written text will also affect the way the story is told; there is more temporal order and coherence, more instrumental rationality, and less vagueness and emotionality in the written report (Jönsson, 1988; Jönsson and Linell, forthcoming). For example, Extract 4.6 involves both stylistic and subtle, though substantial, changes:

> *Extract 4.6*
> (Depressed elderly widow)
> P: (. . .) At what stage eh did you put, did you take the articles from the shopping cart and put them in your own bag? Whereabouts in the department store were you then?

S: (p) It must have been on the way up the escalator I think (P: Yes) don't remember. I think so.
P: (p) You took the articles from the shopping cart and put them in a bag of your own and this took place while you were on the escalator to the upper floor.
S: Mm.

Note that the uncertainty and vagueness of the suspect's statement are eliminated in the police reformulation. Similarly, in Extract 4.7 the suspect has considerable difficulties in expressing her feelings, and nothing of this is reflected in the policeman's rather abstractly formulated summary (in the last line of the excerpt):

Extract 4.7
(Elderly woman)
P: But finally...how long have you been sort of demonstrating against society here? You say that you're sort of demonstrating against society here...
S: Yeah, demonstrating, I don't know if you can say that, but anyway you feel that eh...
P: How shall we expre..how shall we express this do you think?
S: Yeaah eh that I with my upbringing I think that I read so much weird stuff you know (P:Mm) in the newspapers and like that y'know (P: Yes) an 'and eh...
P: You think that society is kind of cock-eyed?
S: Yeah, I really think so (P: Yes) yes. (p) That the ones who eh are are honest they they actually get (p) yes you could...if you say punished or what would you (P: Yes) say. (p) Get stuck in the middle anyway y'know.
P: So you've more or...more or less come into conflict with society we could say here?

Extract 4.8 is drawn from an interrogation, in which the suspect tells a story about having been forced to rent some video-recorders, and then sell them, in order to pay some debts. He claims that he was threatened physically before he agreed to enter the various video shops:

Extract 4.8
S: (---) and then they came here and said that now it's time.
P: Now it's time, Hjalmarsson, for you to pay or I'll be damned, or what did they say?
S: Yes more or less, otherwise the way you look is going to change (---)
P: (---) (into tape recorder:) 'The person understood that he now had to pay back the debt unconditionally and as soon as possible.' Was he the one who suggested that you should go and do this?
S: Well, I don't know if he suggested it exactly but there was, well, he figured that I had some way I could pay (---)
P: (into tape recorder:) 'The person from Bluetown somehow or

another instigated Hjalmarsson and suggested that there was after all a way of getting the money by renting video equipment and directly selling this so that Hjalmarsson could in this way free himself from debt.'

Here, a lot of the dramatic real-life circumstances are eliminated in the neutrally reported sentences (e.g. 'pay back the debt unconditionally and as soon as possible'), which could just as well have referred to much more peaceful events.

A police report is, of course, in a concrete sense a monological text, and it is indeed written by the police officer (for an example, see Table 4.1). Yet, each report in our material has been dialogically produced, and to some extent one can trace several voices in them; in Wertsch's (1991) wording, they are hybrid constructions, the dialogicality of which is largely hidden.

Discrepant relevances: suspect versus police rationalities

The three examples reviewed in the previous sections belong to the category of middle-aged or elderly first-time offenders accused of shop-lifting. It appears that, at least in our corpus, these interrogations provide some of the clearest examples of perspectivity conflicts. While there are many conceivable explanations why these suspects tend to provide a different perspective from the police, we may point to a couple of possibly relevant conditions. In the first place, the triviality of the legally crucial action – leaving a supermarket without paying for a few articles – may lead suspects to say little about it. Moreover, the majority of them admit the offence, which, from an everyday perspective, may mean that there is no point in wasting more words on *that*. On the other hand, it may seem natural that suspects want to provide explanations (Background) and to express their (genuine or simulated) contrition (Resulting Evaluation, Attitude).

At the same time, there is a clear rationality, firmly based in long traditions of professional practice, behind the perspective of the police as well. The task of the police is to take part in the investigation of an apparent case of law breaking, and to present evidence to be assessed by state prosecutors. There is an empiricistic, almost behaviouristic, touch to the policemen's concentration on technical details; actors' behaviours are reported in 'objective' terms. Such 'hard and fast facts' seem to square well with what is otherwise accepted as legal evidence, such as technical evidence like fingerprints, signatures, etc., and eye witnesses' testimonies (i.e. evidence ultimately based on direct sensory perception). In other words, the police perspective is a fairly narrow one, and for good reasons. It should be mentioned, though, that if we look at the judicial system as a whole, there are professionals who pay some, even considerable, attention to what we have termed Background and Resulting attitudes; probation officers, whose reports are read in court trials when the defendant's personal circumstances are reviewed, and defence lawyers, who, in the trials, use arguments based on such information. Thus, the judicial system at large is not totally indifferent to suspects' and defendants' life worlds.

Returning to the discrepant relevances in the police interrogation, we can say that when the police officer issues a general invitation for the suspect to tell his story (e.g. 'Tell me what happened!') or a request for explanation (e.g. 'Why did you do this?'), he would seem to be looking for an explanation in terms of criminal action. Some suspects do indeed comply with this, especially, of course, if they leave it to the policeman to ask specific questions. However, the middle-aged shop-lifters, in particular the three persons in focus here, approached the why question in a rather different way, as a moral issue. They took it to mean 'What circumstances in your life situation made you end up as a shop-lifter?', rather than, say, 'What intent did you have on this particular occasion?' or 'What made you commit this particular act of shop-lifting?'. The three apparently prepared stories in which they tried to explain their conduct as grounded in unhappy life circumstances (marginalization in society, illness, depression, etc.). In terms of accounts (cf. the first section), these three middle-aged or elderly shop-lifters produced excuses; they admitted guilt but provided mitigating background circumstances reducing their responsibility. Other shop-lifters provided no such excuses. Some of them just labelled their actions 'an impulse', 'an idiotic thing', 'don't know myself what made me do it', 'a bloody sick thing' (Swedish *jävla sjuk pryl*), i.e. they confessed without offering rational explanations (they appealed to irrational influences). A few shop-lifters made confessions that included rational explanations ('I wanted that record (i.e. gramophone record)'; 'I did not have enough money and decided to have a try'; but these too wanted to reduce their responsibility by emphasizing that everything happened suddenly and by impulse, when they were already in the supermarket. Both the last mentioned categories of suspects typically took the policeman's perspective in the interrogation, i.e. they simply answered specific questions, while they were sometimes quite talkative about matters unrelated to the case.

Concluding discussion

In verbal interaction, perspectives are set and taken by actors. In general, dialogue as such presupposes and brings about a certain degree of mutuality of perspectives, or else one could hardly talk about a joint discourse (Linell and Luckmann, this volume, Chapter 1). But mutuality may sometimes be only superficial or apparent; although the dialogue may proceed fairly smoothly, the interactants entertain different concerns about and understandings of the topics talked about. Sometimes this can be gleaned from a close study of the dialogue itself. In other cases, it becomes evident from a comparison of the dialogue with, e.g. what the actors say in post-interviews on the dialogue.

In those police interrogations from our corpus in which a real conflict between perspectives seemed to surface, e.g. some of the shop-lifting cases, the suspect's narrative is structured as follows. The background deals with psycho-social circumstances, some complications in the suspect's everyday world. Then comes a train of events in which these complications get condensed or aggravated. Some unlawful behaviour is part of this process, but it tends to be pictured only as a peripheral aspect. A fair amount of space is allotted to the resulting attitudes and emotional reactions (shame, guilt, contrition and finally relief). Together the major topics of Background and Resulting Evaluation deal with the prerequisites and consequences in the context of the suspect's life-world. The policeman's perspective is much more narrowly defined; here, most attention is paid to the central actions, i.e. the shop-lifting in objective terms, all climaxing in the technical completion of the offence (leaving the store with goods without paying for them). There is a background and a resulting evaluation in the policeman's narrative, too, but these tend to be rather strictly confined to the suspect's intention behind the offence and to his or her admission/denial and attitude (repentance) respectively. The climax of the story seems to be the technical completion of the offence in the policeman's professional world, but some abnormal state of confusion and desperation (with unhappy consequences) in the suspects' visions and versions.

Institutional encounters are special in many ways. First, they are asymmetric in that parties differ in responsibilities and the use of background knowledge (professional versus lay perspectives). Professionals and lay persons locate the subject matter in rather different contexts; it is natural for the client to provide a personal ego perspective, and for the professional to adopt a more anonymizing case-type perspective. The layman knows his or her own life conditions, while it is the professional's responsibility to adapt the individual case to the administrative categories available.

Second, as regards the dialogue participation structure, the professional is also the one who defines the conditions; he or she provides the client with opportunities for talking rather than the other way round. Therefore, when we discuss mutuality and shared understanding in actual discourse in social practices, issues of power and dominance must necessarily be introduced. We are then faced primarily with context-determined asymmetries, but there is also, and clearly so in the police interrogation, a margin for variation which is subject to the actors' actual negotiation of topics and social participation (dialogue-produced asymmetries, cf. Linell and Luckmann, this volume, Chapter 1). In the police interrogation the police officer asks questions and the suspect responds on the conditions set by the questions, but the suspect's contributions, of course, also influence the police officer's questioning strategies. On the whole, however, the policeman is the one who sets the overall perspective, and with this the suspect has to comply. The latter can occasionally set his or her own perspective, particularly in long monological turns, and the police officer may then temporarily accept this. Yet this will have limited influence on the final product, in our case the written report. The policeman's responsibility for producing an account that is consistent and relevant for legal purposes implies that he selects certain pieces of information, that he integrates these into a coherent whole, and that he biases the entire narrative to fit the legal perspective. The professional party will 'create a goal-oriented, factual interpretation of often rambling, incoherent, and highly fragmented remarks' (Cicourel, 1981, p. 69). This characterization of Cicourel's referred to another setting, doctor–patient interaction, but it is almost as appropriate for our case (see also Caesar-Wolf, 1984). Yet, as compared to legal professionals' discourse in court, police interrogation practices, at least in our data corpus, allow for a fair amount of understanding on the part of the suspect. Even the reports contain some traces of this; they are sometimes written in a hybrid mode, in terms of both linguistic form and content (Jönsson and Linell, forthcoming). This is perhaps not very surprising, given that police interrogators are not full-blown legal professionals (see note 2).

The heading on the form on which the police reports in our study are typed suggests that it is the suspect's story which is told there. However, our study, and similar studies on reporting procedures elsewhere in modern bureaucracies, shows that this is hardly the case. Rather, the report is the product of interaction between suspect and police officer, where the former is allowed to lay out his story only on the conditions defined by the latter's directives. Furthermore, it is the policeman who writes the report and is responsible for it.

By way of summary, the present study has shown that, on the one hand, there is a dialogicality underlying the police report, and that, on the other hand, the perspective of the report is by and large that of the police. Both the dialogicality and the perspectivity are largely concealed. It is next to impossible to reconstruct a suspect's perspective if, as is indeed the case in normal bureaucratic routines, the report is read without direct access to the underlying dialogical interrogations.

The written police report does *not* have the status of legal proof, according to the present Swedish code of judicial procedure; only evidence presented orally in court counts as evidence (see Bruzelius and Thelin, 1979, p. 140). Nevertheless, the police report plays a very important role in the subsequent treatment of the individual case by the legal bureaucracy. The prosecutor's decision to pursue (or not pursue) the case in a lawsuit is often largely based upon on his or her critical evaluation of the story told in the report, and in the actual court trials prosecutors often explicitly refer to statements found in police reports (e.g. Jönsson, 1988). Therefore, although the police report has no official, privileged status, it nevertheless legitimates decisions in the subsequent treatment of the case. Soeffner (1984), who analyses German data on the treatment of young delinquents (in police interrogations, etc.), suggests that if there is a clear order of actions and decisions in police reports, the order will be reconstructed in an even clearer way when or if state attorneys (in a prosecution) have to maintain or argue that a certain version is true (or at least plausible). In any case, the police report becomes something of an authorized version which stays on in bureaucracy's files, representing, on a rather concrete level, society's collective memory of the suspects' past actions. As a whole, the police interrogation becomes an arena for the authorization of one version of the suspect's alleged criminal conduct.

Notes

1. Work on this paper was supported by grants from the Bank of Sweden Tercentenary Foundation (RJ 83/137 awarded to Karin Aronsson and Per Linell) and the Research Council for the Humanities and Social Sciences (F 402:87 awarded to Per Linell). Insightful comments from the study group at Bad Homburg are gratefully acknowledged. Special thanks are extended to Jan Anward, Jörg Bergmann, Per-Olof Bolding, Carl Graumann, Thomas Luckmann and Roger Säljö.
2. In the case of police officers interrogating suspects, it should be pointed out that, relative to theories of professions and common definitions of professionality (Parsons, 1964; Sarfatti-Larsson, 1977), they are not 'professional' in the strict sense, as are judges and lawyers. Rather, they are 'semi-professional' (Etzioni, 1969); they have received some formal education, often have a good deal of experience and are of course in various ways dependent in their practice on professional legal rationalities. Furthermore, they are, of course, commissioned by society to carry out their specific task in the judicial procedure.
3. Applied to the police interrogation, Mishlerian voice theory would distinguish between the professional voice of the legal system (or of the police) and the lay voice of the everyday life world of the suspect. A more Bakhtinian approach might find several voices in the discourse of both parties. For example, the suspect both voices (or plays) the role of suspect (complying with the conditions defined by the task of the police) and the role of a person with a complex life involving, perhaps, unhappy circumstances. Similarly, the police officer would voice the roles of both an interrogator and a fellow human being. Some individuals would be more multi-voiced in their discourses than others. In this paper, we will not pursue this line much further, and instead adopt a largely Mishlerian outlook.
4. In the extracts, utterances which are considered to be the listener's back-channel items are given within parentheses inside the speaker's turns. (.) denotes a very short pause, (p) a somewhat longer pause. (---) indicates that some words or utterances have been omitted in the excerpt.
5. The distinction between story and narrative parallels that of *histoire* versus *récit* of Genette (1980), or story versus text of Rimmon-Kenan (1983). However, there are numerous terminological variations (see Toolan, 1988), which we will ignore here.
6. Of course, we do not know if the suspects' versions in any of these cases are true. However, the issue of truth or veridicality is immaterial to our analysis, which is 'only' concerned with what is said and written in the spoken dialogue and in the written report.

References

Adelswärd, V., Aronsson, K. and Linell, P. (1988), 'Discourse of blame: courtroom construction of social identity from the perspective of the defendant', *Semiotica*, **71**, 261–84.

Bakhtin, M. M. (1986), *Speech Genres and Other Late Essays*, translated by V. McGee, edited by C. Emerson and M. Holquist, University of Texas Press: Austin, Tex.
Bruzelius, A. and Thelin, K. (1979), (eds), *The Swedish Code of Judicial Procedure*, revised edition, Sweet and Maxwell: London.
Caesar-Wolf, B. (1984), 'The construction of "adjudicable" evidence in a West German civil hearing', *Text*, 4, 193–224.
Cicourel, A. (1968), *The Social Organization of Juvenile Justice*, Wiley: New York.
Cicourel, A. (1981), 'Notes on the integration of micro- and macro-levels of analysis', in K. Knorr-Cetina and A. Cicourel (eds), *Advances in Social Theory and Methodology*, Routledge and Kegan Paul: London.
Clark, H. and Schaefer, E. F. (1989), 'Contributing to discourse', *Cognitive Science*, 10, 259–94.
Cody, M. J. and McLaughlin, M. L. (1988), 'Accounts on trial: oral arguments in traffic court', in C. Antaki (ed.), *Analysing Everyday Explanation: A casebook of methods*, Sage: London.
Etzioni, A. (ed.), (1969), *Semi-Professions and their Organization*, The Free Press: New York.
Genette, G. (1980), *Narrative Discourse*, translated by J. E. Lewin from *Discours du récit*, Cornell University Press: Ithaca, NY.
Goodman, N. (1978), *Ways of World-Making*, Harvester Press: Hassocks.
Goodwin, M. H. (1982), "Instigating': storytelling as social process', *American Ethnologist*, 9, 799–819.
Graumann, C. (1989), 'Perspective setting and taking in verbal interaction', in R. Dietrich and C. F. Graumann (eds), *Language Processing in Social Context*, Elsevier: Amsterdam.
Graumann, C. (1990), 'Perspective structure and dynamics in dialogues', in I. Marková and K. Foppa (eds), *The Dynamics of Dialogue*, Harvester Wheatsheaf: Hemel Hempstead.
Jönsson, L. (1988), *Polisförhöret som kommunikationssituation*, (Studies in Communication 23), University of Linköping: Department of Communication Studies.
Jönsson, L. and Linell, P. (forthcoming), 'Story generations: from dialogical interviews to written reports in police interrogations'.
Labov, W. (1972), *Language in the Inner City*, Pennsylvania Press: Philadelphia, PA.
Labov, W. and Waletzky, J. (1967), 'Narrative analysis: oral versions of personal experience', in J. Helm (ed.), *Essays on the Verbal and Visual Arts*, Washington Press: Seattle, WA.
Linell, P. (1990), 'The power of dialogue dynamics', in I. Marková and K. Foppa (eds), *The dynamics of dialogue*, Harvester Wheatsheaf: Hemel Hempstead.
Mishler, E. (1984), *The Discourse of Medicine: Dialectics of medical interviews*, Ablex: Norwood, NJ.
O'Barr, W. and Conley, J. M. (1985), 'Litigant satisfaction versus legal adequacy in small claims court narratives', *Law and Society Review*, 19, 661–701.
Parsons, T. (1964), *Essays in Sociological Theory*, The Free Press: New York.
Rimmon-Kenan, S. (1983), *Narrative Fiction: Contemporary Poetics*, Methuen: London.

Rommetveit, R. (forthcoming), 'Outlines of a dialogically based social-cognitive approach to human cognition and communication'. To be published in A. Heen Wold (ed.), *A Festschrift for Ragnar Rommetveit*.

Sarfatti-Larsson, M. (1977), *The Rise of Professionalism*, Berkeley University Press: Berkeley, CA.

Schonbach, P. (1980), 'A category system for account phases', *European Journal of Social Psychology*, **10**, 195-200.

Scott, M. and Lyman, S. (1968), 'Accounts', *American Sociological Review*, **33**, 46-62.

Silverman, D. and Torode, B. (1980), *The Material Word*, Routledge and Kegan Paul: London.

Soeffner, H. G. (1984), 'Strukturanalytische Ueberlegungen zur gerichtlichen Interaktion', in J. Reichertz (ed.), *Sozialwissenschaftliche Analysen jugenderichtlichen Interaktion*, Stauffenburg-Verlag: Tübingen.

Spencer, W. (1984), 'Conducting presentencing investigations: from discourse to textual summaries', *Urban Life*, **13**, 207-27.

Spencer, W. (1988), 'The role of text in the processing of people in organizations', *Discourse Processes*, **11**, 61-78.

Toolan, M. (1988), *Narrative: A critical linguistic introduction*. Routledge: London.

Watson, R. (forthcoming), 'Some features of the elicitation of confessions in murder interrogations', to appear in G. Psathas (ed.), *Interactional Competence*.

Wertsch, J. V. (1991), *Voices of the Mind*, Harvester Wheatsheaf: Hemel Hempstead and Harvard University Press: Boston, MA.

5 | Obstruction and dominance: uncooperative moves and their effect on the course of conversation

Marie-Louise Käsermann

Let us initially define dominance as follows. Dominance occurs when A has access to resources *at the expense of* B (Linell and Luckmann, this volume, Chapter 1). This can occur in the following two ways. Although A and B may be equally able and willing to speak about topic X, A speaks more than B. Or, although A may be less able than B to speak about X, she/he speaks more than B. Speaking less on the part of B is but one of several possible *effects* of A's dominance over B. Other effects are less easily identified, e.g. B may speak in a qualitatively different manner when A is present from when A is absent.

It is difficult, from the perspective of an observer, to determine with regard to the above examples whether or not A is dominating B when the latter's contributions are qualitatively or quantitatively restricted in comparison to the former's, for it is unclear whether B would or could contribute more if permitted to do so by A. In order to legitimately interpret a reduced contribution observed in B as an effect of A's dominance, therefore, one has to find a way of making explicit the less directly observable preconditions of motivation and competence of B. This is the purpose of this chapter.

First, I wish to examine a case of reduced conversational participation that has been described elsewhere (Käsermann and Altorfer, 1989) and ask whether this phenomenon can be treated as an instance of dominance. In order to examine competence and willingness to speak I shall then apply the criteria derived from this first study to another corpus of conversational data. This presentation of selected material is thought to be an empirical substitute for an experimental treatment in a field not easily yielding to systematic experimentation (Foppa, 1990).

A case of reduced participation

The case I wish to analyse concerns a conversation between two parents (P) and their son (S) who is diagnosed as schizophrenic. The analysis shows that while all the participants engaged in disruptive communicative behaviour, e.g. interrupting their partners, only when S was the intended victim did this lead to his reduced participation in speaking. S reacted to mild, medium, and strong interruptions from his parents usually by integrating the impediment and by continuing what he was about to say or by repeating the disrupted utterance or by remaining silent. P, on the other hand, responded to a mildly disruptive move from S by integrating and continuing, while after medium and strong impediments P carried on producing substantial utterances which referred exclusively to S's disruptive utterance. Being strongly or moderately disrupted, therefore, did not force P to remain silent. There is still the question, however, of whether the differential effect of presumably equally strong impediments has anything to do with S being dominated by his parents.

One may be able to interpret these differences if one maps the relevant sequences of conversation on to a minimal model of communicative exchange (Foppa, 1984; 1985, Käsermann, 1987). In a sequence of three consecutive utterances $a1$-$b1$-$a2$ from speaker A and B, a functional relation is established if $a2$ is conceived of as an evaluation of how well $b1$ responds to the demands given in $a1$. $a2$ is an *accepting* reaction if $b1$ meets those demands, and $a2$ is an (adequate) *correction/modification* if $b1$ does not fully meet those demands. This functional assumption with regard to the relation between three utterances implies that utterances are used instrumentally to realize certain goals and can, therefore, be judged (and corrected) with regard to how well they serve these goals. It also implies that A's evaluation of the relationship $b1$:$a1$ is essentially a judgement of the extent to which speaker B cooperates in achieving the goals set in $a1$. Not only does $b1$ need to be instrumental as such (e.g. just any answer to a question) but it also needs to be recipient designed. In other words, participants in a conversation should take one another's perspective or should try to set up mutuality (e.g.

Graumann and Sommer, 1988). An a2 correction of b1 depends on two conditions:

- Speaker A sticks to what she/he was unable to achieve in a1 (e.g. being informed by obtaining B's answer to her/his question) and therefore is *willing* to correct a failure in b1 (e.g. by repeating the question after B's unhelpful response).
- She/he is *competent to perform* an adequate correction.

The occurrence of an appropriate correction can be taken as an indication that the correcting speaker is competently sticking to the goals set for the conversation. If, however, under favourable conditions of willingness and competence an expected correction fails to occur or the correction that does occur is inadequate in some respects (see below), one could claim that this impaired performance depended on additional conditions, e.g. on the dominating effect of the conversational partner.

When this analysis is applied to the results of the first study (Käsermann and Altorfer, 1989), the responses of S and of P cannot be interpreted unequivocally in terms of dominance as defined above. This is because the goals of cooperation are unclear, as also are certain aspects of willingness and competence to cooperate:

1. Consider a sequence s1-p1-s2 in which S chooses either repetition or staying silent (s2) after being impeded by his parents (p1). The *occurrence of a repetition* shows that S judges the functional relation of p1:s1 as less than adequate and, therefore, tries to compensate for or correct the parental failure of *topical cooperation*. However, his *staying silent* is neither an acceptance nor a correction. It may occur in lieu of a correction which, in S's view, *should* have taken place and which, therefore, S would be *willing* to make. Yet, whether the failure to make the correction is due to lack of competence or is caused by the increasing strength of parental impediments remains unclear. It is impossible to decide between these two alternatives without further information about S's competence.

2. Consider the sequences p1-s1-p2 where s1 impedes the preceding parental utterance and where p2 is a substantial utterance referring exclusively to s1. Clearly p2 is *not a topically* corrective reaction to a less than adequate s1:p1 (for a discussion of the essentially relational concept of correction, see Käsermann, 1987). However, it may be considered as a positive evaluation (acceptance) of s1:p1; but at a different level than

topic of conversation. For the parent it seems sufficient to take over again the speaker's role regardless of whether what she/he says in p2 bears any relationship to the topical demands initially formulated in p1. It seems more important for the parent to react coherently on a turn-taking as opposed to a topical level. Two interpretations are possible here:
- The parent, following the impediment, makes a qualitative change by lowering her/his level of topical demand, thereby ensuring her/his quantitative participation.
- She/he maintains and is willing to cooperate with goals different from S's right from the start and, therefore, does not experience the so-called disruption as such.

Only in the first instance could one say that the parent was dominated by S because she/he contributed utterances which differed qualitatively from the ones used in less impeding situations.

Conversationally there is no such thing as an impeding utterance in any absolute sense (e.g. defined simply by inherent features of that utterance). Impediments occur, instead, through a combination of violations of the demands on cooperation and the consequent impairment of performance. Only with regard to a given *level of cooperation* is it possible unequivocally to interpret specific a2 reactions (e.g. exclusive reference to b1) either as acceptance (e.g. on a small-talk level, compare Foppa, 1990) or as qualitative change in participation due to dominance. And, only with regard to a set *level of competence* (including linguistic knowledge which is assumed here to be intact) is it possible to interpret unequivocally specific a2 reactions (e.g. silence) as quantitatively reduced performance. Only with regard to these preconditions may the reduced performance be taken as indicative of a lack of cooperation on A's part due to the preceding failure of B to cooperate and, therefore, as dominance in action (= a failure to try to induce cooperation due to being dominated). In what follows possible empirical correlates of the two relevant criteria (willingness and competence to cooperate with set goals) will be proposed.

Reduced participation as a less than optimal conversational contribution

In a dialogue in which, in order to solve a problem, speaker A asks for and speaker B gives advice, the mutually agreed upon goal for both participants is to cooperatively try to realize the given goal. The format may be set up between peers as well as between layperson/expert and it is chosen here because it is thought to guarantee *willingness to cooperate* towards the goals of this format. The cooperation consists in 1) *offering* whatever one knows to be instrumental in order to reach goals set; 2) *accepting* instrumental, cooperative contributions; as well as 3) *correcting* for possibly uncooperative moves. By these three moves the level of willingness to cooperate is defined with regard to a specific format and can be applied formally to the subset of sequences a1–b1–a2 where a1 is a specific contribution of the advice-*seeker*, b1 is a cooperative/uncooperative reaction of the advice-*giver* to a1, and a2 is or is not a corrective attempt.

With regard to criterion of *competence to cooperate* the fundamental problem for the researcher is to discover the distribution of knowledge between the two participants. It is clear that by asking for advice an asymmetry is created which makes the advice-giver superior relative to the advice-seeker. By interacting within the given format the former is in some respects entitled to 'speak more' without being called 'dominant' because she/he is the one who knows what the other is asking for. Besides this central asymmetry, however, there are other aspects of knowledge distribution which play an essential role: in some respects the advice-seeker knows as much or even more than the advice-giver. Take a patient at the doctor's surgery: she/he knows that something is wrong with her/him and in this respect is the ultimate authority, and the doctor's task is to discover just what is wrong in terms of the best scientific knowledge, and so be able to design a treatment. At this point, therefore, the asymmetry clearly works the other way round – indeed in our case it is more so in that the therapist must always offer any diagnosis to the client for adjudication. With this in mind it could be argued that dominance-prone situations may occur in sequences where, embedded within the overall asymmetry (given by the format), there are also instances of an 'inverse' asymmetry created by the advice-seeker's superiority with regard to knowledge of her/his own condition. It may be crucial for the occurrence of phenomena of dominance just how these different layers of knowledge distribution are handled by the participants and, especially, whether sometimes the format-defining asymmetry is unduly overgeneralized. A doctor who is not prepared to listen to and try to understand her/his patient's complaints will most probably make the client feel helpless and stupid if the latter takes the doctor's suboptimal interventions as competent and gives up asserting her/his own knowledge.

For an investigator to discover what the participants of a conversation know at any given point in time is not an easy task. To make sure that the claim with regard to A's being competent at topical corrections is realized, there has to be an attempt at defining A's topical competence as displayed in a1, and at sketching correspondingly possible adequate corrective attempts in a2. Take as an example of this definitional procedure the simple request for information. If someone asks a passer-by what time it is, she/he displays a lack of information and under normal conditions one would not expect her/him to react to even a faulty answer by saying 'I don't believe you'. If, however, the addressee does not perceive the partner's specific lack of knowledge in its relationship to what the latter may already know, and then answers after leafing through a newspaper instead of looking at her/his wristwatch or explains the way to the station, then this *violation of expected procedures* and *types of answers* may cast doubt on the quality of that specific answer and may lead to a corrective 'Are you sure?', etc. This example shows that although it might not be possible to state positively what kind of knowledge someone does have while displaying a specific lack of knowledge, it may be feasible to identify types of reactions (in b1) which violate generalized expectations (in a1) and can be remedied by certain types of corrections (in a2) (compare Garfinkel, 1987; Heritage and Atkinson, 1984).

On this basis I assume that within the chosen format there is a level of exchange at which an adviser's violations of the advice-seeker's expectations should be easily detectable. Consider the utterance 'My problem is X. Can you give me advice as to what I should do about it?' It states in its first part what A knows or believes to be the case and in its second what she/he believes B to know (better). A reply to this question should at least not violate the expectations that the exposed problem will be understood as such and be accepted as part of A's knowledge; and that it will contain – in some form – at least part of the specific knowledge asked for. This knowledge can either be advice or part of it or it can be a preparatory step aimed at reformulating the problem itself. This step, however, can only take place on the basis of previous understanding and acceptance of the advice-seeker's view of the problem. Furthermore, the adviser's violations of these expectations, for example, in denying the truth of the exposed problem or in providing something which is not or not clearly recognizable as advice or part of it, should be easily detected and corrected by the advice-seeker under normal (e.g. not dominance-prone) conditions. This may be assumed because the advice-seeker knows, in principle, the format in which she/he interacts and also knows the specific content she/he is speaking about. Of course, this is just a preliminary outline of what could make up the distribution and structure of knowledge between conversants in the given format of seeking and providing for advice. Nevertheless, I believe that this rough sketch is sufficient to help define the types of possible violations of expectations; and the types of utterances which, under the assumption of a given distribution of knowledge, should occur as corrections of violations of expectations. These two kinds of types can, therefore, act as a kind of standard form or basis for finding out whether occurring violations indeed are corrected as expected. If these corrections, expected within a cooperative format, are not observed their absence may be thought to be the product of dominance.

Material and method

The material of the following analyses are sequences from a psychotherapeutic dialogue (Caspar and Grawe, 1989, transcription by M. L. Käsermann). This particular dialogue has been selected for analysis because the quality of therapeutic relationship was rated very low by both the client and the therapist immediately after the session. Excerpts from the transcripts used as examples are translated from Swiss-German. Within a sequence C-turns are the client's and T-turns the therapist's. They are numbered in the order of their occurrence within the session and are internally structured in accordance with the pragmatic rules for the predicate-centred construction of units of analysis (abbreviated AU: see Moesch, 1988; Foppa, 1990). An AU structure imposed upon a turn is the equivalent of a linguistic sentence-structure but takes care of the various phenomena of spoken discourse (hesitation, stuttering, false starts. etc.). Punctuation is not added in any of the excerpts because this would give the wrong impression of a high standard of grammatical correctness. With regard to the analyses carried out the turns of C and T are projected into sequences of $c_1-t_1-c_2$ t_1 is the therapist's turn. Violations of C's expectations may be committed by T in this turn. Also, if a participant does not take over the speaker's role (criterion: a break of two or more seconds' duration) the silent period is assigned to the speaker. Both interlocutors in this dialogue are male.

The parts of a turn relevant for the given analysis (e.g. C's offering a problem and asking for advice) were distinguished as follows. With regard to c1 it is assessed whether there is any exposition of a problem (EP). If in a c1 one or more EP can be identified it is assumed that C expects T to understand and accept them as correct, and, furthermore, that C is able to detect and compensate for given violations of this expectation. EP is defined by *ostensive reference* to an AU of c1 in which C states that he experiences personal difficulties of a certain kind (compare Extract 5.1, p. 109). Not counted as EP is an AU in which C expresses what is generally accepted as distressful without any sign of negative personal judgement.

With regard to t1 it was recorded, whether it revealed *cooperative understanding and acceptance* (expected reaction) of EP or whether it revealed *uncooperative rejection* (violation of expectation). If in a t1 a rejection of the truth of EP or parts of it occurred it was assumed that C would provide for a correction of this failure. In principle, acceptance is realized if $c1$ is comprised in $t1$ as true/correct, or in other words is affirmed. However, whether this is the case often cannot be derived directly from the linguistic features of t1: meta-communicative statements (e.g. 'You say your problem is X') or explicit repetitions of c1 are rare, and, if the latter are uttered in a doubtful voice, they even amount to a rejection. The same is true with regard to rejection which in an explicit form (e.g. 'No, I do not believe your problem is X; your problem is Y' or the form 'I do not believe that X is a problem at all') occurs very rarely. To solve the problem of identifying acceptance as well as rejection of c1-EP in an actual t1 utterance, therefore, it is necessary to insert an intermediate operation. To get a clearer notion of whether an actually observed t1 is accepting or rejecting EP one may try to make explicit its implications with regard to EP in c1. This can be done by deciding whether a given t1 can be projected on to an (obligatory) affirmative *repetition* of EP with additional (optional) features (such as technical explanation, suggestion). If this operation yields that EP or parts of it are denied or contradicted as to their truth then this amounts to a rejection.

It was also recorded whether T's contribution was or was not easily *understandable* from a linguistic point of view. This was a modest attempt at grasping an aspect of cooperation in the potential advice part of t1. Although the aspect of content may be much more interesting, this is beyond the scope of this analysis.

With regard to c2 it was recorded whether positive evaluations/acceptances expected to occur after a cooperative t1, or corrections expected to occur after specified violations, did or did not occur.

I will now present examples of sequences which proceed either in a cooperative fashion or contain one or more of the defined violations in t1. Their possible effect on c2 is described by contrasting the observed c2 to an expected type of acceptance or correction.

Description of the course of exchange in sequences

Example of a cooperative exchange

In the following extract (5.1) from a psychotherapeutic session, a c1 containing parts in which problems are exposed (EP, underlined and numbered), is followed by a t1 reaction which can be identified as accepting at least one of the EP in c1 and making a linguistically understandable contribution (reformulation/advice).

Extract 5.1

c1 C16
1 well
2 take the last fortnight's stress (1) of writing that paper
3 it (1) partly touches (2) my private life
4 and then my joy of life diminishes (2)
5 I don't enjoy going to work as much
6 as when stress like this is absent
7 and to find a balance (*goldener Mittelweg*)
8 seems to be relatively difficult
9 and that's my conflict

t1 T16
1 well
2 your goal of being appreciated for your work
3 would be in peril
4 if you took it (the job) more lightly

c2 C17
1 that's what I suppose
2 because the goal of being appreciated
3 probably triggers me
4 doing as much as possible
5 having as much output as possible
6 being able to observe deadlines
7 and this is in direct conflict with the other goal
8 of taking it easy
9 of taking life
10 as it happens

1. The identification of EP in c1
   c1 is described here as containing an exposition of a problem

because it explicitly states a source of actual distress of the client together with his experiences or behaviours. It is assumed that the client by uttering EP relates his expectations of receiving (professional) advice or offered reformulation of the given problem.

2. The evaluation of t1

t1 is described as accepting EP because it verbally refers to at least one of the problems in c1 and does so in an affirmative way (AU4 implies the repetition of EP1, in contrast to stating, say, 'You are only saying this' or 'That is quite normal'). Furthermore, in elaborating on one of the possible meaning implications of the problem in a linguistically unambiguous manner (AU2-3), it fulfils that aspect of an advice as an acceptable contribution which is focused on here (another aspect would be 'content', which is restricted in its scope only by the beliefs and fantasies of T). From what so far has been a cooperative course of exchange, it can be expected that c2 will not be a correction.

3. Features of the subsequent c2

c2 can be described as a *positive evaluation* (acceptance) of t1 because there is a verbal reference which elaborates on the personal meaningfulness of t1, thereby expressing that the advice-seeking client has been 'reached' by t1. A positive evaluation may also take the form of an associative chain triggered by t1.

Summarizing, in Extract 5.1 there is a t1 which cooperatively asserts problems exposed by the advice-seeker (client) in c1 and cooperatively contributes by reformulating or reframing them. The reformulation is linguistically understandable, and such as to allow the advice-seeker (client) to accept it and expand on it in c2. The observed c2 reaction is not yet a fully fledged solution of the problem (or 'insight' into), but it shows a certain development in that direction. On the basis of this analysis the course of this sequence could, therefore, be conceived of as an instance of a cooperative exchange where the adviser does not violate the advice-seeker's general expectations.

Direct violations in t1 and their effect on c2

Sequence 5.1 can be used as a standard against which sequences with uncooperative moves in t1 and the effect of these violations on c2 can be described. As stated above it is to be expected that C

Obstruction and dominance 111

will react to a violation by a corrective move which he is topically competent to make. The following sequences give examples of what can actually be observed after a given violation.

Extract 5.2a
```
c1  C5   1    in connection with feeling responsible (1)
         2    among other things it popped into my mind
         3.1  my difficulty (1)
         4    that's to say my feeling responsible (1)
         3.2  is partly influenced by my fear
         5    which I have for some time
         6    whether I am competent at all (2)
t             mhm
c1       7    that this (2) has had a strong influence
         8    and that even now this (2) on an unconscious level is
              still partly influencing me
         9    I also realized
         10   that a lot of this trouble already disappeared by
              experience
t             mhm
c1       11   but every now and then it (2) pops up again
t             mhm
c1       12   and in a wider sense this (2) may also have an
              influence on feeling responsible (1)
              (break 7 sec)
t1  T5        ---
c2  C6   1    furthermore it is a fact
         2    that I always work hard to do a good job
         3    and this may also be hindering me (3)
              (break 7 sec)
```

In c1 the problem of 'feeling responsible' (synonym for 'feeling a failure' as uttered by C in a preceding statement) is described. Instead of taking over the speaker's role, accepting the problem and contributing to its solution, T remains silent. Independent of its possibly strategic therapeutic value, this is a reaction which, within the framework of expectations of C assumed for the given analysis of local dominance, has to be judged as uncooperative and being in need of a corrective move. To grasp a possible deviation of the observed c2 from an expected corrective c2, one may make explicit what kind of reaction to this type of violation could be expected to occur under conditions where C is still able to perform a correction he is competent to make. If one assumes that C cooperatively monitors the overall discussion in the light of the overall goal of getting advice in order to solve a problem, because T has given no sign of having grasped c1, one could expect him to repeat the content of c1, perhaps in other words and an expanded or more concise fashion.

In fact, the *observed* c2 is not such a corrective repetition or paraphrase of the fear of being a failure. Rather, by being a continuation of c1 it could even be taken to show that the missing t1 is not evaluated as uncooperative by C. This may be plausible if one assumes that T's silence is interpreted by C as meaning 'I see', which might at least fulfil the expectation of a general acceptance of EP. Conversely, it might be assumed that C lowers his level of cooperative demand as a consequence of the violation. If this is what happened one would have to say that it was an instance of C's functioning less optimally than he could. However, without additional information this question cannot be decided. It is taken up again with regard to Extract 5.2d, where a corrective c2 restatement of EP occurs, and with regard to Extract 5.3a where c2 contains an interpretation of T's silence.

Following on 5.2a there is an intermezzo 5.2b, with a clarifying question from T, a minimal answer from C, a ratification of that minimal answer by a minimal utterance from T, and a refusal to take over the speaker's role by C.

Extract 5.2
(Continuation of 5.2a)
```
t  T6 1     in feeling responsible
c  C7 1     yes
t  T7 1     yes
            (break 19 sec)
c  C8       ---
```

This part of the exchange is not an instance of the sequence type investigated here because C does not utter any EPs.

In the continuation, 5.2c, T for the first time refers to C's EP from the preceding 5.2a. However, instead of accepting the given EP he rejects it meta-communicatively, suggesting that there has been a misunderstanding, and formulating what he thinks C's problem is or should be.

Extract 5.2c
(Continuation of 5.2b)
```
c1 C5,6
t1 T8  1    now it has just occurred to me
       2    that there may have been some misunderstanding
       3    that by responsible (1) I meant something else (than
            (2), (3))
       4    when we spoke about it
       5    without taking pains to clarify it
       6    without checking
       7    whether you had the same concept as me
       8    when you did your homework on it
c           mhm
t1     9    what I really meant is situations
       10   in which you are criticised without justification
```

```
c           mhm
t1      11  and nevertheless you feel responsible
        12  when there is reason to believe
        13  that you are not to be held responsible (4)
            (break 5 sec)
c2  C9      ---
```

Again, to grasp the possibly differential effect of this kind of violation one may outline the features of an expected cooperation-inducing reaction c2 and compare the observed reaction with it. If one assumes that C is the ultimate authority about his own problems, and if one further assumes that he is still sincerely interested in discussing them with T, then one would expect him to reject T's presumptuousness and to restate his position. In fact C does not take over the speaker's role. As already mentioned this type of reaction is neither the expected correction which should induce T's cooperation, nor does it form an acceptance of t1 whereby it would signal that t1 is not evaluated as uncooperative. If one sticks to the assumption that C *does know* his own problems – this view is also supported by 5.2d (see below) – then his silence here must be interpreted as an instance of local domination by T. One may also speculate that C, although knowing his own problem, being confronted with this kind of uncooperation from an expert may temporarily start getting doubtful about himself.

Consequently T rephrases in 5.2d C's problem as he now perceives it.

Extract 5.2d
(Continuation of 5.2c)
```
c1  C5, 6
t1  T9   1  thus it's somebody else's fault
         2  if deadlines are not met
         3  and nevertheless there is a feeling of responsibility
         4  I am going to be blamed for (4) the job or output
         5  which is delayed and even for the fact of the delay
            itself
c2  C10  1  with regard to this it is important to know
         2  that I have almost no opportunity
         3  to compare with somebody
         4  who does the same job
t           mhm
c2       5  and then I don't have a standard
         6  do I ask too much
         7  or what is demanded of my colleague
t           mhm
c2       8  if I had the opportunity to compare
t           mhm
c2       9  there would be immediate relief (!)
```

	10	if I noticed
	11	'Well from the colleague he asks so much
	12	then he cannot ask so much from me'
t		mhm
c1	13	and because the opportunities to compare are mostly lacking
	14	I am uncertain in my judgement
	15	what belongs to my area of responsibility (5)
	16.1	what do I have to ask of myself
t		mhm
c1	16.2	in the normal (6) case
	17	and when do I really ask too much of myself (7)

As in 5.2c, the *expected* cooperative reaction to this violation in C's side would be a corrective rejection of the problem exposed by T and a restatement of what C thinks his problem is. In fact, this is just about what one really does *observe* in C's reaction: in the given example 5.2d there is first a correcting rejection (c2) followed by a restatement (c1) of the problems exposed so far in 5.2a and 5.2b. With regard to the rejecting part it is, among other things, noteworthy that it is not explicitly marked as a correction of T nor is there any hint as to T's personally not having met C's expectations within the given communicative format. It is conceivable that specific features, such as disguise of a correction as provision of further information (c2: AU1) might turn out to be typical of how under specific asymmetric communicative conditions uncooperative moves by one's, possibly superior, partner, are met by cooperation-inducing corrective moves. With regard to the restating part one should notice the following. First, its occurrence proves C's (assumed) competence, and, second, its form, as compared to 5.2a, seems to be relatively more concise. However, it is to be doubted whether C really means 'because' in Au13 in the sense in which T takes it up later; compare line 4 in 5.2c.

On the basis of the given example, one could surmise that within the format obtaining between a layperson and expert the given type of violation sometimes has a locally dominant effect in that it prevents C from performing according to his knowledge, as is the case in 5.2c. At other times (5.2d) the violation may be compensated for although the features of the correction might not be the same as if the partner was a peer. The fact that the violation has an effect only intermittently shows that something which does not concern C's basic competence and readiness to cooperate within the given format but which is specific to that situation prevents him from optimally reacting. One may venture that it is perceiving his partner as an expert which makes him temporarily unable to perform according to his knowledge.

Indirect violations in t1 and their effect on c2

T's *directly* rejecting the 'truth' of C's EP, as in 5.2, is but one type of uncooperative management of the adviser's task in the given communicative format. Another is demonstrated in the following example.

Extract 5.3a

```
c    C18    EP(1): (because of the tendency to be lazy at work C
                   needs some external pressure)
t    T18    (paraphrase of C18 as a general tendency)
c1   C19    1  there are times
            2  how should I put it (break 6 sec)
            3  where I tend to be lazy (1)
               (break 4 sec)
t1   T19    ---
c2   C20    1  as an example yesterday I went to the office
            2.1 on the basis (break 4 sec, takes breath)
            3  how should I put it
            2.2 with the intention
            4  of taking it easy
t           mhm
c2          5  and then I was about to start writing a new paragraph
            6  and then something was missing
            7  and I started loitering
            8  and after two hours I did not know
            9  what I had done
            10 then I realized what I was doing
            11 and made an effort to start working
            12 and then succeeded
t           mhm
c2          13 and the problem therefore is
            14 it is difficult
            15 to set the appropriate level of demand (1)
            16 to set it not too high
            17 nor too low (1)
            18 for if it is too low
            19 this is not optimal (2)
            20 one is not motivated to start working
            21 and puts it off
```

The sequence c1-t1 in 5.3a is similar to c1-t1 in 5.2a: to C's EP T reacts uncooperatively in not taking over the speaker's role. Unlike 5.2a, however, the expected corrective move in c2 actually occurs, in that C restates his problem by way of a lengthy example (AU1-12) and paraphrases (AU13-21) this restatement by marking its beginning with 'the problem'

(AU13). This shows that after T's silence C in principle is able to correct instantaneously, and therefore silence in this context does not have the effect of a strong impediment. If he did not correct in a similar way in 5.2a then he obviously did not interpret t1 there as an uncooperative move. A possible explanation for the fact that T's silence now, in contrast to 5.2a, is treated as uncooperative may be given in the context preceding the given sequence. The general problem has been expounded by C18 and has been understood and accepted by T18. So a slightly specified version in C19 could now be expected, which would additionally, trigger the advisory part but not, again, a purely accepting response. T's silence in this context, therefore, is not likely to be interpreted as a silent 'I see' but more probably as a lack of readiness to react cooperatively, compensated by the more detailed version C20. With regard to dominance, this event raises the question as to whether one should be prepared to consider as a possible effect not only quantitatively and qualitatively reduced participation but also a quantitatively much enlarged utterance (compare Grice's (1975) maxim of quantity).

Extract 5.3b
(Continuation of 5.3a)
c1 C20
t1 T20   1 I think
          2 this is a typical example
          3 of how this works in your case
          4 but I really wonder
          5 whether it is the low demands of your work
          6 that make you feel fed up with it (break 5 sec)
c2 C21   ---

In the consequent sequence 5.3b T refers to the preceding utterance from C containing an EP in stating in a very general way (AU1-3) that he understands EP. However, if one looks at the understanding of EP which is implied in the advisory/reformulating part (AU4-6) one may note that T interprets C's *subjective* difficulties to set the right level of demands on himself (e.g. 'taking it easy', AU4 and AU15, 18) as *objective* demands given by work, and C's uneasiness with this state as a whole as C's being put off with his work. This equals a rejection of the problem not by substituting something new (as is the case in Extract 5.2) but by *misinterpreting* parts of the given. Under optimal conditions one might expect this rather unexpected reaction to be corrected by C, for example, saying 'Well yes, but that's not really what I was getting at when uttering ...'.

However, under the given conditions C does not correct t1 but remains silent.

In 5.3c T expands on his previous misinterpretation and again does not reach C, who again remains silent after a kind of normalizing interpretative attempt.

> *Extract 5.3c*
> (Continuation of 5.3b)
> c1 C20
> t1 T21   1 I have the same experiences (C20)
>   (break 2 sec)
> c2 C22   ---

In 5.3d the normalization of C's problem is expanded further:

> *Extract 5.3d*
> (Continuation of 5.3c)
> c1 C20
> t1 T22   1 <u>everybody</u> has this kind of experience
> c2 C23   1 sure
>   2 if it is hours and not days
>   3 it is not so bad

Although up to now C has missed two opportunities to insert a necessary correction, this correction could still be uttered in 5.3d after t1, in exactly the same manner as stated with regard to 5.3b. What actually happens is that C accepts the truth of the preceding t by a minimal utterance, thereby overtly treating the preceding t1 as no longer uncooperative. This form of acceptance, however, differs from the one observed in [5]. In addition, c utters something which might be conceived of as a problem, that is, the *duration* of not being motivated, although it is not clearly marked as such. As up to now this topic had not been of any concern to C, one may assume that if he is prepared to regard this as his problem, he has been induced to do so by T.

The gradual break away from C's initial contribution of seeking advice, observed in 5.3a to 5.3c, is topped by the following:

> *Extract 5.3e*
> (Continuation of 5.3d)
> c1 C23
> t1 T23   1 how often did it happen to you last week
> t1   2 that you were lazy at work?
> c2 C24   ---
> t2 T24   1 give me just a rough approximation
> c2 C25   1 approximatively three to four times
> t2 T25   1 three to four times of how many hours
> c2 C26   1 that's hard to say

T quits playing the role of adviser within the given format and sets up a question-answer format. Within this format it is T who actively exposes the problems and does so by an initially unsuccessful (T23) but after a repetition (T24) successful obligation for C to enter that kind of discussion (C25).

Although in many respects they are quite similar, for example, in reducing C's quantitative participation, the sequences composing episodes 5.2 and 5.3 lead up to strikingly different outcomes. There are some possible explanations. First, for C the problem exposed in 5.2 was clearer, right from the start, than the problem exposed in 5.3. The similarity of the structure of the exposed problems speaks against this possibility. Second, the repeated exposition of problem 5.3 before any substantial intervention from T in 5.3 makes it less likely that C is able yet to invent any new corrective version. The fact that this had an immediate local effect, i.e. a different interpretation of T's silence in 5.3 compared to 5.2, makes an overall effect less likely. Third, the degree of uncooperativeness in 5.3 is much stronger and less likely to be remedied by C when conversing with an expert. Support for this tentative interpretation comes also from the next example.

Indirect and linguistically opaque violations in t1 and their effect on c2

Extract 5.4, which partly overlaps with 5.2d shows the effect of a t1 which not only violates reflexively the acceptance-of-EP part of C's expectations but also carries an aspect of prospective violation in being a linguistically strange offer for $c2$.

Extract 5.4a
(Continuation of 5.2d)
```
c1  C10  14   I am uncertain in my judgement
         15   what belongs to my area of responsibility (5)
         16.1 what do I have to ask of myself
t             mhm
c1       16.2 in the normal (6) case
         17   and where do I really ask too much of myself (7)
t1  T10   1   mhm mhm mhm
          2   I do understand you perfectly well
          3   but I wonder
          4   if this is not something
          5   which holds true generally
          6   (which holds true) independently of the work situation
          7   (which holds true independently of) who you work with
```

```
         8   or (which holds true independently of) the kind of
             work you do
         9   that for you there is a tendency
        10   to feel responsible for your work
        11   even if an error has not been caused by you
        12   or you have made the error
c2 C11   1   there is a little of this tendency
         2   there is a little of it
```

In c1 C states that he feels uncertain whether he asks too little or too much from himself with regard to his work. T claims explicitly that he understands EP (AU1–2; compare 5.3b for a similar figure of speech) and goes on with something which seems to be an expansion of EP, i.e. by suggesting that what C has said is true generally, and does not just apply to his own particular situation (AU3–8). This interpretation can be maintained up to the very end (AU9–12). However, it then becomes clear that T is not referring back to C's EP but forward to what he thinks C's problem is, by giving the word 'responsibility' a moral twist as 'responsibility for errors' that was absent in C's words. By this complicated move a delayed and linguistically masked uncooperative rejection of EP is achieved. Under favourable conditions one could expect C to correct such an inadequate interpretative attempt; for example, it would be achieved by the meta-communicative statement 'No, you do not seem to have understood what I was trying to say'. In contrast, what one actually observes is a minimal affirmation of t1, thereby overtly treating it as if it had been a cooperative contribution. It is noteworthy, however, that there are striking differences between this kind of acceptance of t1 and the one observed in 5.1: it is performed by echoing part of the preceding T-utterance and by adding a restrictive particle to the repeated versions, but it does not contain any elaboration of the preceding t1.

In 5.4b T now explicitly utters a contradictory statement:

Extract 5.4b
(Continuation of 5.4a)
```
c1 C10
t1 T11   1   and it would be independent of the comparison or the
             opportunity to compare with others
             (break 6 sec)
c2 C12       ---
```

Again, the same type of meta-communicative correction as in 5.4a could be *expected*. In contrast, one *observes* that C stays silent.

In 5.4c T makes an expanded though somewhat confused reformulation of the contradictory statements of 5.4a and 5.4b.

Extract 5.4c
(Continuation of 5.4b)
c1 C10
t1 T12 1 therefore my hypothesis would be
         2 even if you knew
         3 that others ask less
         4 I think
         5 you would nevertheless feel responsible
         6 or if one did not ask so much of somebody else
         7 this would not be a reason for you to find
         8 in this and this specific case with this problem
         9 where this and this has not turned out the right way
        10 I am not to be held responsible
        11 for it not turning out the right way
            (break 2 sec)
c2 C13 1 yes this might be true
            (break 2 sec)
         2 although it is terribly difficult
         3 to really grasp it

The confusion comes about by T's obvious difficulty in distinguishing between 'demands made by someone' (AU3) and 'demands made on someone' (AU6) and perhaps also by the forms implying specificity (AU8-9) but not in fact referring to anything at all concrete and therefore being absolutely vacuous. The correction which under favourable conditions could be *expected* to be uttered by C does not occur in any direct sense. Instead one *observes* again a minimal though restricted affirmation of the truth of t which is then followed by a statement which meta-communicatively sheds doubt on T's having grasped the point. This, however, is done by blaming not T, but the subject matter's complexity.

It is clear that the analysis of 5.4 is somewhat simplified because it treats the exchange out of the preceding context of 5.2. There is not enough space to make explicit every aspect of T's development of his complex contradictory rejection and the subtle impositions made on C. To elaborate on this one should also take into consideration the content. Nevertheless, this example shows that in contrast to relatively easily detectable violations (extract 5.2, and the slightly less detectable ones of 5.3), violations involving, additionally, linguistic opaqueness diminish the chance of C sticking to his knowledge under asymmetric conversational conditions even more drastically.

Summary and discussion

The analyses should have made it clear that under T's increasing uncooperation (direct, indirect, indirect and linguistically masked, rejection of EP) the likelihood of C's performing according to his knowledge by correcting T gradually diminishes from corrections, to silence, to minimal acceptance as cooperative-uncooperative moves. A systematic comparison of C's performance after T's violations with what one would expect of him under optimal conditions or what one knows he is capable of from undisturbed sequences, for example, extract 5.1 and, to some extent, the correction in 5.2, yields the following results. It becomes clear that C's participation changes quantitatively (i.e. staying silent instead of correcting; speaking more than necessary) as well as qualitatively (corrections with specific features; minimal affirmations instead of corrections, which deviate in form from 'true' affirmations within standard sequences). In other words, although C can be held to be motivated as well as competent in principle to display that part of knowledge on which, under the overall asymmetric distribution of knowledge within the format of seeking advice, he is the authority (Keppler and Luckmann, this volume, Chapter 7), T hinders this display by the way he acts out his adviser's role.

Under the independently given conditions of C's motivation and competence this change can be interpreted as an effect of dominance, that is, as a result of T's having access to resources at the expense of C by being assigned the superior position, even if this assignment is unwarranted. First, by selecting a given format of conversation it can be assumed that there is an overall willingness for the interlocutors to cooperate with each other according to an agreed, defined goal and, therefore, to correct for one another's uncooperative moves. Second, by selecting a type of contribution which belongs within the realm of a speaker's topical competence it is also ascertained that expected corrections *in principle* could occur. If under these conditions they are not actually performed this may be explained by the exertion of interactional dominance. The unfavourable evaluation of the analysed therapeutic session by both C and T is an indirect hint at the legitimation of this interpretation. It is obvious, however, that the argumentation would be more convincing if it could be shown that C in conversing with a peer was able to provide for corrections of comparable violations independently of their degree of strength.

Methodologically it should be noted that, for the detection of differential meaning of similar contributions (e.g. staying silent, accepting a contribution), it is necessary to operate within a functional framework which allows reactions to be predicted and compared with observation. The principle of 'effective functionality' of utterances (Foppa, 1987) by which a non-occurring correction is taken to mean that the preceding sequence is judged to be adequate does not serve this purpose. The analyses carried out point to types of procedures of systematic analysis based on the underlying model of communicative exchange: by outlining a standard course of a sequence of utterances and defining categories of standard units, e.g. (adequate) acceptance, one creates a pattern which allows for the detection and contrastive description of (deviant) subtypes of that unit. It should be noted that formulating such a standard does not amount to making a normative claim or an assertion of adequacy but has a primarily methodological function.

It is obvious that our approach picks out only a few aspects for analysis. Its main limitations are the restrictions to the local management of exchanges and to content only in a very general sense, i.e. broad categories of EP, rejection and so on. The advantage of such a micro-analysis, for me, seems to lie in its potential to help specify possibly relevant questions. One may ask, for example, whether the observed effect of dominance is purely a function of the layperson/expert situation. This question could be investigated by comparing the course of interaction between the same advice-seeker and an advice-giver of peer versus expert status, or by comparing the patterns of conversation of two interactants discussing a subject matter where only one is an expert versus one where both are similarly informed. Another question is whether the observed effect of dominance is a function of degree of clarity and/or personal importance of EP, although in this case it is difficult to imagine a valid empirical approach.

Finally, there are two points which are not touched upon by the given analyses. First, nothing is said about what might be the essence of being domineered or hindered to perform according to one's competence. It is conceivable that C, although being locally aware of the adequate competent move, refrains from behaving accordingly because he tends to globally re-create asymmetries characteristic of a specific institutional setting (Maynard, forthcoming, quoted from Linell and Luckmann, this volume, Chapter 1). Another alternative, however, consists in assuming that while being domineered C's thinking is momentarily blurred. Without actually being able to distinguish between these two alternatives it is, however, noteworthy that there exist (psycho-pathological) settings in which speech oddities as a rule and without further reflection are interpreted as signs of 'thought-disorders'. Second, nothing has been said about the therapeutic implications of the course of these sequences. One may assume that C, in being forced to fight against the resistances of an uncooperative T, is subjected to a consciously applied and perhaps successful therapeutic technique which helps him clarify his problems. However, helpful therapeutic resistance should perhaps show different features from the ones observed and lead to at least minimal satisfaction in both C's and T's judgement of the session. In any case, it would be interesting to find out whether the observed lack of cooperation of T could be used deliberately in the sense of a successful technique to ultimately help clarify C's problems.

References

Caspar, F. and Grawe, K. (1989), 'Weg vom Methoden-Monismus in der Psychotherapie', *Bulletin Schweizer Psychologen*, 3, 6-19.
Foppa, K. (1984), 'Redeabsicht und Verständigung', *Manuskripte*, 23 (84), 73-6.
Foppa, K. (1985), 'Negotiating meaning in conversation'. Paper presented at the symposium *The Social Constitution of Meaning in Interpersonal Communication*, Werner Reimers Stiftung, Bad Homburg, 4-7 December.
Foppa, K. (1987) 'Dialogsteuerung', *Schweizerische Zeitschrift für Psychologie*, 46, 251-7.
Foppa, K. (1990), 'Topical progression and intention', in I. Marková and K. Foppa (eds) *The Dynamics of Dialogue*, Harvester Wheatsheaf: Hemel Hempstead.
Garfinkel, H. (1987), *Studies in Ethnomethodology*, Polity Press: Cambridge.
Graumann, C. F. and Sommer, C. M. (1988), 'Perspective structure in language production and comprehension'. *Journal of Language and Social Psychology*, 7, 193-212.
Grice, H. P. (1975), 'Logic and conversation', in P. Cole and J. L. Morgan (eds), *Syntax and Semantics*, Vol 3, *Speech Acts*, Academic Press: London.
Heritage, J. and Atkinson, J. M. (1984), Introduction in J. M. Atkinson and J. Heritage (eds), *Structures of Social Actions: Studies in conversation analysis*, Cambridge University Press: Cambridge.
Käsermann, M. L. (1987), 'The analysis of dialogues with a schizophrenic patient', in R. Wodak and P. van de Craen (eds), *Neurotic and Psychotic Language Behaviour*, Multilingual Matters: Clevedon PA.
Käsermann, M. L. and Altorfer, A. (1989), 'Obstruction in conversation: a triadic case study', *Journal of Language and Social Psychology*, 8, 49-58.
Moesch, K. (1988), 'Prädikatzentrierte Einheiten als Basissegmente zur Analyse von Diskursen: ein pragmatischer Lösungsversuch', unpublished manuscript.

6 | Dialogue between expert and novice: on differences in knowledge and their reduction

Margret Wintermantel

A common event in verbal interaction is the transfer of knowledge by one dialogue partner to another. These communicative events make up the broad class of instructional exchanges which vary in their content and in their length according to the characteristics of the material which is to be transferred. The research reported here addresses the issue of how particular knowledge areas are verbalized and comprehended in instructional dialogues between experts and novices. This special knowledge concerns the carrying out of concrete actions like using a camera, repairing a bicycle tyre, or building a model with building blocks. The sum of what is said by the expert within these instructional dialogues will be called instruction and it contains utterances about the action itself and about the situational determinants, i.e. objects, relations, etc., from which the single action-steps evolve. The dialogical task of the novice is to grasp the meaning of what is being said by the expert and to bring together the concepts, facts and relationships that comprise the relevant action knowledge. Instructions are usually delivered over serially connected utterances which are interrupted by the recipient's contributions, as in the following example (dialogue between an instructor (I) and a recipient (R) in a driving lesson):

> *Extract 6.1*
> I: First of all, declutch
>   as if you wanted to start
>   But now, don't put in the bottom gear
>   but the reverse gear
> R: How?
>   Like this?
> I: Yes, very nice

> now do not let go of the clutch pedal
> turn around
> support your right arm on the headrest
> and look out through the back
> stay seated like this as long as you
> are driving backwards
R: Like this?
I: So, you've got your left foot
> on the clutch pedal,
> the right one
> over the accelerator
R: M/hm.

Depending in part upon the features of the action to be learned, the instruction can be more or less extensive. Within the instructional dialogue, the whole action sequence which is to be learned is broken down into its smaller component parts which are presented successively by the instructor. Usually, the recipient does not play the role of a passive listener, but contributes to the dialogue in an active way. S/he shows that s/he understands (or does not understand) by certain signals, as in the example above.

At first sight the question of dialogical dominance in these kinds of instructional situations is apparently quite clear. It is apparently a consequence of unequal knowledge distribution leading to a particular asymmetry in the verbal exchange. In terms of the conceptualization proposed by Linell (1990), this is clearly an asymmetry with regard to domain. The asymmetry of knowledge is characterized by one party lacking knowledge possessed by the other (Drew, this volume, Chapter 2). The dominance is on the side of the expert who, because of her/his knowledge superiority, designs and controls the knowledge transfer in different ways, whereas the novice follows it and is brought from low to higher competence. This particular dominance relation, due to knowledge superiority, provides a regularity which is accepted by both participants at the outset. For the one who is delivering the instruction it should be clear that s/he is ready to transfer her/his knowledge; for the one who wants to learn in the course of the dialogue it implies acceptance of the dominance of the expert.

Both participants, the instructor and the recipient, bring this pragmatic knowledge into the instructional dialogue as knowledge which is common ground (Stalnaker, 1978) of the dialogue partners. The common ground includes world knowledge as well as pragmatic knowledge in the sense of knowing about situations and about adequate language use within these situations (Graumann and Wintermantel, 1984).

Belonging to this common ground is the knowledge 1) that there is a particular dominance relation between instructor and recipient; and 2) that there must be reciprocal acceptance of this relation. We can therefore take the unequal distribution of knowledge and the resulting asymmetry in verbal exchange as a first characteristic feature of instructional dialogue.

Casual inspection of examples of instructional dialogues and dialogue fragments leads us to postulate a second characteristic feature, i.e. their goal directedness. This does not mean that other verbal interactions are not goal directed, but instruction dialogues differ from the others because of the explicit intentions of the two participants to contribute to a common goal, namely that of equalizing the initial unequal knowledge distribution.

To summarize the global description of the particular constellation which is prototypical for the instructional dialogues we are studying: there is an expert who knows how to carry out a concrete action, like repairing a bicycle tyre or paddling a canoe, and there is a novice who does not yet know how to do it, but who wants to learn the skill. The expert knows how to verbalize his/her action knowledge and the novice knows that he or she must extract the meaning from the expert's verbal utterances in such a way as to understand the new information and incorporate it into his/her existing pre-knowledge.

The conceptual prerequisites of instructional exchanges

An instructional exchange is a course of action in which knowledge is effectively transferred from one participant to the other. From a psychological perspective the crucial processes that occur in this transfer are cognitive processes operating on concepts and relations between concepts, taking place in the minds of the participants. From a socio-psychological perspective the crucial processes are social interactions, embedded in particular social situations and characterized by particular communicative practices.

In the asymmetrical situation of the instructional dialogue communication depends in part on the fact that critical knowledge of one participant has to be brought into meaningful speech in a partner-oriented and context-sensitive way to the end that the other participant may share that knowledge. Thus, the description of the dynamics of knowledge transfer should take into consideration both the psychological and the social-interactional perspective. We must next consider whether theoretical concepts referring to knowledge representation and cognitive processing are relevant factors in the analysis of the purposeful interactions of two actors, the expert and the novice, in an instructional dialogue. Beginning with the view of verbal communication as based on purposeful other-related speech of two actors who use their cognitive resources, we can test the limits of the cognitive conception with regard to the analysis of instructional dialogues. Taking into consideration the psychological 'micro' aspect as well as the socio-psychological 'interactive' aspect, the following questions must be answered:

- What does the expert know about the concrete action to be instructed, about the novice who is the other participant of the interaction, and about the communicative situation?
- How is the conduct of the dialogue related to this particular knowledge and what kinds of processes are responsible for the transformation of action knowledge into other-related speech in the course of the instruction dialogue?
- What are the processes which govern the dialogic actions on the side of the novice who is engaged primarily in the process of understanding what an instruction is about?

The following three processual aspects of the situated expert-novice dialogue as a speech exchange are included in these questions:

- Production and understanding of a discourse as a set of connected utterances referring to some concrete action.
- Representation of action knowledge as the conceptual basis for verbal instruction.
- Constitution of, and contribution to, the dialogue by both instructor and recipient.

Producing and understanding of discourse

Verbal instructions for carrying out certain practical actions with varying degrees of complexity consist of connected utterances that are semantically coherent, i.e. they refer to concrete action sequences that lead to particular ends. In linguistic terms an instruction is a special sort of discourse which can be defined as an account of an action sequence attached to certain situational states. The beginning and the end of the instruction are fixed by the limits of the real action sequence, and the single utterances are connected because, taken all together, they refer to the action sequence as a whole.

Although the expert's part of the instructional dialogue is much more than the production of a discourse and, on the recipient's side, much more than a case of discourse understanding, it is important to consider the textual character of the instruction because it may be worth drawing attention to three features of the instructional dialogue. First, the single utterances gain their proper meaning only as parts of the whole discourse. This may become clear when looking at an utterance the meaning of which depends upon the linguistic context. Utterances like 'turn the top round' or 'brush it away' could, in different instructions, refer to quite different action sequences and thus have different meanings. Second, the order in which the information is given is important. Usually, the temporal order of single actions as parts of concrete action sequences is fixed; this order must be recognizable in the sequential order of the instructional utterances. And third, the text is important for understanding what can be called the 'referential movement', that is, the speaker's movement through the system of concepts and relations between concepts that make up his/her understanding of the crucial action sequence.

Instruction is a complex communicative task which requires the presentation of a particular domain of knowledge in a form of connected utterances which the recipient must understand, put into use, and carry out the particular action (Suchman, 1987, pp. 100–2). Thus, the produced discourse should be adequate with regard to the 'objective' action sequence, i.e. it should be exhaustive, correct and easy to understand by the novice. To determine what in this sense makes an instructional discourse easy to understand presupposes that we have sufficient knowledge of the cognitive processes that govern discourse understanding and subsequent acting. A number of recent empirical studies seem to show that discourse understanding begins with the construction of some hypotheses as to what the discourse is about, and includes a process of continuing verification and modification of these hypotheses. These hypotheses are continually checked against the incoming discourse information. If the new pieces of information fit, then the hypotheses will be elaborated; if not, they will be modified.

In psychological explanations of what discourse comprehension is, the interpersonal aspect of discoursive talking between two persons is not usually analysed. Instead stress is laid on the 'interaction' between some pre-existing general world knowledge and new information. Pre-knowledge is used, together with linguistically conveyed information, to construct a mental representation of what the discourse refers to in reality. Virtually all modern psychological models of discourse comprehension conceptualize this as a constructive process. They have included explanations of how this constructive operation might occur. Theoretical concepts like 'situation model' (Van Dijk and Kintsch, 1983), or 'mental model' (Johnson-Laird, 1983; Garnham, 1987) are introduced to refer to the mapping of text meaning on to some corresponding segments of reality.

In applying this theoretical approach to the activities on the recipient's side, we get a picture which reduces his/her participation in the dialogue to processes of speech comprehension in his/her mind. In particular the participation of the recipient is conceptualized as follows: within the instructional dialogue, the textual information is taken in order to construct a mental model of the relevant action sequence. Constructing a mental model requires continual interaction between the text and the recipient's knowledge; both kinds of information, the old and the new, are used for model construction, elaboration and differentiation.

As long as the construction does not end up in a mirror-like representation, in contrast to a somewhat abstract and oversimplified picture of the sequence, we may talk about a model. It would therefore seem that if the mental model which the novice constructs does contain the most relevant features of the real action sequence, then the instruction has been efficient; if it contains features which are irrelevant for the carrying out of the action sequence, then the instruction did not really succeed.

This view of what happens in the mind of the novice seems to be plausible, especially with regard to the constructive activity which leads to a mental representation of the instructed action. However, the formation of a mental representation is just one part of the dialogic activities within the instructional interaction. Instead of being passive as a dialogue partner and active only as an information processor who takes the presented pieces of information as single building blocks out of which an efficient mental model is constructed, the recipient is engaged in a social interaction as an active participant. In the ongoing instructional dialogue s/he is active in showing signs of understanding or misunderstanding, posing different kinds of questions, givings comments, repeating parts of the expert's speech, etc. In each case s/he plays a part in maintaining and designing the dialogue. Thus, the cognitive dimension of constructing a mental representation of the action-knowledge is embedded in communicative activity. There is not only a series of actions carried out by two individuals but joint action composed of speaking and listening (Schegloff, 1982).

So far we have considered the comprehension of the person who is instructed, and must now turn to the question of production. According to the cognitive approach the expert already has a representation of the crucial action sequence before instruction begins. This knowledge need not be complete or consistent with regard to any 'objective' criteria, as long as it provides a coherent and interconnected set of concepts and facts which has been tested somehow in reality. This knowledge structure can then provide the basis of what is called the conceptualization process (Levelt, 1989) as the first part of speech production. Thus, on the part of the expert, it is the more or less complex knowledge concerning the concrete action to be instructed which has to be transformed into speech and delivered in the instructional dialogue.

The expert will not automatically reproduce his or her knowledge to the novice. Instead, like any other participant in a dialogue, he or she will choose between different options of verbalizing the knowledge in question. Given the particular knowledge structure that has to be transformed into speech, the expert has a choice with respect to movement through the conceptual system, the terms to use for concepts, word order within single utterances, the level of detailing, etc.

The 'design' of the instruction by the expert is primarily dependent upon his/her interpretation of the communicative situation. This interpretation is, at least in part, dependent upon the recipient's contributions. Thus, the interpretation of the situation is not static but changes in the course of the dialogue. The dynamic structure of changing interpretations of situations can be explicated in terms of the perspectival or horizon structure of all perceptual and cognitive experience (Graumann, 1990). In the course of the instructional dialogue the participants start from different points with different purposes and they have to come together by coordinating their individual perspectives.

The expert tries to find out what relevant pre-knowledge the novice has of the domain to which the instruction belongs, whether s/he understands the words which are used and whether s/he is able to organize the information given – in short, what the horizon structure of the novice is. It depends upon the expert's interpretation of the horizon structure of the novice what lexical, grammatical and organizational options s/he will choose in using language for the transfer of knowledge (Wintermantel, 1990). This holds true also for complex instructions in the form of extensive sequences of single utterances relating to complex patterns of states and changes of states.

Thus, partner-oriented speech in the instructional dialogue requires more of the participants than merely adjusting single utterances to each other; they must design and produce a complex sequence of utterances which refers to knowledge of the action sequence and takes into consideration the perspective of the novice. In the following section we shall take a look at action-knowledge.

Representing action knowledge as a conceptual basis for verbal instructing

The giving of adequate instruction presupposes some pertinent knowledge on the part of the expert. In the case of instruction for concrete actions, it should include the correct order of the single action steps, the precise ways of acting them out, the logic of the 'in-order-to' relations, and the real objects which have to be handled in the course of action (Vallacher and Wegner, 1987). That is, knowledge structure includes declarative, procedural and even motor components, which function together as the conceptual basis for the instruction.

It seems reasonable to assume that different experts may have different knowledge of the same action sequence, including the connected objects. In the case of the technical procedure called distillation, for example, we might find that chemical engineers differ from technical designers with regard to their model of the distillation process. However, the degree of knowledge can vary too: the expert can know how to utilize objects/machines to her/his greatest advantage without actually knowing how they function technically. For example, one could be an 'expert' in driving a car without knowing how it actually functions mechanically; similarly one can be an 'expert' photographer without knowing the technical aspects of a camera.

On the novice's side the background knowledge can vary as well. One can imagine a novice who knew nothing about photography being well informed about the physical laws governing the optical qualities of camera lenses. The potential variation in knowledge background between expert and novice is large and an instruction dialogue must be seen as dependent on this constellation. As such, it is not the real difference in knowledge background that determines what is relevant with regard to the situation interpretation. Rather, it is the assumed difference in knowledge background concerning the task and subject matter which is of central importance for the course of interaction.

From the side of the novice, the dialogue can be seen as successful when an adequate understanding of the concrete action as an organized structure of single action-steps is achieved. Again, we must note that this understanding can be correct or incorrect, adequate or inadequate, leading to more or fewer correct steps in the carrying out of the relevant action. The quality of the product of understanding has to be seen with regard to the function it has been given, which is to make the overall action possible. This quality is dependent on the mapping of the instruction onto the novice's previously existing knowledge.

Given an instruction as referring to a particular concrete action, what distinguishes actions from random physical activity? The characteristic feature of actions is their goal directedness (von Cranach et al., 1980), the action components being steps on the way to a specified goal. Action theorists usually describe the relations between single action-steps and the goal as hierarchically organized, the lower levels relating to the higher ones in a number of means–end relationships. When carrying out a particular action sequence, the hierarchy has to be worked through. With regard to the verbalization of the action knowledge, the expert can choose the level which s/he assumes to be adequate for what is needed by the novice.

The option which will actually be chosen is primarily a function of the expert's assumptions with regard to the novice. As this process seems to be first and foremost a searching for different means and deciding upon the right one, we can infer that this is a type of problem-solving.

Constituting the dialogue and contributing to it on the instructor's as well as the recipient's side

Why can the problem-solving paradigm, which originates from an individual-oriented cognitive approach, be applied to the description and explanation of instructional dialogues? Usually, a problem is defined as follows (Duncker, 1935; Newell and Simon, 1972). An undesired initial state is to be changed by operators into a desired final state. The means by which this transformation from one state to the other is to be effected is not obvious. Between the two states there are barriers of quite varying natures which must be overcome if the problem is to be solved. In contrast to tasks which can be classified as demands for which routinized achievement strategies are provided, problems are characterized by the absence of previously developed accomplishment strategies.

The conceptualization of problem-solving as information-processing is based on two separate cognitive structures: the epistemic (knowledge of the facts) and the heuristic, the second consisting of the transformation operators (Dörner, 1976). Among the transformations, complexity-reducing operations turn out to be essential. Aside from abstraction and reduction, the formation of complexes seems to be an important strategy as it determines the level of detailing with which a problem situation can be seen. The formation of complexes means the combination of elements into wholes: e.g. learning how to ride a bike or how to ski implies the combination and coordination of single movements into an integrated process. With actions, one can differentiate between various levels of complexes. The level of complexes chosen determines the level of detailing at which an action sequence will be viewed. To find an adequate level of detailing is an important factor in successful problem-solving. A high degree is as inefficient as a low degree, because a high degree leads to a situation where the problem-solver gets lost in detail, whereas a low degree gives no chance of making the relevant differentiations.

To find the right operators to reduce the complexity of the situation should be central for the instructional dialogue as well. The expert must take the perspective of the novice with respect to the knowledge to be instructed, the situation, and the expert her- or himself. The first decision s/he has to make concerns the level of detailing on which to start the instruction and how to verbalize. Accordingly, we can try to apply the problem solving paradigm to instructions in the following way. The primary condition for the expert is that the novice is unable to carry out the relevant action because of insufficient knowledge. The novice wants to accomplish the action, however, and the expert ought to be of assistance. With the help of her/his knowledge s/he must overcome the obstacles created by the insufficient knowledge of the novice. The novice also has a problem to solve

Table 6.1 Relationship between two problem-solvers

	Expert	Novice
Initial state	Structured knowledge about the action	No action knowledge
Barrier	Knowledge transfer	Understanding
Goal	Knowledge transferred	
Common goal	Equalizing of knowledge distribution	

as s/he has to proceed from the undesired initial condition of having no knowledge at all about the action sequence, to the desired final state of knowledge. In the course of the instruction dialogue the novice has to overcome barriers of non-understanding with the help of the expert's statements. Thus, mutual problem solving is acted out in a coordinated verbal exchange.

The adequacy of the verbal presentation is only partly a question of combining information pieces, the other part being on the more pragmatic side of putting the information into the appropriate linguistic forms (Suchman, 1987, Chapter 5). In conclusion, it can be considered characteristic of the instruction situation that highly dynamic and complex mutual problem-solving takes place.

The relation between the two problem-solvers, as involved in the instructional dialogue, is presented in the schema shown in Table 6.1.

The instructional dialogue as mutual problem-solving

Adjusting to the novice's competence by modifying the level of detailing

In a first study we tried to find out whether the paradigm of problem-solving, and in particular of the complexity-reducing strategy of constructing part–whole relationships, would be fruitful for describing and explaining the dialogical processes within the asymmetric interaction taking place in an instruction situation. The crucial action knowledge which had to be transferred was the building of an object with building blocks.

In the learning context the task was to build a fantasy object made up of twenty-seven small coloured building blocks (Lego). This fantasy object bore no resemblance to any familiar object and was called Imarello. It consisted of four parts which had to be made out of single lego blocks. These four parts looked like familiar objects (bridge, stairs, springboard and platform). The instruction was given in a non-verbal, graphic format. After having learnt how to build the fantasy object, each subject ($N = 20$) had to instruct another person how to do the same. This instruction had to be delivered in a dialogical situation.

It was found that eighteen of the twenty instructors took the opportunity to refer to the parts looking like familiar objects by naming them (as 'bridge', 'stairs', 'springboard' and 'platform') instead of describing one single action-step after the other.

Thus, they broke down the total action into meaningful parts. In cases of recipient non-understanding, however, the instructors moved to the lower levels of the action hierarchy, as in the following example.

> *Extract 6.2*
> I: Now take all the red ones and put them together so that it looks like a platform.
> R: Like a platform?
> I: Yes, take one of the red blocks, put it in the middle of the desk, and then take another and then a third and put them . . .

Moving to a lower level of detailing as a response to a sign of misunderstanding given by the recipient seems to be a speaker strategy of adjusting the speech to the recipient's assumed horizon structure. To find out whether instructions with changing levels of detailing (referring both to single blocks and to blocks forming meaningful parts of the model) would be more effective than instructions with a high level of detailing (referring only to single blocks), we compared two, suitably formulated, instruction versions with regard to the time needed for making up the Imarello. The results show that the version with changing levels of detailing led to much shorter 'building' times than the version with a high degree of detailing.

Changing the level of detailing within the instructional discourse means reducing the complexity of the whole action sequence by decomposing it into part–whole relationships. This strategy, showing variability in choosing adequate operators, clearly indicates the importance of adequate conceptualization of the particular knowledge represented in dialogical speech.

Adequacy is determined by the characteristics of the action knowledge and by the assumed perspective of the recipient.

Turning now to the information about the recipient which is utilized by the instructor, how is it given and how does it influence the instructor's speech? In a second study we analysed instructional dialogues with regard to the recipient-related level of detailing chosen by the experts in presenting the critical action sequence (Wintermantel and Siegerstetter, 1988). The experts were thirty-four car mechanics who were asked to instruct novices in an aspect of the servicing of a car, namely 'timing of ignition'.

The hypothesis was that in the course of the dialogue the car mechanics would change their level of detailing according to the contributions of the novices. In particular, when the novice signalled to the instructor that s/he did not understand what was being said, the instructor would have to change his/her answer to a different level of the action hierarchy. In the course of the instruction the novice asked questions such as 'how?' and 'to what purpose?', which the instructor answered accordingly.

In order to analyse the 'movements' of the expert within the action hierarchy, we first had to construct a hypothetical schema representing the critical action complex (Figure 6.1). We did this with the help of other car mechanics. In a second step, we decomposed the instructions into nuclear sentences so that we could localize each single nucleus within the hierarchy, and pursue the course of the presentation.

We found that the car mechanics did change the degree of detailing of their instructions according to the hearer's questions. With 109 questions in the authentic dialogues, a change of levels took place in 97 cases. The level remained the same in only 12 cases. An important difference was noted between the 'to what purpose' questions on the one hand and the 'how' questions on the other. It was found that the instructor moved downward within the action hierarchy after a 'how' question and upward after a 'to what purpose' question. These results show that our instructors took the opportunity to design the dialogue. They not only gave a precise and exhaustive description of the action sequence but, instead of taking into consideration the novices' contributions, the instructors were oriented towards the novices in a much more dynamic interactive sense. They changed their instruction plans and adjusted their way of organizing information throughout the interactions whenever they seemed to be getting signs of non-understanding from the novice's side. And they modified it in a systematic way, which

On differences in knowledge and their reduction 137

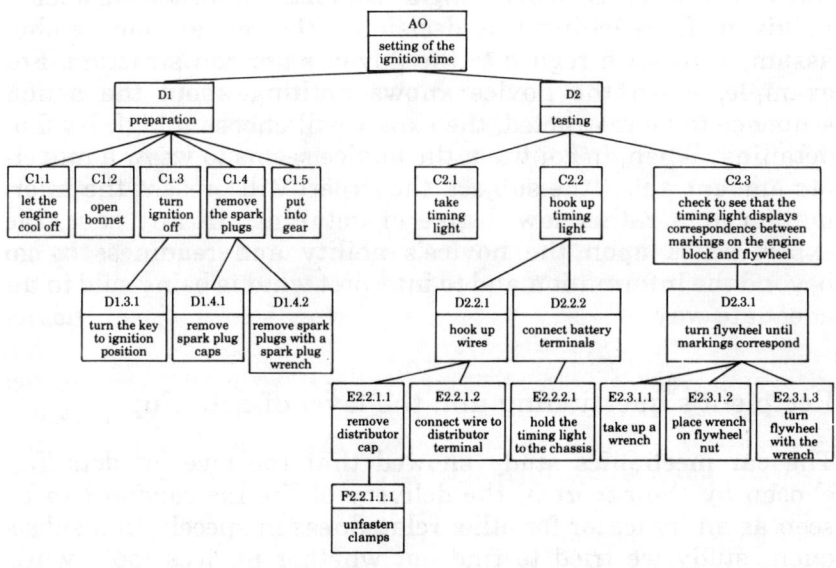

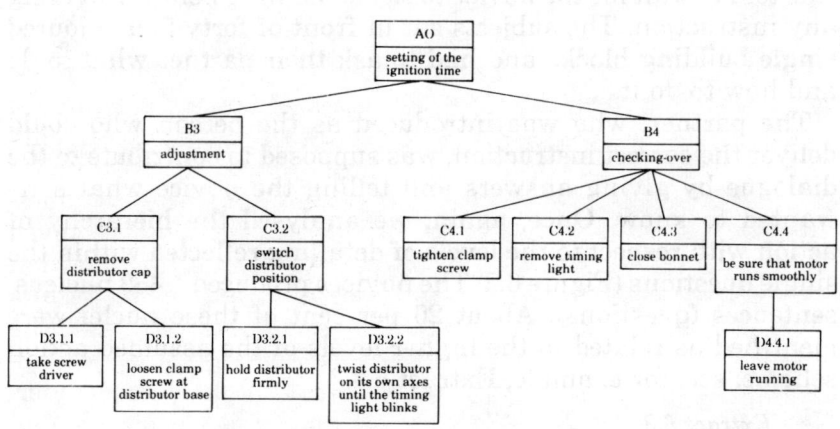

Figure 6.1. Hierarchical scheme of 'timing of ignition'

can be explained in the context of the problem-solving paradigm as follows. When planning the verbal presentation of the real action sequence, the first decision the instructor has to make concerns the degree of detailing at which the information should be given. In reaching this decision, s/he makes some global assumptions with regard to the novice's horizon structure. For example, when the novice knows nothing about the action sequence to be instructed, the expert will choose a high level of detailing. When, in contrast, the novice seems to know a moderate amount about the subject, the expert will present the information at a rather low degree of detailing. In any case, the expert relies upon the novice's ability and readiness to go beyond the information and to interpret what is being said in an adequate way.

Recipient's questioning and the level of detailing

The car mechanics study showed that the level of detailing chosen by the expert in the delivery of the instruction can be seen as an indicator for other-relatedness in speech. In a subsequent study we tried to find out whether novices too – while being instructed – ask for information that is located on different levels of detailing. To test this question we again let novices make a construction out of building blocks. This time the expert was told to wait for the novice to say something before providing any instruction. The subjects sat in front of forty-four coloured single building blocks and had to ask their partner what to do and how to do it.

The partner, who was introduced as the person who could deliver the correct instruction, was supposed to contribute to the dialogue by giving answers and telling the novice what s/he wanted to know. Once, again, we analysed the hierarchy of action with respect to the levels of detailing reflected within the single questions (Figure 6.2) The novices produced 1,489 nucleus-sentences (questions). About 20 per cent of these nuclei were identified as related to the higher levels of the assumed action scheme: see, for example, Extract 6.3.

> *Extract 6.3*
> R: The white ones also go on one another?
> I: Yes
> R: Like a tower?
> I: Yes
> R: Do I need all white ones for the tower?
> I: Yes

This fragment shows a novice's attempt to understand a particular action through its relationship to a whole hierarchical organization of complex action instead of staying at the highest level of detailing where only the smallest action steps are located. These results, although gained in rather restricted experimental settings, indicate the mutual recognition by expert and novice of the asymmetry in the interaction. In spite of this asymmetry there is mutual dependence of the two participants. The expert needs signals of understanding or misunderstanding from the novice in order to decide what information should be given, and the novice needs to have an adequate presentation of the information in order to incorporate it into her/his pre-knowledge and to construct a knowledge basis for carrying out the practical action.

In terms of the perspectival or horizon structures of the participants we can now say that successful instructional dialogue is progressive approximation of individual horizons. That is, the expert learns to take the perspective of the novice and thus s/he is able to follow the individual informational needs of the novice. On the other hand, the novice also has to take his/her partner's perspective. This implies that s/he knows that the expert not only can choose between different options of verbalizing the action complex but that s/he can also refer to different levels of detailing of that action complex and stress different aspects of it. Instructions for action sequences always rely upon some implicit knowledge about actions in general. A good instructor knows how to set the perspective in such a way that the novice can use old and new information in order to come to the correct understanding.

Conclusion

The theoretical framework of our studies includes the assumption that dialogical speech in instruction situations is the result of a problem-solving process. Unlike individual cognitive processes which are described in the textbooks of cognitive psychology, we conceptualize problem-solving as joint action. It is a dynamic and complex process, for it is a speaking and listening activity in which knowledge has to be presented in a way that is adequate and purposeful for both the expert and the novice.

In the course of the dialogue, the expert finds her/himself in a

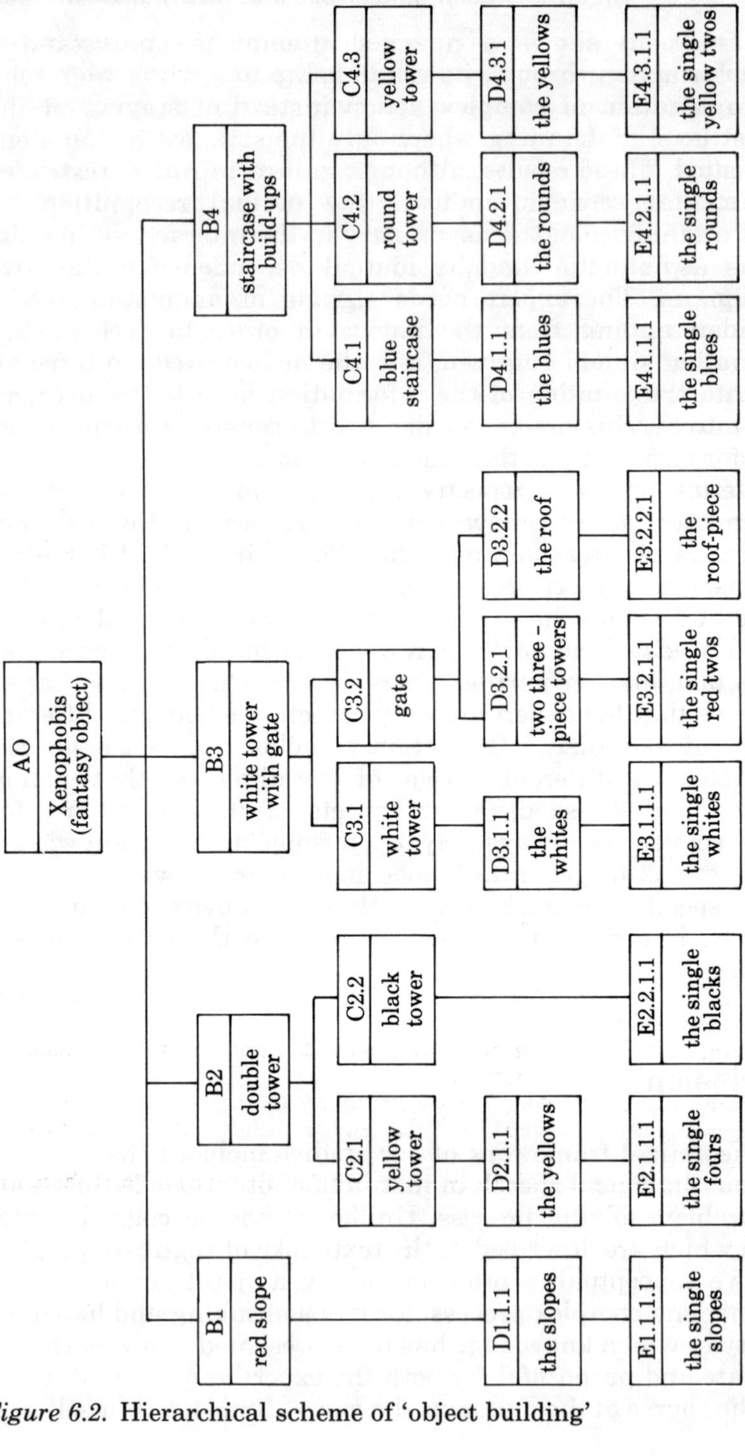

Figure 6.2. Hierarchical scheme of 'object building'

dominant position. Primarily, s/he has to refer to the hierarchically organized action complex and find the right degree of detailing and an adequate means of verbalizing. In the course of the instruction, the instructor has to take the novice from an initial state of no-knowledge to a final state of knowledge. The dominance relation within this situation determines that the expert normally is the leading problem-solver, as s/he has to deliver the instruction and adjust to the novice's horizon. In this situation, specific problem-solving strategies are used by both participants together in a context-sensitive way. In the context of our research they appear to be based only in part in cognitive resources, the other part being interactional.

The expert and the novice are jointly engaged in constructive interaction, success depending upon both participants. If the expert does not act in an adequate way then the novice cannot be effective. If the novice cannot get what s/he needs for understanding and for correct interpretation of what has been said, then the instruction is also inefficient. Thus a reciprocal recognition of the different horizon structures of the partners engaged in instructional dialogues involves the recognition of a mutual dependence upon one another.

References

Cranach, M. von, Kalbermatten, U., Indermühle, K. and Gugler, B. (1980), *Zielgerichtetes Handeln*, Huber: Bern.

Dijk, T. A. van and Kintsch, W. (1983), *Strategies of Discourse Comprehension*, Academic Press: New York.

Dörner, D. (1976), *Problemlösen als Informationsverarbeitung*, Kohlhammer: Stuttgart.

Duncker, K. (1935), *Zur Psychologie des Produktiven Denkens*, Springer: Berlin.

Garnham, A. (1987), *Mental Models as Representations of Discourse and Text*, E. Horwood: Chichester.

Graumann, C. F. (1990), 'Perspectival structure and dynamics in dialogues' in I. Marková and K. Foppa (eds.), *The Dynamics of Dialogue*, Harvester Wheatsheaf: Hemel Hempstead.

Graumann, C. F. and Wintermantel, M. (1984), 'Sprachverstehen als Situationsverstehen', in J. Engelkamp (ed.), *Psychologische Aspekte des Verstehens*, Springer: Heidelberg.

Johnson-Laird, P. N. (1983), *Mental Models*, Cambridge University Press: Cambridge.

Levelt, W. J. M. (1989), *Speaking: From intention to articulation*, MIT Press: Cambridge, MA.

Linell, P. (1990), 'The power of dialogue dynamics', in I. Marková and K. Foppa (eds), *The Dynamics of Dialogue*, Harvester Wheatsheaf: Hemel Hempstead.

Newell, A. and Simon, H. (1972), *Human Problem Solving*, Prentice-Hall: Englewood Cliffs, NJ.

Schegloff, E. (1982), 'Discourse as an interactional achievement: some uses of "uh huh" and other things that come between sentences', in D. Tannen (ed.), *Analyzing Discourse: Text and talk* (Georgetown University Round Table on Language and Linguistics), Georgetown University Press: Washington, DC.

Stalnaker, R. C. (1978), 'Assertion', in P. Cole (ed.), *Syntax and Semantics: Pragmatics*, Academic Press: New York.

Suchman, L. A. (1987), *Plans and Situated Actions*, Cambridge University Press: Cambridge.

Vallacher, R. R. and Wegner, D. M. (1987), 'What do people think they are doing? Action identification and human behaviour', *Psychological Review*, **94**, 3–15.

Wintermantel, M. (1990). 'Sprechen und Verstehen im Dialog: Eine sprachpsychologische Analyse', in M. Herzog and C. F. Graumann (eds.), *Phänomenologische Methoden in den Sozialwissenschaften*, Asanger: Heidelberg.

Wintermantel, M. and Siegerstetter, J. (1988), 'Hearer questioning and instruction', *Journal of Language and Social Psychology*, **7**, 213–27.

7 | 'Teaching': conversational transmission of knowledge

Angela Keppler and Thomas Luckmann

Asymmetries of knowledge in dialogue

Participants in dialogue proceed upon two complementary assumptions concerning important, communicatively relevant traits of the persons with whom they are engaged in dialogue, even though they may not be continuously and clearly aware of such assumptions. First of all, until they have proof to the contrary, they apply the general principle of the reciprocity of perspectives[1] by assuming that others enter into dialogue with the same kind of basic knowledge about the world as they have themselves, and that they also possess similar if not identical means with which to act communicatively on the basis of such knowledge. At the same time, they also know that the operation of this first basic assumption is empirically restricted because of systematic as well as fortuitous inequalities in the social distribution of knowledge. In other words, past experience has taught participants in dialogue to be prepared for culturally, socially and individually determined differences in knowledge and in means of communication between themselves and others. Just as they know that the elementary components of a given social stock of knowledge are normally within the reach of, and possessed by, 'everybody', they also know that normal conditions do not always prevail. In addition, they are also aware of the fact that certain parts of knowledge and of communicative repertoires are unequally distributed among their fellow human-beings, who are experts in some areas and laypersons in others.

Asymmetries of knowledge are a universal aspect of human social life. Indeed, in some cases the basic principle of the reciprocity of persons' perspectives, and the elementary assumption that they share knowledge of the world and the means of communication about it, only apply with such severe empirical restrictions that communication between them is almost impossible. On the whole, this is of little practical consequence. Persons belonging to radically different cultures rarely find themselves in situations in which they are forced to communicate. In fact, a society can be defined by the absence of such radical differences among its members.

Less radical asymmetries of knowledge in dialogue often remain unnoticed. For one thing, differences in the level or in particular items of knowledge may be sufficiently irrelevant to dialogue so as not to form serious obstacles to 'successful' communication and therefore escape notice without much consequence. On the other hand, some asymmetries may be serious enough to prevent, objectively, an adequate understanding among the participants. Under some circumstances they may still remain unnoticed. The consequence may be a shared delusion of 'successful' communication. Furthermore, even if specific asymmetries of knowledge are perceived by one or all participants to be relevant to the course of the dialogue, they may be allowed to subsist. Topics, formulations and the like are individually and collectively adjusted in such a way that the obstacles are circumnavigated rather than removed. After these adjustments, dialogue may proceed on its original course.

However, specific asymmetries of knowledge often become interactively relevant.[2] They become obstacles which cannot be ignored unless the direction of the conversation is changed from its original course. Even then they may be allowed to stand, even though the participants are aware that an adequate continuation of the intended course of dialogue will not be feasible. Among several reasons for this the most important is probably the tacit knowledge of the participants that obstacles to understanding can be turned into interactional assets. Both 'superior knowledge' and 'ignorance', whether real or feigned, can be made to serve tactical and even strategic purposes.

These possibilities of ignoring asymmetries of knowledge, of circumnavigating them or of putting them to good use by failing to remove them, are no doubt important aspects of human communication and deserve to be investigated systematically. None the less, the *removal* of such specific asymmetries of knowledge as are considered actual or potential obstacles to successful communication is surely an even more important component of dialogue and is likely to occur more frequently in ordinary conversation.[3] Normally, participants in dialogue will try to remove situationally relevant asymmetries of knowledge whenever they hinder the satisfactory continuation of the communicative processes in which they are engaged.

In the following we will analyse one kind, and one kind only, of communicative procedure by which specific asymmetries of knowledge are removed. We shall not be concerned either with the general sociological problems of the unequal distribution of knowledge in society or with the variety of institutionalized procedures by which societies distribute the common elements of their stock of knowledge to all members of society and restrict other elements to specified groups.[4] The 'teaching' which we are about to analyse is not done by institutionally defined instructors, it is done by situationally selected 'teachers'. In other words, we are not going to investigate socially organized pedagogical communicative processes, nor shall we study the various genres of formal instruction.[5] We shall analyse 'teaching' in ordinary conversation. The most frequent structural variant, 'factual' instruction, will be described *in extenso*. By way of contrast, a less frequent but interesting variant, the transmission of 'wisdom', will be briefly considered at the end.[6]

The structure of conversational teaching

A change of style[7]

When a communicatively relevant specific asymmetry of knowledge is noticed by one or more of the participants in conversation, its removal usually becomes a task which they feel obliged to attend to immediately. For the duration of this task, an important transformation in the nature of dialogue occurs. In conversations participants normally have roughly similar chances of joining in and saying something – whether they in fact make use of this chance or not. Whenever a teaching sequence is in progress, the 'egalitarian' style which characterizes informal dialogue is temporarily replaced by a 'hierarchical' one. This does not mean that conversation yields to another genre of communication – if, indeed, conversation may be considered a genre in the first place.[8] Conversational teaching remains an enclave *within* conversation. It does not adopt the form of an institutionalized pedagogical enterprise. In conversation no one is authorized *in advance* as a teacher nor does he or she remain one beyond the clearly circumscribed teaching sequence. Nor is anyone's role pre-established socially as that of a pupil. In principle, teachers may turn into pupils and pupils into teachers within the same conversation, although not within the same teaching sequence.

However, one participant *is* selected as a temporarily privileged speaker for the explicit purpose of conversational teaching, and another, to whom the teaching is addressed, as the recipient. The recipients are assigned the relatively passive dialogical role of having to show that they are attending to what they are being taught and of indicating that they understand – or do not understand – any of the steps taken by the 'teacher' to convey to them the knowledge they are assumed to lack.

In a dyad, this aspect of the teaching procedure is relatively simple. Temporarily, one of the two is the 'teacher', the other the 'pupil'. If more than two persons are engaged in conversation, the situation is significantly more complicated. Typically, in the course of conversation one of the participants has shown that he or she lacks an item (or set of items) of knowledge relevant to the topics of conversation. Again, typically, it is this first 'ignoramus' who is selected by the 'teacher' as the main (or, possibly, only intended) recipient of the teaching sequence. (We shall return to the issue of teacher/pupil selection shortly.) As a rule, the other participants are not marked (by gaze, by being addressed by the 'teacher' by name, etc.) as intended recipients. However, everyone involved in the situation is evidently aware that they cannot help being co-recipients of the teaching. This raises for them a point of interactional etiquette. For one thing, there may, objectively, be additional 'have-nots' who should be aligned with the first ignoramus. Are they then to declare themselves as also being in need of the knowledge about to be imparted, and define themselves as additional 'pupils'? Or should they 'dishonestly' suppress their lack of pertinent knowledge and take a chance on acquiring it as free-loaders? On the other hand, they may be as well informed as the teacher candidate. Are they to indicate that they could join in the teaching, or even join it in fact? Would that not be showing off unnecessarily? Or should they 'modestly' accept the role of automatic co-recipients, with their status as potential 'pupils' or 'teachers' remaining undecided? But this again raises a point of interactional etiquette: is it proper to leave other participants in the dark on a matter of potential interactional relevance?

Rather than continuing with speculation on the delicate problems of interactional propriety which are generated by communicatively relevant asymmetries of knowledge, we shall look at some transcripts of conversation in which 'teaching' occurs.[9]

Openings of teaching sequences: 'pupil' initiatives

Even a cursory inspection of the data shows that there are fairly obvious differences between openings in which the 'teaching' is initiated by the 'have-nots' (participants who do not know what is, or seems to be, pertinent to that juncture of dialogue with respect either to the dialogue itself or to the non-verbal components of the ongoing interaction) and those initiated by the 'haves' (participants who *do* know). As a rule, the 'have-nots' show their wish to acquire the pertinent item of knowledge by the simple device of a question or a query. On the other hand, the 'haves' who wish to transmit their knowledge to someone who lacks it must first engage in a certain amount of manoeuvring in order to secure for themselves the right to teach. In other words, potential 'teachers' must acquire some sort of authorization, whereas no particular negotiations are required in order to become a 'pupil'. As we have just said, 'pupils' to be usually initiate a teaching sequence by a question or a query. (For the sake of a simple terminological distinction, we shall call a demand for information pertaining to the ongoing interaction a 'question', a request for knowledge thematically relevant at a particular juncture of dialogue a 'query'.) Questions and queries may concern simple information items as well as 'knowledge' of a more general kind. Asking for the exact time, for example, or requesting the speaker to repeat a word one has not understood for acoustic reasons implies neither knowledge that goes beyond the self-contained item of information nor a genuine asymmetry between the speakers. Whether a teaching sequence is initiated by a question or query can be decided only after looking at its further conversational treatment.

    Extract 7.1 'Soße' [For transcription convention key see Appendix, p. 272-3]

```
→  1 Emil:    mit so ma Gla:sschä:le ⌈ond ma Handdüchle-⌉
→  2 Ute:                            ⌊Papi wi-wi-pas-   ⌋
   3          siert n des emmer daß bei dir bei de Soßa
   4          (-) des Dicke, vom Dünna so absezd,
   5                         (0.5)
   6 Vater:  ⌈M::hh-
   7 Emil:   ⌊Des Dünne-
   8                         (0.5)
   9 Vater:   S:: isch norma::1- normalerweise nicht,

             Sauce (translation)
   1 Emil:    with a glass bowl like that⌈and a hand towel     ⌉
→  2 Ute:                                ⌊Daddy, how-how- does ⌋
   3          it always happen with you that in the sauce
```

```
    4            (-) the thick separates from the thin,
    5                          (0.5)
    6 Father:  ⌈M::hh-
    7 Emil:    ⌊The thin-
    8                          (0.5)
    9 Father: It's:: norm::al - not normally,
```

In this example (a family dinner-table conversation), the topic pursued by Emil (1) is interrupted by a question directed by Ute (2-4) to her father about his success in keeping the 'thick' and the 'thin' apart in his sauces, a question presumably generated by Ute's interest in the sauce before her rather than the conversational topic at hand. It is interesting to note with regard to the speculations at the end of the previous subsection that in this example the father is directly authorized as the 'teacher-to-be' and, even more interesting, that while he is signalling his preparations to respond (6), Emil indicates that he, too, is a 'knower' rather than a 'co-pupil'.

In the next example (a conversation between a father and his two sons about cars and costs of car repairs) Hugo is engaged in explaining certain details of car servicing and repair when he uses a term (1) which, as it turns out, Karl does not understand. But Karl puts in his query after leaving ample time for Hugo to volunteer information about *'Bremsen komplett'* (i.e. the full brake job). The example nicely illustrates some general points about communicatively relevant asymmetries of knowledge.

Extract 7.2 Bremsen komplett
```
      1 Hugo:  Also d Brems komplett machä dürft scho so
      2         auf °fünfhundert kommä°.
      3                          (2.5)
   →  4 Karl:  Was isch d Brems komplett?
      5                          (0.5)
      6 Hugo:  Neu belegä d Bremsflüssigkeit wechslä

             Full brake job (translation)

      1 Hugo:  Well to do a full brake job might easily
      2         °run to five hundred°
      3                          (2.5)
   →  4 Karl:  What is a full brake job?
      5                          (0.5)
      6 Hugo:  New linings changing the brake fluid
```

Queries are typically a consequence of asymmetries of knowledge between a speaker and a listener inadequately taken into account by the speaker. More specifically, whenever a speaker overestimates the amount of knowledge possessed by the listener, the listener may repair the situation by a query.

The general principle of the reciprocity of perspectives of fellow participants in dialogue never applies without empirical restrictions. These help to adjust communicative perspectives and to design utterances for particular recipients.[10]. Knowing what the others know and what they do not know with regard to the topic at hand depends on adequate awareness of the distribution of knowledge in that society at the time. It also depends on satisfactory identification of the social and social-biographical characteristics of the listeners and, for certain kinds of conversation, even on considerable personal knowledge of the fellow participants. Evidently, such knowledge is hardly ever present in full measure. Sometimes it is lacking to such an extent that the recipient design of utterances by the speaker may be inadequate. Are there typical ways of overcoming the potentially ensuing interactional problems?

It has been shown that speakers, at least in conversations in our kind of society, tend to proceed 'politely'.[11] They prefer to over- rather than to underestimate the listeners or, rather, the knowledge on the part of the listeners which they deem necessary for an understanding of the utterance. A maxim of conversational etiquette against 'talking down' seems to operate in ordinary conversations in our society. Thus speakers will generally avoid potentially unnecessary explanations (e.g. of what is involved in a 'full brake job'). If such knowledge should be found to be lacking after all, the speaker is ready to supply it on demand. The giving of potentially necessary information creates a *fait accompli* which is beyond repair if it proves, in fact, to be unnecessary. The withholding of potentially necessary information, however, can easily be corrected.

In the two preceding examples the 'teacher-to-be' was directly or implicitly selected by the 'pupil-candidate'. If a 'teacher-to-be' accepts the invitation, as he or she usually does, he or she typically becomes the main speaker for the duration of the teaching sequence.[12] If, for one reason or another, he or she declines the invitation, other participants may vie for that position. But unless one of them is eventually accepted as the 'teacher' and thus main speaker, successful teaching is unlikely to take place.

Openings of teaching sequences: 'teacher' initiatives

Earlier we said that teaching sequences initiated by 'teachers' to be are opened by more complicated procedures than those started by future 'pupils'. Whereas the latter merely need to ask a question or put a query, the former are obliged to engage in preliminary negotiations in order to acquire the 'right' to teach. However, these preliminaries may range from relatively simple gambits to complicated manoeuvres.

Incidentally, there are openings of 'teaching' sequences which are neither those of the 'teacher-to-be' nor fully 'pupil' initiated. They are presented as corrections of statements made by a previous speaker. In our society there is a notable reluctance to engage in conversational disagreement with others.[13] If such disagreements occur, they tend to be indirect and 'buffered' by various well-known procedures. As a rule, speakers are expected to justify any disagreement – especially one that involves matters of fact. Explicit justifications of this sort typically take the form which characterizes teaching sequences. The 'right' to teach is thus acquired by the disagreement on the part of the 'teacher-to-be' with someone who does not yet know that he or she is a 'pupil-candidate' but who contributes to the opening of the teaching sequence in consequence of the fact that he or she 'must' be granted the right to be given an explanation of the disagreement.[14]

There are more obvious, relatively simpler procedures by which a would-be 'teacher' invites others to invite him or her to 'teach', as for example in 7.3:

Extract 7.3 Kamin

```
   1 Vater:   Und doa:
   2                       (1.0)
   3          is ein (-) Kamin (-) hochgegangen,
   4                       (1.5)
   5          doa ham mer also echt klettern müssn=
→  6 Anne:    =°Was is ⌈des en Kamin?°
   7 Peter:           ⌊Ja ja
   8 Vater:   Bitte?
→  9 Anne:    Was is des en Kamin?
  10 Mutter:  Bloß e so e schmals ⌈Deng.
  11 Chris:                        ⌊Felsspalte.
  12 Vater:   E FELSSPALTE on doa musch doa
```

Chimney (translation)

```
   1 Father:  And the:re
   2                       (1.0)
   3          a chimney (-) led up,
   4                       (1.5)
   5          there we really had to climb=
→  6 Anne:    =°What's ⌈this chimney?°
   7 Peter:           ⌊Yes, yes
```

```
 8 Father: Sorry?
→ 9 Anne:   What is this chimney?
10 Mother: Such a narrow ⌈thing.
11 Chris:                ⌊crevice.
12 Father: A CREVICE where you've got to go
```

By means of pauses and intonations, the speaker sets a word ('chimney') off from the remainder of the utterance and marks it as having a communicatively especially relevant status (3).[15] After a slight delay, one of the listeners takes up this opening gambit and puts the query (6) which was 'invited' by the speaker. The latter does not launch into the teaching sequence directly. He insists on a repetition of the query (9) and thus, whatever his motive, draws attention to the query and makes doubly sure of his 'right' to teach. In fact, he successfully maintains that 'right' (12) against the interference of two other 'teacher'-candidates (10, 11) who, however, at least have thereby managed to declare themselves as being in possession of the relevant knowledge rather than as being free-loaders.

The speaker may be said to have 'try-marked' the concept in his utterance instead of assuming that the concept is known *or* not known to the participants. By *not* volunteering potentially *un*necessary information, he avoids 'talking down' to them. By referring to a communicatively relevant asymmetry of knowledge obliquely, he invites an invitation for necessary teaching without breaching communicative etiquette. It is a relatively safe dialogical procedure to leave the description of their own knowledge status to the listeners and to indicate that he or she, the speaker, is, in fact, leaving it to them.

The following example illustrates well the somewhat problematic nature for a 'teacher-to-be' as well as for potential recipients of self-initiated 'teachings'. It combines several features of simpler opening manoeuvres.

```
→ 1 Otto:  Ja! Un das is am Tschenny Läke
  2              (0.5)
  3        des sin die Gränd Ti:tens!
  4              (1.0)
  5        °Die Gränd Ti:tens:°
  6              (2.0)
  7 Ida:   °Da gibts Grizzlibärn und andre ⌈Bärn°
  8 Otto:                                  ⌊hh Des
  9        is Tschäkson Houl
```

```
       21 Otto:    Zuerst wohl erforscht von französisch
       22          sprechenden Kanadiern und deswegn (-)
       23          Gränd Ti:tens
       24                              (2.0)
    →  25          Weiß nicht ob du soviel französisch kannst
       26          Chris was (-) Töton heißt,
       27                              (2.0)
       28 Chris:   Was heißts? Ich kann jednfalls nix=
       29 Otto:    =Das sin zwei Berge und die s(t) ehn danebn
```

Grand Tetons (translation)

```
        1 Otto:    Yes! And this is at Jenny Lake
        2                              (0.5)
        3          these are the Grand Tetons!
        4                              (1.0)
        5          The °Grand Tetons°
        6                              (2.0)
        7 Ida:     °There there are grizzly bears and other⌈ bears°
        8 Otto:                                            ⌊.hh that's
        9          Jackson Hole
```

```
       21 Otto:    First probably explored by French
       22          speaking Canadians and therefore (-)
       23          Grand Tetons
       24                              (2.0)
    →  25          Don't know whether you speak enough French
       26          Chris what (-) teton means,
       27                              (2.0)
       28 Chris:   What does it mean? Anyway I can't=
       29 Otto:    =These are two mountains and they stand together
```

By virtue of the fact that he is showing travel slides to a group of relatives, the 'would-be-teacher' is already the principal speaker. None the less, he does not launch directly into a topically 'legitimate' teaching sequence. (Perhaps this is due to the somewhat titillating nature of the historical/geographic/linguistic knowledge he would like to impart.) The first gambit consisted, in a similar manner to the previous example, of 'try-marking' the *'Grand Tetons'* by stress and syllable-stretching (3). After a pause, created by the refusal of the audience to accept the gambit (4), he repeats the words, still stressing them, although at a lower volume (5). Another pause shows that the gambit is definitely rejected. Another potential 'teacher', Ida, (Otto's travel companion) starts to comment on the slide (7), but Otto successfully re-establishes himself as principal speaker (8). He does not give up. Soon (23) he marks his 'Grand Tetons' again, again without success. But after a two-second pause (24), he engages in a more obvious manoeuvre than the previous one ('try-marking' 'Grand Tetons') and 'nudges', perhaps rather obviously, one of the viewers into declaring his knowledge-status. Most probably the speaker assumes that the latter is deficient (25, 26), but characteristically he addresses the selected 'pupil-to-be' or, one is tempted to say, 'victim', by name. After another two second, i.e. rather lengthy, pause, Otto's prompting is crowned with success and Chris complies with the invitation to ask (28). Only then does Otto embark upon his ('*les-voyageurs*-seeing-impressively-pointed-peaks-and-thinking-of-the-obvious') explanation.

The transfer of knowledge

Although there is a change in communicative style when 'teaching' sequences are opened in ordinary conversation, they, as shown, remain embedded in its overall dialogical structure. In the *openings* of conversational 'teaching' shifts in recipient design on the part of the speaker (from the taken for granted, elliptical to the explicitly pedagogical style) are either self-initiated-but-other-ratified or even other-invited. Despite the fact that a 'teacher-candidate' is selected in an opening sequence, the transfer of knowledge which occurs in the next and main phase of conversational 'teaching' does not turn into genuine monologue but retains manifestly dialogical features.

Successful *transfer of knowledge* presupposes the participation of the recipient. More than that (or, rather, more precisely) it requires that the recipient *show* his participation.

Extract 7.5 Prallhang-Gleithang
→ 1 Otto: Gleithang wird ähm (-) ⌈akkumuliert akkumuliert
→ 2 Ida: ⌊und abgelagert
→ 3 Otto: am Prallhang wird erodiert, (-) äja?
→ 4   (1.5)
→ 5   Dadurch ä (-) durch die Schuttmassn die abgelagert
→ 6   werdn ä hh wird dann der <u>Mäander</u> des Flusses immer
→ 7   stärker, ja::,
→ 8 Chris: mhm
→ 9 Otto: Bis es dan zum Zwangsmäander dann kommt wenn des
→ 10   Gelände sich hebt so wie am Mittelrhein;
→ 11   (0.5)
→ 12   Das is n sogenannter Zwangsmäander der wenn der Fluβ

	13	nicht mehr frei, (-) sondern durch die Hebung, (-)
	14	wird er gezwungen sich einzuschneidn
	15 Chris:	ja
	16 Otto:	Während hier am Oberrhein des sin freie Mäander,
	17	(0.5)
	18 Chris:	ija:.
	19 Otto:	die also sichtlich weiter sich ausgestaltn

Undercut bank/slip-off slope (translation)

→	1 Otto:	slip-off slope is where it hhm (-) ⌈accumulates
		⌊and deposits
	2 Ida:	
	3 Otto:	undercut bank is where it erodes, (-) yes?
	4	(1.5)
	5	Because ah (-) of the gravel which is deposited
	6	there are aahh there is an increase in the <u>meanders</u>
	7	of the river, yes::,
	8 Chris:	mhm
	9 Otto:	Until it then comes to a forced meander when
	10	the land rises just as on the middle reaches of the Rhine;
	11	(0.5)
	12	This is a so-called forced meander which happens when the river cannot
	13	wander freely anymore, (-) but because of the steepness, (-)
	14	⌈it is forced to carve its own way
	15 Chris:	⌊yes
	16 Otto:	Whereas here on the Upper Rhine there are free meanders,
	17	(0.5)
	18 Chris:	ye:s.
	19 Otto:	which therefore can still be seen forming today

At first sight, this example seems to illustrate something like 'monological' teaching. But a closer look at lines (8, 15, 18) shows the participation of the listeners – it is, after all, a dialogical enterprise. The example also shows the pedagogical step by step procedure followed by the speaker.

Conversational 'teaching' sequences are evidently recognized by the participants as a conversational sub-species which may operate with its own rules for some time but which will eventually be replaced by the rules of ordinary conversation. For the duration of such sequences there is a modification of the 'normal' turn-taking procedure. By observing the modified procedure, the participants demonstrate their awareness of the special features of 'teaching' sequences. The principal speaker need not worry about losing his or her turn when pausing. Within this phase, the speaker typically only relinquishes his or her turn for a clearly delimited purpose: an acknowledgement by the 'pupil' that he or she had recognized the preceding utterance as the first step of a knowledge-transfer sequence. Such pauses invite positive or negative feedback signals by the recipient. An assenting 'mhm' or 'yes', a dubious 'hm', etc., serve as 'behavioural tokens' which are offered to the 'teacher' in the appropriate slots.[16]

In general, pauses by the principal speaker seem to be rather direct invitations to the 'pupil' to acknowledge successful or unsuccessful 'receipt' of the preceding 'teaching' step. Another, less direct method is the 'try-marking' of concepts. Evidently, first 'try-marking' a word and then pausing is a particularly insistent invitation to the recipient to respond in one way or another.

Just as there are several ways of 'inviting' recipient acknowledgement, there is a substantial repertoire of 'behavioural tokens' for responding to the invitation. The absence of any recipient signal is, of course, a powerful indication of inattentiveness or failing interest. And the monotonous repetition of an 'mhm' rather than an inventive use of the repertoire of recipient signals is likely to signal such lack of interest.

Terminations of 'teaching'

It has already been noted that the dialogical character of 'teaching' can be impaired by an absence of recipient signals. Such a *show* of inattentiveness, or even of complete lack of interest, typically leads to a termination of the attempt to transfer knowledge. A monological continuation of 'teaching' sequences is probably extremely rare, at least in contemporary Western conversational 'cultures'. On the basis of our data we suggest that a more likely outcome is a return to the ordinary style of conversation in which the unsuccessful 'teaching' sequence was embedded. The turn-taking modifications which mark 'teaching' sequences are cancelled, the authorization of the principal speaker no longer seems to hold, and other participants frequently re-enter conversation by introducing new topics.

The following example shows one possible ending of a 'teaching' sequence:

Extract 7.6 Kernfusion
```
  1 Kurt:   Die Sonne is kein Atommeiler in unserm
  2         jetzigen Sinn sondern im Sinne der Kern-
  3         fusion ⌈ja,
→ 4 Lilo:          ⌊Ja ja ich weiß ⌈schon;
  5 Kurt:                          ⌊Un diesn Prozeß:=
  6 Lilo:   =diese Zukunftsener ⌈gie
  7 Kurt:                       ⌊die jaja;
  8 Lilo:   ja:.
```

Nuclear fusion (translation)
```
  1 Kurt:   The sun isn't an atomic reactor in our
  2         present sense but in the sense of nuclear
  3         fusion ⌈yes,
→ 4 Lilo:          ⌊Yes yes I know ⌈already;
  5 Kurt:                           ⌊And this process:=
  6 Lilo:   =this energy of the fu ⌈ture
  7 Kurt:                          ⌊which yes yes;
  8 Lilo:   yes:.
```

This way of ending a 'teaching' sequence indicates that the transfer of knowledge was unsuccessful or, at least that it could no longer be successfully continued. One may speculate that entirely unsuccessful transfers of knowledge are most often due to a 'teacher's' pedagogical inadequacy. Unsuccessful continuations of the transfer of knowledge, however, are probably attributable to the 'teacher's' undue extension of his privilege as principal speaker.

As in all 'teaching' phases, the termination of (presumably) successful transfers of knowledge is a dialogical affair, i.e. it requires the participation of both 'teacher' and 'pupil'. Such participation is not necessarily on terms of equality. Thus, it is typically the 'teacher' who signals the end of the knowledge-transfer phase. He does this by a summary 'formulation',[17] or by non-verbal means as, e.g. by lowering the intonational contour or by slowing down as shown in the following extract.

Extract 7.7 Mission
```
→  1 Nonne:  Dominikaner is ein (-) vorwiegend ein Prediger-
             orden
   2                               (0.5)
   3 Hr B:   °aja°
   4 Nonne:  Während Franziskus ah die Predigt (-) °scho au°
   5         er hat- er hat die Laienpredigt,
   6                               (0.5)
   7         also jeder soll predigen muß ⌈predige
   8 Hr B:                                ⌊hmhm
   9                               (0.5)
→ 10 Nonne:  Aber sogar noch mehr mit seinem Leben als
  11         wie mit Worten;
```

Mission (translation)

```
 1 Nun:   Dominicans are a (-) mainly a preaching order
 2                 (0.5)
 3 Mr B:  °oh yea°
 4 Nun:   While Francis ah the sermon (-) °also already°
 5        he has- he has done lay preaching,
 6                 (0.5)
 7        well everybody should preach must ⎡preach
 8 Mr B:                                    ⎣hmhm
 9                 (0.5)
→10 Nun:   But even more with his life than
 11       with words;
```

But in some instances 'pupils', too, take the initiative to close the knowledge-transfer phase by saying or demonstrating that at that juncture they have already assimilated the items of knowledge (Extracts 7.8 and 7.9) which are being transferred to them.

Extract 7.8 Mission
```
 1 Nonne:  Herrgott wenn du mich etz wirklich
 2         noch brauchn kannsch odr willsch ((schnell))
 3                 (0.5)
 4         dann zeig mir des deutlich
→5         °°ond klar.°°      ((langsam))
 6                 (1.0)
 7 Hr B:   aja:.
```

Mission (translation)
```
 1 Nun:   Lord now if you really
 2        still can or wish to use me ((fast))
 3                 (0.5)
 4        then show me distinctly
→5        °°and clearly°°    ((slow))
 6                 (1.0)
 7 Mr B:  aja:.
```

Extract 7.9 Post
```
 1 Berta:  Weil die tragn das nur einmal aus:
 2         sobald das dann vorbei is s wird nich
 3         zweima ausgetragn (-)
→4         .hh So läuft das ab.
 5                 (3.0)
 6 Arne:   ehmhh;
```

Post (translation)
```
 1 Berta:  Because they deliver only once:
 2         as soon as that is over it won't be
```

```
         3             round a second time (-)
→        4             .hh that's how it works.
         5                      (3.0)
         6 Arne:  hmhh;
```

Incidentally, merely *saying* that one 'has got the point' need not necessarily suffice, and the 'teacher' *may* continue. *Demonstrating* that one has acquired the knowledge in question, however, seems to be a definite method to stop further 'teaching'. (In Extract 7.9 the principal speaker even stops 'teaching' in the middle of the sentence.)

Once the transfer of knowledge has been terminated successfully, i.e. in the sense of joint ratification that the transfer has taken place, there is no further reason to maintain the modifications of conversational style. The designation of one participant as principal speaker is invalidated, just as the relative 'passivity' of the 'pupil' is replaced by fully-fledged 'rights' of participation in the turn-taking 'machinery'. Once the communicatively relevant asymmetry of knowledge is overcome, the 'egalitarian' style of dialogue prevails again. The 'teaching' sequence in ordinary conversation is typically a 'side sequence within an ongoing sequence'.[18]

Information, knowledge and wisdom in conversation

There are evident and significant differences between communicative interaction in socially defined and institutionally organized pedagogical enterprises such as schools and apprenticeships on the one hand, and conversational 'teaching' on the other. The most obvious differences concern the ways in which time is budgeted for pedagogical purposes. In the former, substantial blocks of time are allotted for such purposes according to socially defined and institutionalized schedules which determine an individual's 'budgeting' of her or his course of life; in the latter, 'teaching' sequences are opened and closed within 'dominant' conversational sequences. In the former, momentary interests and motives are subordinated to overarching biographical ones; in the latter, interest is generated in a situation and also satisfied in it. Teaching and learning are planned in advance, 'teaching' sequences arise *ad hoc*.

Allowing for such differences, one may none the less say that almost any kind of knowledge, using the term in its broadest, unspecific connotation, can be transmitted in conversation. However, the relatively elaborate dialogical procedures and interactional manoeuvres which are normally necessary for conversational 'teaching' are not required in the transfer of simple *information*. In ordinary question and answer sequences, for example, the 'normal' conversational turn-taking 'machinery' remains in operation. Asking the time and getting an answer does not change the general conversational style. It is therefore useful to distinguish between simple, item-bound information and other kinds of knowledge which have an implied or, sometimes, articulated significance as constituent elements of overarching bodies of knowledge.[19] Only the latter are transmitted in relatively lengthy, embedded sequences whose features have been described in the preceding sections.

An important implication of the distinction between 'mere' information and items of knowledge which have a meaning beyond the individual instance is that the successful transfer of items of knowledge (in this narrower sense) involves the placement of the items in a larger context. This requirement may be met implicitly by both 'teacher' and 'pupil'. Thus, when seemingly item-bound, individual instances are introduced into 'teaching' sequences, they will serve as examples.[20] In this case the 'teacher' may simply assume that the interpretive rules for this genre are known to the recipient, whereas the 'pupil', seeing the point, will not demonstrate that fact. On the other hand, 'teaching' may include explication of the 'larger meaning' of an item of knowledge which the 'teacher' imparts to the pupil in the recipient design of the 'teaching'. The 'pupil' demonstrates 'having got the point' by enlarging upon it in the closing phase of the sequence.

It may be assumed that placement in a larger context of knowledge-items transferred in a 'teaching' sequence is a pervasive characteristic of the conversational 'teaching' procedure. Thus highly specific information on how father prepares sauces may be linked to a folk theory about curdling substances. Items about the annual income of professional tennis players may be related to hypotheses about career earning expectations, and remarks about starving children in the Third World may be interpreted in the light of a Christian theodicy. Such placement may not be articulated. Sometimes it would appear cumbersome or even pedantic and then it is likely to be avoided for reasons of conversational etiquette. However, there does seem to be a tendency to articulate the place of a particular item of knowledge in a larger scheme, even if that item was communicatively relevant only when the 'teaching' was initiated. This tendency, noticeable in our data, is probably one of the reasons why 'teaching' sequences extend over several turns, forming sequences within sequences.[21]

It is easy to show the difference between information and knowledge in the narrower sense by the way in which their transfer is treated in conversation. However, even knowledge in the restricted sense is by no means homogeneous. It includes knowledge about the multiple domains of reality, about nature, technology, human beings, and lexical knowledge. It is knowledge both of matters of fact and matters of 'ought'. There is one important kind of knowledge which spans several domains and includes both matters of fact and matters of 'ought'. It is wisdom. This is knowledge accumulated over the generations about the course of human life, its sense and nonsense, its problems and possible solutions to the problems, its good and its bad sides. Such knowledge has a long and hallowed history in many cultures. Several oral and literary genres, some religious but some also quite secular, have emerged in the course of history.[22] The reason why we single it out in the present analysis of inequalities of knowledge is that its transfer in conversation shows certain important deviations from the general structure of conversational 'teaching'.

It was noted earlier that being the *recipient* of 'teaching' is not a favourite pastime in modern conversational 'cultures'. Correspondingly, would-be 'teachers' must avoid giving the impression that 'teaching' is *their* favourite pastime.[23] They must therefore carefully prepare the ground before launching into 'teaching' on their own initiative. As was noted, matters are somewhat simpler in the case of 'pupil-initiated' 'teachings'. It is noteworthy to repeat that there is a strong preference for 'pupil-initiated' 'teachings' in our conversational culture. This, however, does not hold for the transmission of wisdom. True, instances of the transmission of wisdom are not only much rarer in our data than 'teaching' involving other kinds of knowledge; it may be assumed that in this respect our data mirror the prevalent conversational culture. But *if* transmission of wisdom is initiated at all, it is initiated by the 'teacher', not the 'pupil'. If there are seekers of wisdom, they do not invite its teaching in conversation (going to seminars on transcendental meditation, surely, is another matter). Thus the first noteworthy deviation in the structure of 'teaching' is already apparent in the opening phase.

Extract 7.10 Stalingrad
→ 1 Vater: Ja Carl du mußt doch auch- Carl
    2   du mußt doch auch davon ausgehen

Conversational transmission of knowledge 161

```
 3                    (0.5)
 4           daß
 5                    (1.0)
 6           so langs's (-) den Leutn gut geht do
 7           denken se net an Gott. Do denkn se auch
 8           nicht ans Betn (-) ans Betn denken se ersch
 9           dann, wenn's ihnen dreckig geht

19 Vater:    Wenn's oim gut geht do denkt doch gar
20           niemand an Gott.
21                    (3.0)
22 Carl:     °Des isch sicher en Fehler des schtimmt;°
23                    (2.5)
→ 24 Vater:  Des hot scho mancher;
25                    (0.5)
26           Atheist.
27                    (0.5)
28           und so weiter (-) in Stalingrad; (-)
29           wenn er an der Front war und seine
30           Ka:- Kameraden um ihn um- umenander
31                    (0.5)
32           HIE waren und=so=weiter. Dann hat
33           er auch so: gemacht.
34                    (1.0)
```

Stalingrad (translation)

```
→  1 Father: Yes Carl you've also got to- Carl
 2           you've got to suppose
 3                    (0.5)
 4           that
 5                    (1.0)
 6           as long as (-) people are doing fine then
 7           they don't think of God. And they don't
 8           think of prayer (-) they think of prayer only
 9           when the going gets tough.

19 Father:   When one is doing fine then
20           nobody thinks of God
21                    (3.0)
22 Carl:     °This is certainly wrong that's true;°
23                    (2.5)
→ 24 Father: That's what many a;
25                    (0.5)
26           atheist.
27                    (0.5)
28           and so forth (-) in Stalingrad; (-)
29           when he was at the front and his
```

```
30          co:-comrades round him round- all around him
31                       (0.5)
32          dropped DEAD and=so=forth. Then he too
33          did tha:t.
34                       (1.0)
```

In this example, a family dinner-table conversation between father, mother, three adult sons and a daughter, two significant features appear at the very beginning (1): the direct address (Carl) and the normative appeal ('you've also got to'). The authority of the father to present his 'wise summary' of human behaviour in stress cannot be derived from a claim to have personally witnessed what he reports (24–33). It is the experience of his *generation* which he presents as evidence for the generalization that people only turn to God when the going gets tough. As a member of the war generation he shares – vicariously – in the experience of a significant portion of its members. This authorizes him to see that piece of evidence in support of the initial general insight into human behaviour.

In this case, too, one may still speak of a sort of inequality of knowledge between the 'teacher' and the 'pupil(s)'. But here the speaker's advantage over the listeners is based on experience, an experience of human nature which cannot be 'learned from books', an experience acquired in 'the tough school of life'.

The structure of this sequence differs significantly from that of the 'teaching' sequences analysed earlier, not only in the opening phase but also in the transfer phase. The salient fact is the changed function of pauses. They do not invite recipient signals but are, as it were, an integral part of the speaker's turn. Characteristically, in many instances, the intonation sinks rather than rises. This sets off the constituent parts of the utterance from each other. The rhetorical purposes seem obvious: the message is allowed 'to sink in'.

Correspondingly, the listeners need not acknowledge 'receipt' by a stream of 'behavioural tokens'. On the contrary, it seems as if the absence of such signals indicates the 'sinking in' of a serious message, a process which is not to be distributed by trivial 'hms' and 'yesses'.[24]

This should not be taken as a sign that the dialogical procedure which characterizes the removal of communicatively relevant inequalities of knowledge in conversation is abandoned in favour of a full-fledged monologue, thereby ending conversation and beginning another kind of communication. The transmission of wisdom, too, occurs in sequences firmly embedded in conversation. However, the dialogical aspects of the structure underlying the transmission of wisdom are, on the whole, less obvious. The interplay of utterances, invitational pauses and 'behavioural tokens' does not cease entirely but is supplemented by the characteristic 'sink in' pauses on the part of the speaker and, correspondingly, the avoidance of superficial 'receipt' signals on the part of the listener. Dialogue can be maintained in the silences, too.

Notes

1. Schutz and Luckmann, 1973, pp. 84 ff.; see also Litt, 1926, pp. 109 ff.
2. Drew shows in a detailed manner how asymmetry is generated out of interactional moves. His analysis of asymmetries in ordinary conversations highlights the ways in which asymmetries of knowledge have a demonstrable relevance to the participants in the design of their talk. See Drew in this volume, Chapter 2.
3. On 'dialogue and conversation' see also Luckmann, 1990, especially pp. 55 ff., where conversation is defined as a 'historical subspecies of dialogue in which a relatively high degree of specifically communicative symmetry, typically as equality, prevails.
4. For a general treatment of these issues, see Berger and Luckmann, 1966.
5. For an analysis of asymmetries in institutional settings see e.g. Linell and Jönsson's, and Käsermann's contributions to this volume. Linell and Jönsson show in their analysis of narratives produced in police interrogations that 'on the one hand, there is a dialogicality underlying the police report, and on the other hand, the perspective of the report is by and large that of the police' (Linell and Jönsson, this volume, Chapter 4). Käsermann, in her analysis of psychotherapists' sessions, is interested in the consequences which an unequal distribution of knowledge has for the speech exchange system. She is especially concerned with those communicational moves which are associated with the position of one participant being regarded as an 'expert', e.g. the therapist in relation to a client in psychotherapy: see Käsermann this volume, Chapter 5.
6. The analysis is based on a substantial corpus of recordings of family table talk, of social occasions organized for the purpose of showing slides to friends or family members and various other materials from a research project on reconstructive genres of everyday communication (directed by Jörg Bergmann and Thomas Luckmann, Department of Sociology, University of Konstanz, financed by the German Science Foundation from 1984-9). The present paper is based in considerable part on analyses published in Keppler, 1989; Keppler and Luckmann, 1989; see also the two forthcoming publications by Luckmann and Keppler.
7. One could also speak of a change in 'footing' (Goffman, 1981, p. 128).
8. See Luckmann, 1984.

9. Because the data which we used for this analysis do not include video-recordings, we cannot consider mimetic 'questions' and 'queries' such as raised eyebrows, looks of puzzlement, etc.
10. On receipt design, see Sacks and Schegloff, 1979.
11. See Schegloff, 1979.
12. On the concept of the main or principal speaker, see Wald, 1978, p. 152.
13. See Pomerantz, 1984.
14. For a detailed analysis of a pertinent example, see Keppler, 1989.
15. Following Sacks and Schegloff (1979, p. 18) we may describe this procedure as 'try-marking'. They use the concept in a somewhat narrower sense to describe a speaker's reference to a person, whenever he or she was uncertain whether he or she was known to the addressee, by means of a specific pronunciation: 'with an upward intonational contour, followed by a brief pause'.
16. 'Behavioural tokens', a term introduced by Schegloff (1982) to describe utterances which, in addition to showing recipient participation as acknowledgements of having understood the preceding step of the knowledge-transfer, may also function as 'continuers' (Sacks, 1971, p. 4), i.e. as dialogical ratifications of the pseudo-monological transfer of knowledge by the principal speaker.
17. On 'formulations' in their original sense, see Sacks, 1971. For an extended employment of the concept, see Luckmann, 1988.
18. See Jefferson, 1972, p. 294.
19. Such bodies of knowledge need not have the form of systematic theory, folk or scientific. They may be as modest as the inventory of mountain-climbing techniques or consist of an account of the elementary geology of erosion or describe the complex functioning of the mail service.
20. See Keppler, 1988.
21. There is an exception to this tendency. When knowledge is articulated in minor genres or genre-like forms such as sayings, proverbs, stereotyped formulations, etc., its introduction in conversation may occupy a single turn.
22. In our limited corpus of data there are many instances of the main variants of teaching but relatively few examples of the transmission of wisdom and even fewer such of a purely secular nature.
23. The 'schoolmaster' and 'pedant' stereotypes are negatively loaded in our, and earlier times.
24. Incidentally, but not fortuitously, a similar method is likely to be employed, in combination with other methods, in key phases of the narration of religious conversion: see Ulmer, 1988.

References

Berger, P. and Luckmann, T. (1966), *The Social Construction of Reality*, Doubleday: New York.

Goffman, E. (1981), 'Footing', in Erving Goffman, *Forms of Talk*, Blackwell: Oxford.

Jefferson, G. (1972), 'Side sequences', in D. Sudnow (ed.), *Studies in Social Interaction*, The Free Press: New York.

Keppler, A. (1988), 'Beispiele in Gesprächen. Zu Form und Funktion exemplarischer Geschichten', *Zeitschrift für Volkskunde*, 84, 39-57.
Keppler, A. (1989), 'Schritt für Schritt. Das Verfahren alltäglicher Belehrungen', *Soziale Welt*, 40, 538-56.
Keppler, A. and Luckmann, T. (1989), "Weisheits' - Vermittlung im Alltag. Wer in den Augen eines anderen weise ist, ist weise', in Oelmüller; W. (ed), *Philosophie und Weisheit*, Schöningh: Paderborn.
Litt, T. (1926), *Individuum und Gemeinschaft. Grundlegung der Kulturphilosophie*, G. B. Teubner: Leipzig.
Luckmann, T. (1984), 'Das Gespräch', in K. Stierle and R. Warning (eds), *Das Gespräch* Poetik und Hermeneutik, Fink: Munich.
Luckmann, T. (1988), 'Alltägliche Verfahren der Rekonstruktion kommunikativer Ereignisse', unpublished manuscript, University of Konstanz.
Luckmann, T. (1990), 'Social communication, dialogue and conversation', in I. Marková and K. Foppa, (eds), *The Dynamics of Dialogue*, Harvester Wheatsheaf: Hemel Hempstead.
Luckmann, T. and Keppler, A. (forthcoming) 'Lebensweisheiten im Gespräch' in H. G. Petzold and R. Kühn (eds), *Psychotherapie und Philosophie*, Junfermann: Paderborn.
Luckmann, T. and Keppler, A. (forthcoming) 'Weisheit im modernen Alltag', in H. Flothkötter and B. Nacke (eds), *Zeichen der Zeit*, Regensberg: Münster.
Pomerantz, A. (1984), 'Agreeing and disagreeing with assessments: some features of preferred/dispreferred turn shapes', in J. M. Atkinson and J. Heritage, (eds), *Structures of Social Action: Studies in conversation analysis*, Cambridge University Press: Cambridge.
Sacks, H. (1971), 'Spring Lectures', No. 5, unpublished manuscript.
Sacks, H. and Schegloff, E. A. (1979), 'Two preferences in the organization of reference to persons in conversation and their interaction' in G. Psathas (ed.), *Everyday Language: Studies in ethnomethodology*, Irvington: New York.
Sacks, H., Schegloff, E. A. and Jefferson, G. (1974), 'A simplest systematics for the organization of turntaking in conversation', *Language*, 50, 696-735.
Schegloff, E. A. (1979), 'Identification and recognition in telephone conversation openings', in G. Psathas, (ed.), *Everyday Language: Studies in ethnomethodology*, Irvington: New York.
Schegloff, E. A. (1982), 'Discourse as an interactional achievement: some uses of "uh huh" and other things that come between sentences', in D. Tannen (ed.), *Analyzing Discourse: Text and talk* (Georgetown University Round Table on Languages and Linguistics), Georgetown University Press: Washington, DC.
Schutz, A. and Luckmann, T. (1973), *The Structures of the Life-World I*, Northwestern University Press: Evanston, IL.
Ulmer, B. (1988), 'Konversionserzählungen als rekonstruktive Gattung. Erzählerische Mittel und Strategien bei der Rekonstruktion eines Bekehrungserlebnisses', *Zeitschrift für Soziologie*, 17, 19-33.
Wald, B. (1978), 'Zur Einheitlichkeit und Einleitung von Diskurseinheiten', in U. Quasthoff (ed.), *Sprachstruktur - Sozialstruktur. Zur linguistischen Theorienbildung*, Scriptor: Königstein.

8 The taming of foes: The avoidance of asymmetry in informal discussions[1]

Hubert Knoblauch

Although the data of the following investigation stem from what may be called 'argumentation' in everyday family dinner talk, the problem of dialogical asymmetry does not arise in the way one would usually expect, and it is rather this lack of conspicuous asymmetry that is in question here. True, local asymmetries, as descried by Linell and Luckmann (this volume, Chapter 1), are a ubiquitous phenomenon in verbal exchanges. But if one expected everyday argument in family talk to be a field of speakers' attempts to exert dominance, as in, say, institutional dialogue (Linell and Jönsson, this volume, Chapter 4; Drew, Chapter 2), one would be disappointed. Dominance, as we found in our investigation, seems, rather, to be the very feature speakers in dialogues try to evade. And oddly enough, they seem to circumnavigate this by using a format which is traditionally taken to be the very basis for the exertion of dominance: disagreement.

The use of disagreement, of course, is not a tool for the ultimate establishment of an 'ideal speech situation', which may be characterized by communicational equality. The 'irreparable rhetorical character of everyday talk', frankly admitted by Habermas (1981; 1984, p. 179), allows at best for what Rommetveit (1974) calls *complementarity*. Complementarity designates forms of verbal exchange which are based on reciprocity, more exactly – on reciprocity of motives (of, to use Schutzean terms, in-order-to and because), e.g. in buying and selling, asking and answering and so on. One aim of this paper, therefore, is to give evidence for the fact that speakers produce disagreement collaboratively in a way which evades dominance, especially by avoiding both the abyss of conflict talk and the byway of instruction. Disagreement may thus be regarded as complementary verbal interaction which establishes a dialectical relation between utterances and speakers.

The complementarity of this dialectical relation between utterances and speakers does not, however, pertain to all contexts of conversation. I assert neither that it is a feature of all categories of argumentation nor that it is typical of discussions in general nor of all those family discussions in our investigations which have been subjected to detailed scrutiny. On the contrary, this complementary relation in argumentation only comes up in certain kinds of conversation, in what Goffman (1981) has called a *form of talk*. Thus the second goal of this paper is to outline the elements of this form of talk which I would like to call *informal discussion*. Even if informal discussions can be said to form long sequences of conversation, i.e. what Bergmann (1987) has called a *communicative aggregate*, one salient feature of this kind of discourse is the frequent use of disagreement.

Although I shall present only a few examples of such informal discussions, there are two reasons for assuming that these cases exhibit patterns of a more common form of talk. One reason is intuitively found in our common everyday experience; the second reason can be seen in what appears to me to be shortcomings of previous research on argumentation.

First, we are all acquainted with those heated debates in pubs, those often sophisticated discussions on such important questions as the form of the latest sporting idol, or whether the newest film isn't just too boring. From our own experience we may remember two things. On the one hand we usually debate, that is, we disagree about something unproblematic; on the other hand we never arrive at answers to those very important questions with which we started our debate. The very opposite is the case. Our discussions ramble from one subject to the other, we talk on and on; we order a beer while thinking about an argument, and having been served we realize that we are too late, the discussion has arrived at a different topic, the point cannot be made any more because, for example, X suddenly tells one of his most amusing jokes. There is no doubt that in this way informal discussions account for a certain degree of sociability; they provide us with topics and, moreover, with the tension and the thrill of pursuing these topics; and they make us continually change the topic. As we usually do not know how this happens, as conversation may go on against our will, one of the interesting questions of this chapter is - aside from demonstrating the complementarity of disagreement – to hint at how (and why) we do this.

Even though argumentation has long been a topic of academic interest, I felt at a loss when trying to use concepts of argumentation theory to analyse these informal discussions. No doubt, one can find something in them which takes on the status of an argument (by means which are described later). And, no doubt, persuasive techniques, as have been described thoroughly by Perelman and Olbrechts-Tyteca (1970), are employed continuously.[2] But in informal discussion, logical truth seems only of minor importance. Instead of using the formal structure of an argument – be it a 'tree of arguments' or the so-called T-scheme as proposed by Toulmin (1983) – the speakers seem to be driven by the dynamics of dialogue, by the stepwise transition of verbal action in performance (Linell, 1990).[3] That previous analyses of argumentation do not provide us with sufficient instruments to investigate such informal discussions is easily seen. First, few investigations are concerned with naturally occurring argumentational data. And even where this is the case they mostly rely on argumentations which are produced in institutional contexts, which exercise heavy restrictions on the performance of arguments.

Argumentation has been investigated in multiple ways. Nevertheless most of the data analysed stem from argumentation in *institutional* settings (which are more readily accessible). Parliamentary debates, public discussions on the radio, on television or in public places, therapeutic conversation and court trials are but a few examples of such settings. If, however, one were to accept the scientific commonplace that informal discussions form the somehow 'original', non-contaminated paradigm for discussion, or if one just wished to study naturally occurring informal argumentation, it is obvious that these settings differ in significant ways from anything one may conceive of as informal discussion: speech and individual contributions are often planned and projected in advance; the rules of talk, the distribution of proponents' and opponents' roles are fixed and organized beforehand, and often even the formal role of a chairman is pre-established. It is hardly necessary to stress that these precautions do not hold for informal argumentation (which can take the form of informal discussions). But it does seem necessary to draw attention to the fact that systematic contortions can arise if features of institutional argumentation are simply transferred to informal settings.

Take, for example, the lore that argumentation starts usually with a 'problem', the 'quaestio' or 'validity claim'. In this version argumentation can then be defined as the process of solving the problem posed in the 'quaestio'. Given the quaestio, this process is conceived of as a kind of logical calculus. Even if some unspecific interactional concepts (as, e.g. some notion of 'challenge')[4] are included, argumentation is seen to be amenable to analysis in terms of, e.g. a 'deep structure of a tree of arguments' which are organized along a problem with which the speakers are preoccupied the entire time (Miller, 1984, pp. 222 ff.). If one, however, takes a close look at these investigations, one finds that it is exactly the quaestio which is pre-given by scientific investigators themselves who impute a 'problem' to be argued about by their subjects, and then find (surprisingly enough) that their subjects' argumentation resolves around this 'problem' (Miller, 1984).

On the other hand, the very definition of informal discussions entails the fact that 'problems' are not given in advance. Precisely the opposite: informal discussions are the processes by which 'problems' are constructed. That is, the 'problem' is not to be seen as a singular utterance (as seems to be taken for granted in speech-act theoretical approaches) but is constructed interactively by the use of disagreement. Faced with such apparently 'non-logical' procedures, some analysts have misconceived this form of talk as unregulated, the usual rules of turn-taking and of speech etiquette being continuously broken (Schank, 1987, p. 34). In this perspective dialogical argumentation turns out to be a kind of continuous reparation procedure. What I want to show is that the apparent violation of rules, the seemingly redundant constructions of disagreement and the incessant interruptions, are instead vital constituents of argumentation in informal discussions. They provide argumentation in a dialogical, dialectical way which does not in any way lack rationality – only the rationality differs from that of more institutionalized forms of argumentation. In order to describe the form of conversational argument involved, I will draw on Coulter's notion of argumentative sequences (Coulter, 1979), to designate series of disagreements.

Thus the 'validity claim' made in argumentation does not pertain to singular utterances. It is rather a collaborative accomplishment of the speakers brought about by means of disagreement. What is at issue in an argument is not 'self-evident', seen by just looking at the words. Nor is it something one speaker alone can intentionally bring about. Rather it seems as if it were the machinery of argumentative conversations, the form of talk, which produces and transforms the claims and counter-claims of the individual actors, almost unwillingly on their part. The issue is constructed by all the participating speakers, and their ways of producing it, the manner of their disagreement, become part of the issue itself. Thus an argument only becomes a conversational 'problem' if it is established interactively, that is if the speakers produce a disagreement which is perceivable to both parties. This social reality of argument depends, as I will try to show, on the interactive construction of its observability which thus renders it effective as disagreement.

Although I do not agree with Habermas's notion of 'validity claim', he was the one to stress the necessity of argumentation in modern society, argumentation being the way in which the differences of knowledge, values and identities, based on the plurality of life worlds, become an enduring problem for social action. Opposing the harmonistic view held by Pomerantz (1984; see also Jacobs and Jackson, 1982), which states that disagreement is a 'dispreferred activity', informal discussions provide one example of the frequent and even cherished use of disagreement. The machinery of argumentation works on the ground of continuous disagreement, both with respect to the organization of turns, and to the thematic organization.[5] Instead of being dispreferred, disagreement is – under certain conditions – a mechanism to produce topical relevance, to provide for thematic progression, for entertainment and thrill.

Moreover, the situation in our family dinner talk structurally very much resembles the 'ideal speech situation'. The family members are all adults, leading (on the whole) economically and socially autonomous lives; no blatant asymmetry in the distribution of power is discernible,[6] there is no pressure of time, and there is no need for immediate action, no urgent decisions have to be made. The family members have, so to say, all the time in the world to present their attitudes, to argue and to catch on.

Nevertheless, these informal discussions are not guided by the unauthoritative 'power of the better argument', as Habermas lets us so convincingly hope. (It is the speakers' attempt to avoid asymmetry of knowledge which prevents this power exerting its influence.) Two reasons for this are suggested. First, the asymmetries underlying all social action especially endanger the fragile complementarity of disagreement. By hinting at two possible dangers, I will show how speakers accomplish argumentation in pursuing what metaphorically may be called well-tempered disagreement. Second, all communication takes place in specific social situations, characterized by setting, timing and types of actors. A form of talk as vulnerable as argumentation relies heavily on communicative routines which safeguard it from the explosiveness implied in disagreement. Argumentation, or informal discussion at least, seems a more routinized endeavour than the self-reflection of social consciousness.

Informal discussion can also be found in family dinner talk, which has been recorded 'naturally' for the Constance research project on 'communicative genres'.[7] Having finished dinner, the members of the family are sitting together, drinking some domestic red wine, talking about the soup and the grandmother who is absent – and suddenly they are involved in a heated debate. This happens on several occasions even at consecutive dinners, and in all subsequent years of recording. And these discussions are mostly very lengthy. The family may be debating for hours and hours on their different religious attitudes, on sports, on Marx and the Pope, on the German New Rightists and on the new occultism. Family members' folk category for this is 'argumentation' or 'discussion', and their utterances are 'arguments', 'points' or 'assertions'.

It was a debate on Boris Becker which first turned my attention to these conversations. After an opulent meal the family talked about some athletes, above all Boris Becker, who then, in 1984, was the focus of public interest in Germany. This topic turned into a busy quarrel of a kind which I found in later years when we recorded the family's conversations on tape.

The building blocks of disagreement

Some of the most pervasive elements of argumentative sequences in informal discussions may be detected from a small excerpt, the Gienger argument which comes from what I call the Boris Becker discussion. This excerpt takes a prominent position as it was here that the conversation turned into an informal discussion.

The family members had been talking for quite a while, mostly about gymnastics, a sport into which several members are or have been involved. It is this topic which triggers off an argumentative sequence. Christian has stated that one cannot earn a lot of money by doing gymnastics; then he continues:

Extract 8.1 Boris Becker [For transcription convention key see Appendix, p. 272-3.]

```
 1 C:  (Ye and this guy Gienger, what does- what money does he
        have now?)
 2 C:  (He- he's a referee now)
 3 M:  'Uhm,'
 4     (--)
 5 U:  Look ⌈ how (simple minded this ⌈ Gienger is)
 6 M:       ⌊(At the cost of his health)⌋
 7 F:                                   ⌊ O:h well he
 8 F:  has- he's saved enough [hat seine Schaefle scho im Trock-
       ene].
 9 C:  No:; but not like some others.
10 F:  =Listen, these advertisement contracts; and so on;
11     if his name is printed on a product
12     somewhere; (hh)
13 M:  That's right; but not to the extent as say ⌈for example
14 F:                                             ⌊but sure
15 M:  in tenni ⌈s with this guy:: Boris
16 F:           ⌊ (that is- that is-)
```

Christian asks a rhetorical question in line 1, and answers it immediately in line 2. Referring to Gienger, a former world champion in gymnastics, who now is (only) a referee, he supports the view that gymnastics is an unprofitable sport. I will try to account for this rare formulation of a 'quaestio' later. Let us first turn to what follows. After the comments of Ursula (line 5) and mother (line 6), it is father (line 7) who, overlapping with Ursula's turn, makes a consequential utterance. It is this utterance which meets with Christian's explicit contradiction (line 9). And now father goes on, providing something which can be understood as an argument - even an elliptical one (lines 10 ff.). Mother first sounds as if agreeing with father (line 13); then, however, she goes on to say something which rather backs Christian's assertion. Father tries to interrupt her (line 14), but she persists and goes on with the comparison to Boris Becker.

Instead of well organized and clear statements, we encounter a confusing succession of statements of different speakers. The rhythm changes from slow (1-3) to fast (10 ff.), and there are obtrusive overlaps and interruptions (5-7). Instead of one argument there is a succession of disagreements, instead of clear pros and cons different speakers express their positions, the meaning of which is hardly understandable (10 ff.) at first glance. We are dealing here with an argumentative sequence. None of the speakers is able to obtain a privileged right to speak, each has to risk losing his or her turn. One of the essential motors of this argumentative sequence is to be seen in the contradiction which develops between Christian and father (and then mother).

Contradictions

When Christian poses his rhetorical question, his mother agrees, and Ursula squeezes in an assertion. Just like her mother, she also seems to go along with Christian. Their father then interrupts the two of them quite rudely (something which he is not in the habit of doing). It is here that disagreement's shadow looms. But it is only the subsequent utterance by Christian which recognizably takes on the features of what may be called contradiction. The same holds for father's next utterance, something like an insisting backing, and also for mother, who seems to be contradicting her husband. This is quite a lively conversational phase, no pause is left open, the utterances follow each other in a hurry. The issue itself seems to change, starting with Gienger's earnings and ending with Boris Becker's. But before we can go into this, we must clarify what is meant by contradiction.

It is not Christian's 'contradiction' which starts the argument. Already the father's first statement (lines 7-8) is a clear reference to Christian's initial question (1). This reference to Christian's answer is not at all a mere semantic accomplishment. In fact, there is a very open anaphorical relation:

> *Extract 8.1b*
> 1   C: He- he's a referee now
> 7f. F: Oh well he has- he's saved enough [*Schaefle scho im Trockene*]

The anaphorical reference is not only a guess. Note that it is Christian who immediately responds to his father's utterance (line 9). It seems as if there were a disagreement before Christian himself states the blatant 'No'. Following Spranz-Fogasy's definition (1986, p. 28), I shall use the term 'contradict' when speakers reject the other's assertion, opposing it with an alternative assertion, or reasserting their own point of view. Within the organization of verbal exchange, contradiction is, according to Spranz-Fogasy, the second part of an adjacency pair. It thus establishes a conditional relevance for a more extensive treatment of what is contradicted in the two turns. The term 'contradiction', however, does not seem to cover all forms which function as 'disagreement tokens' (Coulter,

1979). Only by using a number of 'presuppositions' could one reconstruct a logical opposition between 'referee' (*Kampfrichter*) and 'saved enough' (*Schaefle im Trockene*), thus making a case for maintaining that Extract 8.1b constitutes a contradiction. That is why I prefer using disagreement as the overall term. 'Disagreement' designates non-accordance of a speaker's statement with a preceding speaker's utterance, thus establishing a conditional relevance for the following turns. Disagreement is based not so much on the incompatibility of validity claims (i.e. semantic contents) or on 'hidden dissent' (as, e.g. in 'sharp remarks' or implicit contradictions). Disagreement may be regarded as interactive accomplishment of speakers' utterances. That is, whatever speakers may say and however contradictory their utterances may be from a logical point of view, disagreement only has argumentative consequences for the participants if the dissent produced is recognizable by them.

Let us turn back to the Gienger argument. Shortly after father's delayed disagreement '*Schaefle im Trockene*', Christian follows with a disagreement token: 'No; but not like the others'. This is in essence a simple *negation* (I will come back to the additional 'not like . . .'). Negations using 'no', 'nope' as well as confirmations such as 'certainly', 'but sure', etc. (taken that a negation had already occurred) are very common and well-known means of disagreement (Vuchinich, 1984). They can be enforced somewhat more emphatically by means of repetition, stress, etc., as in the following example where Christian counters Ursula's personal reproach with a fast series of 'no's':

Extract 8.2 Boris Becker
1 U: Ye 'pposed the text from the beginning cause I have been reading it.
2 C: No=no=no=no it was . . .

A contradiction can be brought about also by *calling in question*. Calling in question consists of a question which does more than just require an answer. It requires justification of the preceding utterance. This questioning seems to be marked prosodically in a specific way, not always as marked as in one example in which, in response to an assertion of Christian's, Ursula produces the very strongly stressed exclamation 'WHA::T?'.

Another widely used building block of disagreement is applied by mother in the Gienger argument. It is her 'that is true but not to the same extent as . . .' which bears a very strong resemblance to the 'Yes-but' (Koerfer, 1979). The structure implicit in the 'yes-but' can be produced in such a way that it also holds for longer statements:

> *Extract 8.3 Christianity*
> 1 C: It's all right to think that way
> 2   but look, (-) ehm it is not my own decision . . .

Christian first shows agreement with Ursula's preceding utterance (1); then, however, he adds a 'but' which establishes a contradiction. The 'yes-but', of course, entails a double structure, allowing for agreement and at the same time for continuing disagreement. In these exchanges, this well-known double structure forms the starting point for a whole range of argumentative techniques, like comparisons, contrasts, distinctions and dissociations, as have been described for monological arguments by Perelman and Olbrechts – Tyteca (1970).

There is another, very frequent, type of contradictory 'technique'. Alluding to a well-known rhetorical pattern, one could call it *negated parallelism*.

> *Extract 8.4 Christianity*
> 1 C: That's a reproach
> 2 U: No:; that's no reproa:ch . . .

The negated parallelism entails simple negation but also repeats the contradicted utterance almost word by word. This repetition is striking. Why should a speaker produce such a redundant reproduction if the first simple 'no' has already done the work of disagreement? First, there is, of course, the possibility of different placements for the negation. 'That is not a reproach' would do a very different job from what Ursula really says. That is, the repetition enables us to point out what it is in an utterance that is contradicted. I would like to call this *the disagreed aspect*. Second, this redundancy in disagreement is by no means rare. Speakers do not ashamedly or anxiously hide their contradictions away. They rather seem to stress them.

The rhetoric of disagreement

Disagreement can take on much more complex forms than those mentioned under the heading of 'contradictions'. These forms of disagreement are characterized by what appears to be *redundancy*. To get an idea of what I mean by this notion, take a look at a scene where a real conflict started.

Extract 8.5 Geschmack
```
1 M:   There are few people who can in- in a short moment
2      such wrong – do such wrong as you do (. . .)
3 F:   There are few people; who lack any humour but this
4      is the case today.
```

Mother relates her general statement (line 1f.) to her husband; and some turns later he returns this reproach in an anaphorical way (3f.). In terms of content, there is no contradiction between 'doing wrong' and 'lacking humour', but the participants are well aware that there is a strong disagreement here. The pertinent feature of such a construction is redundancy; speakers use more words than necessary in order to express their disagreement. If we are not to cast the speakers as fools we should assume that this redundancy does a good job. The redundancy not only makes the disagreement obvious to the participants; it can also be seen as a recipient design. Anyone present knows which utterances are at stake; one easily understands who it is who is contradicted. This device is especially important in multi-party conversations.

This interpretation may at first seem too bold; but, as mentioned before, these constructions are by no way exceptions in informal discussions. They already form part of a lot of parallelisms, as, for example, in the following extract.

Extract 8.6 Christianity
```
1 U:   Christian one must be able to believe such things.
2 C:   Why should one? One must not be able to believe them.
3 U:   I do not believe in spirit, so I . . . either . . .
```

Christian questions Ursula's utterance (line 1) and then adds a negated parallelism in which he repeats her utterance (2). This is not intended to be a logical argument. The construction is that of a disagreement, as is evident from Ursula's response (3). This use of rhetorical formats like anaphors or parallelism gives the impression that the speakers valued such sophisticated disagreement (Loveday, 1983).

In the argument about Boris Becker, a dispute starts up between Christian and his father on 'top athletes'. In order to demonstrate my point, I will reproduce this longish construction (it takes over three pages of transcription) in a simplified way:

Extract 8.7a Boris Becker
```
1 C:   [The problem with these athletes] is solved better in East
        European countries
2      than in our country
3      those athletes make big money here in a single stroke,
4      and what is left to them in the end?
```

5   Whereas in the Eastern block athletes have security for the
6   whole of their lives. (. . .)

This rough reconstruction shows that Christian is producing a chiastic structure which is built on the opposition between East (line 1f.) and West European athletes (2), exemplifying first the West (3f.), then the East Europeans (5f.). Even in this simplified transcript this may strike one as a very sophisticated construction. Let us turn to father's response:

Extract 8.7b
1 F: The Eastern block athletes are plain professionals.
2   They are hired by enterprises. But they do not work.
3   Whereas our athletes. They have to work for their
4   living on their own.

It is remarkable that father not only produces another chiasm, but carries out a genuine chiastic counter-movement to Christian's statement. Evidently, a simple 'no' is often not deemed sufficient to clear up a controversy. It would leave too vague what it is that is 'challenged' and, moreover, it would not accomplish what this redundancy does: make disagreement observable to the co-participants, even, as we have seen, in cases in which there is no discernible 'contradiction in terms' between utterances of the two opponents.

There are, of course, cases where speakers' first utterances can be understood as controversial assertions. Even if one would call them arguments, they nevertheless cannot produce argumentative sequences only by virtue of being stated controversially. Take the following excerpt. The family's discussion of Christianity has been interrupted by a joke. Then Christian takes the floor again:

Extract 8.8 Christianity II
1 C: Well, to my mind there are- are hm really two spheres here.
2   ( ) the' are two different spheres. ((He explains the
3   Christian teaching of the two worlds.)) Ther' it's already
4   th' Good and the Bad. In every human being. That already
5   in every part.
6 U: no one says- no one is contradicting this.

Christian's voice already gives the cue that he is trying to take up the interrupted discussion again. Then he presents something which can be read as an argument (lines 1–5), presenting it as his view (1). But unexpectedly he does not meet with disagreement. Moreover, at the point where disagreement might be produced, Ursula states explicitly that she will not contradict.

So Christian continues presenting his idea of the two worlds in the sequence following this extract.[8]

The generation of argument through the spirit of disagreement

The assumption that argument starts off from an explicit 'assertion', therefore, does not hold for these informal discussions. On the contrary, disagreement may turn up at places which do not seem to be marked as claims or assertions:

> *Extract 8.9 Spiesser*
> (Willie reports that his Grandmother has asked him to stop the tape recorder in order not to waste energy.)
> 1 W: and that tape recorder ⌈that takes 3.2 watts
> 2 M: ⌊(   )
> 2 W: therefore you'd need to ⌈you would need to–
> 4 H: ⌊NO:nononono::: – that's not true.

This short fragment shows[9] how an utterance becomes an assertion only by virtue of a second turn of disagreement. It shows also that disagreement may crop up at any possible place in a conversation. Disagreement comes about in a second turn. There, contradiction is pointed up in a way which brings out the reference to the corresponding utterance. The fact that disagreement can happen at any possible place (not only, as we see from the examples, in slots) accounts for the seemingly rule-breaking character of these conversations. Instead of disorder, however, a new structure becomes established: disagreement establishes a conditional relevance for the next turns.

Disagreement thus has a topical potential for rendering certain utterances problematic. The topical focus ('aspect') established in the tension of the two utterances is not restricted to them but makes necessary what Jacobs and Jackson (1981) call an 'expansion'. By means of the second turn, the previous utterance or a part of it (the 'aspect') becomes the topic of the third turn. So, for example, Herbert stresses that a tape-recorder does not consume 3.2 watts, then he claims that it must be more than this, and so on. Expansions may be 'arguments', 'backings', 'warrants' – utterances which seem to be defined rather by their relation to the interactive production of disagreement than by their logical relation to the contracted 'validity claim'. Therefore I will not dwell on the logical structure. Instead I would like to hint at two other possibilities derived from this conditionally relevant 'expansion'.

Conflict and the ping-pong rule of evidence

If an utterance is contradicted, there is, of course, a simple possibility: continue with the contradiction!

> Extract 8.10 Broesler
> 1 W: When we went in the blue- the blue suits
> 2   both of us; didn't we?
> 3 M: =Blue sui:ts? You never had any.
> 4 W: =Sailo:rs suits.
> 5 M: You NEVER had any.
> 6 W: =S:ure.
> 7 H: I didn't.
> 8 W: ⌈You too
> 9 M: ⌊No you only had bei:ge waistband trousers ...

Willie's reminiscence of the 'blue suits' (1f.) is interrupted by mother who denies it resolutely (3). Although Willie restates his assertion (3), mother repeats her disagreement emphatically (5). Again Willie insists on his view (6) when suddenly Herbert contradicts him; overlapping with Willie's second attempt to insist (8), mother finally produces a correction which ends the disagreement on the 'blue suits'.

As this example shows clearly, one possible way to 'expand' does consist in the repetition or continuation of disagreement, that is by denying, insisting and so on. This can result in a series of virtual 'couplets' of 'yes', 'no', 'sure', etc.

> Extract 8.10b
> Nannen   : I refer here to ((name))
> Maier   : No, I am sorry, that is not true. No.
> Nannen   : Sure, you have to deny this.
> Maier   : No, we do not have to, but, no.
> Loewenthal: No, no, no

This fragment, which stems from an analysis of conflict talk (Apeltauer, 1977), illustrates the dynamics of disagreement. There is no simple 'monological' rule like, e.g. the 'general rule of evidence': that the one contradicted should give evidence.[10] What we find is a little like passing over the obligation or right to give evidence, and continuing with the disagreement instead. This right or obligation goes back and forth like a ping-pong between the opponents. This ping-pong strategy reflects simply the conversational turn-taking basis of these discussions. The game may continue for a while, and in fact we find this structure in conflict talk among children who playfully produce long series of disagreement, raising their voices step by step until a 'winner' takes the highest or loudest step (Boggs, 1978; Lein and Brenneis, 1978).

As in children's conflict talk, adults may take an ironical stance and imitate this playful character. If, however, irony is not marked phonetically and if the discussion tackles 'serious' topics, there is a *critical limit* built into the ping-pong rule. The charge to provide evidence may be passed over several times, so that speakers can check the other's 'in-order-to' and 'because' motives. The disagreement-expansion format restricts the ping-pong rule in such a way that repeated disagreement can be seen as refusal to expand.[11] The ping-pong enables the speakers to check their motives, that is who it is who has to provide an argument. It is obvious that by pure continuation of disagreement, speakers would enter a dead end. The communicative problem of solving disagreement by expansions would turn into a serious interactional problem of reciprocity, given that no party could assume more than the other was willing to cooperate with, that is, produce something like an expansion (which could be challenged again). It is not surprising that this critical limit can be regarded as one reason which gives rise to conflict talk. The refusal to cooperate may be accompanied by rising voices or threatening gestures. In addition, conflict talk involves a shift to the personal level (which is implied in the demonstrated unwillingness to cooperate).[12] Thus informal discussions always face the danger of conflict talk. How do speakers avoid this danger?

One possibility is already mentioned: stick to the critical limit of the ping-pong rule. To cite an example:

Extract 8.11 Christianity
1 U: A truly believing Christian must object to military service.
2 C: .=No,
3 U: Sure
4 C: No::, [a believing Christian, must, must go into the army
5 U: (Sure)

Both parties have refused to offer an argument although both disagree. Having produced disagreement tokens twice, the situation seems hopeless. Obviously both speakers are aware of this unpromising situation, so Christian immediately adds an expansion to his disagreement token (4). As Ursula overlaps exactly at this point (5), she seems to recognize the problem too (and to withhold, realizing that Christian's second disagreement token is but an introduction to his expansion). If Christian were bluntly to say 'no' again, he would not be accepting that Ursula is asking for a reason, which is rendered possible only by her insisting after his disagreement token. (It is hardly necessary to add that these series can apply to other forms of disagreement, e.g. parallelisms, too.)

Avoidance of conflict thus works out by means of the limitation of the ping-pong rule giving way to complementarity. This rule, however, holds only if disagreement is bluntly continued. As already mentioned, speakers may also produce an expansion. But the expansion itself gives way to another form which leads out of argumentation.

On the fringes of instruction

The expansion itself may become the subject of a disagreement.

> *Extract 8.12 Christianity*
> 1 M: First we have to be desperate; so that we ⌈then-
> 2 U: ⌊'Ye'
> 3 C: =because desperate people are more easily
> 4   ma- manipulated. Tha- that's how I understand the matter.
> 5 U: HOW THAT? No:::

Christian's utterance (3) is just an expansion of a preceding disagreement. He simply takes up the formulation of his mother – his opponent – and gives her something like a reason for his position (3f.). He has hardly finished his sentence when Uschi disagrees again expressively (5).

We can already guess from this example how this argumentative sequence will progress: one party puts forward an expansion which can be regarded as an argument – and which meets again with disagreement. Progression by means of an expansion, however, is not always open to further disagreement. There is another possibility, which is evident in the next example:

> *Extract 8.13 Boris Becker*
> (M talks about her gymnastics training group)
> 1 U: Perhaps they don't know⌈it any more.
> 2 M: ⌊Su:re, they know (it).
> 3 U: 'Hmh.'

Ursula suggests that the girls in her mother's sports group do not know 'it' any more (1). The disagreement is formulated anaphorically by mother (2). Here, however, Ursula replies by only murmuring an accepting 'Hmh'. There is no further disagreement and no further expansion, as the topic over which there was disagreement has come to an end. The reason for this argumentative 'shortcoming' is easily understood. Mother is talking about 'her girls'. Even if Ursula suggests something, she does not know the girls (as is clear from the preceding talk). Mother has privileged access to the knowledge on this subject matter – and no disagreement series is produced. Although this example is but a short disagreement episode, we could now assume that asymmetries of knowledge may obstruct the development of such argumentations. Analysing similar texts, Keppler and Luckmann (this volume, Chapter 7) found that in everyday conversations teaching is introduced by a phase in which asymmetries of knowledge are established interactively between the speakers. Teaching may be initiated by the speaker; it may also be initiated by the recipient of the expected teaching. And one of the ways for the 'teacher' to initiate the instruction is – disagreement. This 'rectification' (*Richtigstellung*') takes the following form:

>   Speaker 1 : Utterance
>   Speaker 2 : Contradiction
>   Speaker 2 : Teaching

If asymmetries of knowledge are once established, the teachers-to-be get the floor. They have the 'ticket' for a unit of talk which they understand as being lack of knowledge of the other interlocutor. 'The right to teach' is thus acquired by the 'teacher-to-be's disagreement with someone who does not yet know that he is a 'pupil'-candidate but who contributes to the opening of the teaching sequence in consequence of the fact that he 'must' be granted the right to be given an explanation of the disagreement' (Keppler and Luckmann, this volume, Chapter 7, p. 150). Instruction is segregated from the main flow of talk, and the 'teacher' becomes the principal speaker for the duration of the teaching sequence.

According to the classical *Contra factum non valet argumentum*, we thus find teaching also starting off from disagreement, somehow neutralizing the ping-pong rule: the teacher gets the floor upon contradicting and holds it until having 'unloaded' the better knowledge announced in disagreeing (Keppler, 1989). With respect to the continuous flow of disagreement this functions like an interruption or at least like a 'side-sequence'. Being involved in a series of argumentative

The avoidance of asymmetry in informal discussions   183

sequences, a speaker, however, tries to avoid establishing the implied asymmetries of knowledge. If one speaker assumes the role of a teacher too often, the right to disagree is endangered and the other speakers are likely to be degraded to recipients of the teacher's knowledge. The establishment of topics in argumentative sequences helps to prevent this. Sometimes the avoidance of instruction becomes quite obvious:

    Extract 8.4 Boris Becker
    1 C: . . . a kid like this Boris Becker (hh) makes such a lot
    2   of money without- any taxation like ⌈(
    3 U: ⌊not no: taxation
    4   (0.5)
    5 U: ⌈Twenty four perce:nt he has to pay. ⌉
    6 C: ⌊ I don't know how   ⌋ in any case
    7 C: they should impose much higher tax rates.

Having disagreed with Christian on the tax rates Boris Becker has to pay, Ursula presents her better knowledge about the exact figure (5). But before she has even made her most important contribution Christian interrupts her (6), going on with his argument. The asymmetry of knowledge is evident. Christian wants the tax rates to be raised, but he does not even know, as Uschi shows, the existing tax rates. But as is usual in these arguments, no one bothers about better knowledge. Surely, the 'ways' of argumentative sequences and of teaching are not too different; each expansion includes an element of knowledge. But in argumentative sequences speakers hesitate to install this asymmetrical form:

    Extract 8.9b Broesler following the 'NO:nononono::: that's not true' in 8.9a
    1   (1,0)
    2 W: this small tape recorder,
    3 H: No tape recorder works on 3.2 watts.
    4 W: = So it uses 7.

Being contradicted, Willie apparently waits for teaching – but there is a long pause (1). As we now see, Willie himself does not know much better, so he just repeats his assertion with marks of uncertainty (2). But Herbert, too, only reformulates his disagreement. At this point it is clear for both that they will not engage in any teaching: Willie 'offers' a first alternative (4); in a few turns they 'raise the ante': Herbert proposes 20, and finally they agree on 20 watts. Only now Willie can go on with his criticism as 20 watts is so little as to demonstrate the ignorance of both of them with respect to energy consumption.

    This example demonstrates how near teaching can be to

argumentation. But in this case, too, both speakers try to avoid the asymmetry of knowledge. Both speakers are right in a certain way. Willie was not too wrong and Herbert's contradiction turned out reasonably. Argumentative sequences thus not only face the problem of conflict; they also flee the byway of teaching which would leave the floor to one speaker only, leaving the path of precipitated, hurly-burly disagreement.

So far I have tried to show how speakers get around possible asymmetries hidden in the structure of disagreement. This mainstay of my argument, however, relies on the affirmation that there is a specific form of talk in which such disagreement occurs. Therefore I would like to sketch some other features of this form of talk.

Informal discussion as a communicative aggregate

The informal discussions analysed in this chapter are mostly multi-party conversations. Four, five, up to fifteen people are sitting around a table while three, four or five are continuously talking. This poses the problem of the organization of talk: who disagrees with whom and what is the position of the third, fourth, etc., speaker? This problem has a surprising solution. The artful construction of disagreement not only signifies what it is that is not agreed to; it also shows whom the speaker is opposing and, if several speakers are talking, it also indicates who is opposed to whom and who agrees with whom.

The construction of what we may call *oppositions*, that is of speakers' local relations to one another in disagreement, is complemented by the use of 'agreement markers'. They can be very explicit, saying 'this time you are right' or 'that is true'; they may be more restricted like 'yah yah', 'hmm', or they may be constructed like parallelisms or anaphors, repeating the preceding utterance of another person. Agreement markers not only indicate what and whom the speaker agrees with, thus establishing coalitions (speakers' momentary positions of consent); they also provide for the positioning of speakers' utterances. If W and Z are disagreeing, X, agreeing explicitly with W, might well meet with disagreement from Z. Thus, the series of disagreements establishes a *dialectical relation* of speakers in terms of proponents and opponents. By means of this dialectical relation (the social correlate of complementarity) the utterances of each speaker are located on one side or the other. Only by virtue of this dialectical relation is it possible for speaker X to contradict Y during Y's turn even if X does not yet know what Y will say; for X it may suffice that Y has uttered a token of agreement to Z – the one X had contradicted before.

The local character of disagreement also accounts for the dialectical positions. Situationally there is a pro and a con – but there is hardly a third position in arguing (that is unless speakers do interrupt, head for some byway like teaching or change the form) as will become clear below.[13] Suppose someone tried to mediate. In this case the mediators would have to agree with one and then with the other of the preceding speakers. He or she would already run the risk of being disagreed with in between – i.e. at a point where he or she had just agreed with one speaker. And even if he or she succeeded in referring to both positions – the next speaker could (and really would) contradict the attempt of conciliation, thus involving the mediator him- or herself in the dialectical stream of disagreement, opposition and coalition.[14]

This dialectical structure has an impact even on the logics of conversational argumentation. Of course we could try to reconstruct the deep structure of, for example, the Gienger argument, and arrive at something similar, such as Toulmin's scheme. This, however, could only be brought about if we included elements which are not spoken explicitly. Apparently, the logic is rather dialectical, and it follows a dialogical rather than a monological pattern.[15]

This has two consequences. On the one hand the speakers add to their disagreement tokens, which themselves already require some art: argumentative means, such as, e.g. logical particles (because, so, thus). In the Gienger argument Christian alludes to an 'argument of distinction' which becomes fully realized by mother, introducing an example which, (along with his distinctive 'not as much as', then becomes the topic). Similar techniques to those found in these disagreements have been described by Perelman and Olbrechts-Tyteca (1970) as comparisons, dissociations and so on. Given the continual disagreement, these techniques lead to ongoing change of the 'quaestio'. What is disagreed with at one moment may be expanded by an example, and the example again may meet with a disagreement. It is in this way that the question of Gienger's income turns into the question of Boris Becker's income taxes.

Informal discussions, however, do not consist exclusively of series of disagreements. On the contrary, disagreement may come to a sudden end. There are several typical ways of ending a series of disagreements or argumentative sequences.[16] Although the features of such sequences do not have the rigidity of communicative genres, they form an 'event' (Gumperz and Berenz, forthcoming) within a social encounter; they show visible boundaries and a specific sequential organization. The social encounter itself, family discussion, can be described by a loose but recognizable concatenation of different communicative forms, that is, an aggregate.

If argumentative sequences in informal discussions come to an end, they may be followed by very different communicative forms. Some of them seem to be spontaneously produced 'flying stretches' of hectic conversational activity; others bestow the impression of resting places, e.g. when speakers are given the floor. In any case, informal discussions do not at all consist exclusively of argumentative sequences. Even if they return to argumentation once in a while, on the whole they appear as something of a communicative pie. Speakers may tell jokes and funny stories, paranormal stories, memories and so on. Some of the intermingled forms have already been analysed in some detail, so it may suffice just to mention them: situative resources may interfere, like pets or the practical requirements of dinner table sociability (wine, food, etc.); argumentative sequences may turn into the reconstruction of medial experiences, or they may be interrupted for the telling of wisdom (Bergmann, 1988; Keppler and Luckmann forthcoming; Ulmer, 1988). The attempt to look for some systematical concatenations between typical forms, however, seems a vain enterprise. It may be that the very informality of an event is made up by the broad variety of communicative forms. Mixed as the communicative pie of informal discussions may be, it always tastes like argument. To state it less metaphorically: it is always dominated by argumentation. This implies that even if other forms are hooked in, speakers frequently return to argumentative sequences.[17]

Whereas continuous disagreement accounts for the intrinsically motivated shift of topics, the informal character enforces this in allowing for departures from argumentation to other communicative forms.[18] This is one explanation of the trait we all know so well: its never-ending character. As opposed to formally institutionalized discussions (Berthold, 1982), informal discussions are communicative aggregates which derive the very essence of their informality from this freedom to select forms and to argue, too. Instead of pursuing a topic straight ahead, speakers may talk about contraception, go on to celibacy and finally turn to religious cults. And they may finally come to an end when the participants get tired, when it is time to sleep – and when no speaker disagrees any more.

'Don't shout!': conflict and argumentation

Facing the problems of conflict, of asymmetries of knowledge, of shifting topics and their never-ending character, why do speakers indulge in informal discussions at all? The reason for this seems quite obvious if we look at the – admittedly fragmentary – excerpts. Argumentation turns out to be a machinery to produce topics which, on the one hand, provide for a thrill by means of disagreement and, on the other hand, maintain a high degree of sociability exactly in getting around asymmetries and in allowing for other communicative forms, bestowing a non-binding, almost playful character on them. The sociability of well-tempered argumentation confers some kind of equality on the participants. Participants may feel free to disagree at any point, they feel free to introduce some other form of discussion at any time, they may even abstain from discussing if they are not in the mood to do so. In the manner pointed out above they may just obstruct any attempt to bring forward better knowledge (or 'better argument'). Thus they cherish discussion almost for its own sake – and for the sake of maintaining the conversation. Despite the equality of sociable argumentation, informal discussions are subject to strong restrictions. Apart from speakers' unwillingness to pinpoint notions and utterances to a degree which would allow for the notion of validity claim (which would in any case be counteracted by the ongoing disagreements), the thrill of the dialectical complementarity of disagreement always faces dangerously in two directions: disagreement may lead to the establishment of asymmetries of knowledge (thus depriving 'ignorants' of the right to disagree and thereby ruling out the equality of the ping-pong); and disagreement may lead into the troubled waters of conflict talk, ending up with the opposite of sociability: shouting, crying and quarrelling.

In fact, speakers not only pay attention to the overt communicative etiquette of well-tempered disagreement. Formulations of manners of speaking like, e.g. 'now let him finish' or 'don't shout' may be indicators of this. There are even more enduring 'shelters' built in these discussions which not only prevent them from driving into these byways; they also have results which are not intended. Namely, these discussions often start off from topics which are of personal interest, be this just the personal reproach of one child against another which prompts the discussion, the moral personal attitudes of family members, like Christian's Catholicism, the interruption of the sons' gymnastic careers, or Ursula's atheism. The family members seem quite likely to discuss these personal questions but, paradoxically, they do not succeed in accomplishing this in a direct way. In fact, as soon as these topics get into the machinery of disagreement, they become immediately transformed into topics of much less personal concern and of much broader interest. Actually, the Gienger argument is exactly one point where such a transformation occurs. The family had been talking about gymnastics, and at several points serious attacks against the two sons who had interrupted their careers had been brought forward.[19] The conversation then even included some moral sentences,[20] slowly turning away from the sons and introducing other examples (two elite gymnasts in the village, a successful gymnast from the neighbourhood). It was only when the Gienger argument started that the conversation turned into a discussion and lingered on with the next, the well-known example of Boris Becker.

This turn is significant also for other discussions. They start off with topics of personal concern, but immediately these topics become transformed into topics of more general interest. There are good reasons for this, which are already built into disagreement. As the avoidance of conflict talk may be one reason for this turn to impersonal topics, the topics are at the same time of such generality as to allow anyone to make contributions. The differences of knowledge – be this mother's knowledge of the local gymnasts or Ursula's knowledge on literature – are overcome in choosing topics of general interest.

All of the family's informal discussions thus tackle problems of general interest in order to keep the harmonious balance of well-tempered disagreement.[21] This conflict prophylaxis leads to an interesting paradox. Apparently the family members liked to talk about personal problems – at least most of their informal discussions started with such topics. In order to avoid conflict and avoid asymmetries of knowledge[22] they turned to commonplace topics, and thus they had to get clear about personal problems (religious, political, moral, attitudes in some cases) arising from the most trivial and popular topics around.

Even if one of the families analysed in this chapter seems to have cherished this kind of talk, one cannot assume that all families engaged in informal discussion. On the contrary. As already mentioned, a second family rarely engages in informal discussions, and if they did, they were seriously in danger of conflict (which in fact did happen). The family in question, on the other hand, not only had this notion of argumentation, but interviews with family members showed that they knew about the peculiarity of this kind of argumentation. Ursula, for example, recalled that these discussions were common among her parent's generation when she was a child, 'that the old sat together, they sent us children to the play room and discussed – something we children found most boring'. Discussion – 'that was a notion among us children. What are the old people doing? They are discussing again. We found that deadly boring'. 'Discussion', however, could mean two things. 'Father's relatives often met too. And they were always shouting. Obviously they called it discussing too, but they only shouted that is what my father's relatives were like.' Compared to her family, father's relatives were extremely 'vindictive', they quarrelled all the time. One could argue that her family is an exception, but other research hints at the possibility that there might be something like a certain communicative culture which allows for informal discussion.[23]

Thus, informal discussion seems to depend on what Gumperz (1982, pp. 43 ff.) calls 'conventions' which develop on the basis of social networks. Families cherishing such discussions are certainly an example of such networks. But this communicative form necessitates a kind of network of social relationships which is not found only in families. Certainly, more investigations of different settings, contexts and aggregations would be required. But it is safe to assume that informal discussions can be characterized by what Simmel (1970) has called *sociability*, that is, they are social encounters in which certain elements of the outer social structure are disregarded (power, status). The sociability of non-dominating argumentation is, however, not devoid of all inequalities. Communicative cultures that cherish informal discussions have to handle the explosiveness of disagreement in such a way as to allow for complementarity, both by instruction and by the avoidance of conflict. Still, members do not form a circle of naive philosophers, unknowingly guided by the 'power of the better argument'. In fact, they just like to have arguments without getting into conflict, and in the end they talk as usual. And I hope at least to have hinted at one of these 'habits of the heart' which, if I am not mistaken, most of us pursue once in a while.

Notes

1. I am indebted to Allison Wetterlin who helped me to anglicize the text and to avoid referring only to male speakers. I would also like to thank Cathryn Houghton for her help and Ivana Marková for many comments and corrections.
2. Cf. Perelman and Olbrechts-Tyteca (1970). I will hark back to the rhetorical techniques described there.
3. Quasthoff (1978, p. 27) has already shown that 'natural argumentation' is much more complex than Toulmin's scheme projects.
4. Take, as an example, Toulmin's phases of argumentation (1983, p. 16): 'There must be an initial stage at which the charge or claim is clearly stated, a subsequent phase in which evidence is set out or testimony given in support of the charge or claim, leading to the final stage'. Maas (1974) and Klein (1985) also take the 'challenged' (*das Strittige*) to be presupposed in argumentation.
5. Harvey Sacks (1987, p. 66) has used this metaphor of the machinery leading from disagreement to consent.
6. For structurally accidental reasons the father is less important than the children, and the only daughter contributes more to the conversation than three of the four sons taken together.
7. The material stems mainly from dinner-table talk of one family in several subsequent years which is part of the data of the Constance research project. Material from other families and other settings are also included. At the risk of some distortions I have translated the excerpts, which were originally in Swabian, a south-west German dialect, and Standard German.
8. It is only after about half a minute that he triggers a disagreement which takes up one of his examples. And, as we may gather from what has already been said, the example becomes the topic of the argument rather than Christian's thesis on the two worlds.
9. Willie and Herbert had for some time been maligning the technical ignorance of their fellowmen when Willie introduced his grandmother as another example. Here he meets with Herbert's contradiction, surprisingly because what later turns out to be at issue (the number of watts consumed) is but a subordinate point which was formulated in passing and in a rather casual way.
10. For the *Beweislastregel* and the *allgemeine Begruendungsregel* cf. Kopperschmidt 1980, pp. 64 ff.
11. If a second speaker questions an utterance by disagreeing, the first speakers may continue disagreement because they either do not know what they disagree about or what reasons the second speakers have in mind. Thus they require the second speakers to give a reason. If they again continue disagreeing in their subsequent turn, second speakers may show that they do not want to put forward evidence (if they did, the ping-pong would come to an end) but want the first speakers to back, explain, justify, etc., what has been disagreed on. The second speakers would thus indicate that they were not willing to provide reasons but only to challenge the first speakers. One more disagreement token by the first speakers would amount to a blunt refusal to give evidence, knowing that the second does neither. Apart from accidental deviations (e.g. embedded clarifying question–answer pairs), no speaker would seem to be

willing to give evidence, so that the disagreement-expansion pattern would not work any more, the complementarity, or reciprocity, underlying the ping-pong rule would be shattered.
12. In fact, the above cited example of continued disagreement (Extract 8.10b is one prominent example of conflict talk.) One of the families (Extract 8.5) also engaged in conflict talk after the discussion had turned to the very personal level of the parents reproaching each other. In any case it can be said that disagreement is a structural prerequisite for conflict.
13. This holds even for semi-formalized legal mediation where the establishment of a third party remains fragile: cf. Nothdurft (1989).
14. When I first formulated this idea I did not anticipate that it would be accidentally verified. During a discussion in 1988 the father suddenly proposed that he be referee of the discussion. All agreed and so he organized the turns. But it took only five minutes for him to become involved again in the discussion as a member who immediately was disagreed with by Adi – and who contradicted again ...
15. Thus different aspects of utterances rely on the correspondent opposing part, which should be connected crosswise:

>Challenge: Gymnastics is a non-profitable art
>C: Gienger earns little money   F: G. has enough savings
>C: Not like others   F: The advertisement contracts
>M: Not like Boris Becker   F: But sure
>C: Becker earns millions

16. One is to drown out the speaker. Several times two, three or even four speakers just consented, very obviously, e.g. in saying 'certainly' (*doch*) at the same time or just by repeating the utterance of the preceding speaker. Opponents would appear very offensive if they continued the argument. A second way of ending an argument is consent. Consent rarely needs ratification of the thesis but just implies an (at least partial) acceptance of the last argument ('surely, but ...', '*ja, aber* ...'). In several cases one can hardly tell consent from a pure stop, the third form. The opponent or proponent simply stops disagreeing. The fourth form, interruption, is the most frequent. While arguing, suddenly the girlfriend of one son leaves, prompting a series of good-byes, comments, etc. Or one speaker takes his glass of wine and shouts, loudly, 'Cheers' while another is about to develop a thesis about the conflict between Marxism and Catholicism. Interruptions, stops, consent and drowning out do not necessarily mean that the argumentation has come to an ultimate end. Often they are a kind of thematic association, they pick up the thread of the argumentative topic in order to tell a funny joke.
17. I found several typical ways of returning to argumentation. First, a speaker may explicitly reformulate the problem after the argumentation has been interrupted. Interestingly enough these reformulations rarely reproduce exactly what has been said; they say it in a few words, thus posing a new problem. A special kind of reformulation is the invitation. Once Ursula, having seen that her opponent, Christian, had been interrupted by a bad joke from Detlef, asked the other participants to listen to Christian. Another

way is to formulate what may be called a real assertion. Christian, e.g. announces that he will now state his opinion on contraception, and so he goes on: 'I would like to make an important comment on ...'. As we have seen, this must not lead to an argumentative sequence. In order for it to become an assertion a speaker depends on the fourth form which may be produced at any time: disagreement as a second turn.

18. The notion of 'argumentative *Dialogsorte*' asserts exactly the opposite, that is: that there is an argumentative character throughout argumentations: cf. Jaeger (1976).
19. After Detlef has explained why he could not continue gymnastics, Uschi accuses him of never finishing anything he has begun. Now it is the family's second former gymnast, Christian, who is defending. But he is interrupted by the attacked, Detlef, who justifies himself: he did not have the same chances as others. Then we hear father's sceptical 'Hm', followed by a long pause. Father seems then to expand his sceptical remark, but lets it go. The next pause is followed by a long turn by mother who tells of two elite children gymnasts of the village, a story which is linked by a comparison ('they too'). Neither Detlef nor Christian become topics again; but there is constant allusion to their broken careers.
20. 'You are always starting something and then leaving it'/'99 per cent is hard work - the rest is talent.'/ 'Either you decide to do it or you leave it altogether'. The sentences which follow in quick succession all consist of two parts, and the two parts are contrasting (start-stop; work-talent; decide-or leave it). The third sentence is followed by what has come to be known as the Gienger (and later the Boris Becker) argument. Christian's affirmation 'gymnastics is a lost art' then, cannot be looked at in isolation. It appears to be motivated by a topic of some relevance to the past family history, and it is also motivated by the reproach in the preceding talk.
21. The long discussion on Christianity, e.g. sets in with a personal reproach:
    Christianity
    1 M: Didn't you talk about the article.
    2 U: =Christian didn't understa::nd, that's all.
    3 C: I understand it quite well. (0,5)
    4 C: It was mostly almost plain blasphemy.
    5 U: What; not at a:ll.
    Directly the theme has been initiated by mother (1), Uschi starts with the reproach that Christian did not understand (with the connotation: has been too stupid) the afore-mentioned article. Christian, of course, immediately disagrees. There is a short gap - obviously Uschi does not insist and leaves space for Christian's next move. But he does not enlarge on his ability to understand but turns to the article itself; and Uschi hurriedly disagrees with his assertion, so that both can now engage in a discussion of the article and not of Christian's ability to understand it. For reproaches in families, see Frankenberg (1976).
22. Most family members live most of the time on their own in other cities. Thus the family shares few of the experiences which are commonplace for normal members of society.

23. It is no novelty to argue that there are certain milieus which are more prone to argument than others. Schiffrin (1984) also points at the 'argumentative' culture (of Jews in Philadelphia).

References

Apeltauer, E. (1977), *Elemente und Verlaufsformen von Streitgespaechen*, dissertation, Münster.
Bergmann, J. (1987), 'Gattungsfamilien und Gattungsaggregationen', unpublished manuscript, Konstanz.
Bergmann, J. (1988), 'Haustiere als kommunikative Ressourcen', in H.-G. Soeffner (ed.), *Kultur und Alltag*, Schwartz: Göttingen.
Berthold, H. (1982), 'Der Sprachgestaltungsprozess im Kommunikationsereignis Diskussion', *Zeitschrift fuer Phonetik, Sprachwissenschaft und Kommunikationsforschung*, 25, 1.
Boggs, S. T. (1978), 'The development of verbal disputing in part Hawaiian children', *Language in Society*, 7, 325-44.
Coulter, J. (1979), 'Elementary properties of argument sequences', unpublished manuscript, Boston.
Eemeren, F. von and R. Grottendorst (1983), *Speech Acts in Argumentative Discussions*, Cinnaminsson: Dordrecht.
Frankenberg, H. (1976), *Vorwerfen und Rechtfertigen als verbale Teilstrategien in innerfamilialen Interaktionen*, Haag and Herchen: Dusseldorf.
Goffman, E. (1981), *Forms of Talk*, Blackwell: Oxford.
Gumperz, J. (1981), *Discourse Strategies*, Cambridge University Press: Cambridge.
Gumperz, John and Norine Berenz (forthcoming), 'Transcribing conversational exchanges', in J. A. Edwards and M. D. Lambert (eds), *Transcribing and Coding Methods for Language Research*, Lawrence Erlbaum: Hillsdale, NJ.
Habermas, J. (1981), *Theorie des kommunikativen Handelns*, Vols I and II, Suhrkamp: Frankfurt.
Habermas, J. (1984), 'Wahrheitstheorien', in *Vorstudien und Ergaenzungen zur Theorie des kommunikativen Handelns*, Suhrkamp: Frankfurt.
Jacobs, S. and S. Jackson (1981), 'Argument as natural category. The routine grounds for arguing in conversation', *Western Journal of Speech Communication*, 45, 118-32.
Jacobs, S. and S. Jackson (1982), 'Conversational argument: discourse analytic approach', in J. R. Cox and A. Willard (eds), *Advances in Argumentation. Theory and Research*, Southern Illinois University Press: Carbondale.
Jaeger, K.-H. (1976), *Untersuchungen zur Klassifikation gesprochener deutscher Standardsprache. Redekonstellation-stypen und argumentative Gesprächssorten*, Hueber: Munich.
Keppler, A. (1989), 'Schritt für Schritt. Das Verfahren alltäglicher Belehrung', *Soziale Welt*, 40, 538-56.
Keppler, A. and T. Luckmann (forthcoming), 'Lebensweisheiten im Gespraech', in H. G. Petzold and R. Kühn (eds), *Psychotherapie und Philosophie*, Junformann: Paderborn.

Klein, W. (1985), 'Argumentationsanalyse', in J. Kopperschmidt (ed.), *Argumente-Argumentation*, Munich.
Koerfer, A. (1979), 'Zur konversationellen Funktion von "ja aber". Am Beispiel universitaerer Diskurse', in H. Weydt (ed.), *Partikeln der deutschen Sprache*, Berlin.
Kopperschmidt, J. (1980), *Argumentation. Sprache und Vernunft II*, Stuttgart.
Lein, L. and D. L. Brenneis (1978), 'Children's disputes in three speech communities', *Language in Society*, 7, 299-323ff.
Linell, P. (1990), 'The power of dialogue dynamics' in I. Marková and K. Foppa (eds), *The Dynamics of Dialogue*, Harvester Wheatsheaf: Hemel Hempstead.
Loveday, L. (1983), 'Rhetoric patterns of conflict: the sociocultural relativity of discourse-organizing processes', *Journal of Pragmatics*, 7, 169-90.
Maas, U. (1974), 'Argumentationshandlung', in D. Wunderlich (ed.), *Pragmatik und sprachliches Handeln*, Athenaeum: Frankfurt.
Miller, M. (1984). 'Zur Ontogenese des koordinierten Dissens', in W. Edelstein and J. Habermas (eds), *Soziale Interaktion und soziales Verstehen*, Suhrkamp: Frankfurt.
Nothdurft, W. (1989), 'Interaktive Paradoxa konsensueller Konfliktloesung', in L. Hoffmann (ed.), *Rechtsdiskurse. Untersuchungen zur Kommunikation in Gerichtsverfahren*, Narr: Tübingen.
Perelman, C. and L. Olbrechts-Tyteca (1970), *Traite de l'argumentation*, Presses Universitaire de France: Brussels.
Pomerantz, A. (1984), 'Agreeing to disagree with assessments: some features of preferred/dispreferred turn-shapes', in M. Atkinson and J. Heritage (eds), *Structures of Social Action*, Cambridge University Press: Cambridge.
Quasthoff, U. (1978), 'The uses of stereotype in everyday argument', *Journal of Pragmatics*, 2, 1-48.
Rommetveit, R. (1974), *On Message Structure*, Wiley: Chichester and New York.
Sacks, H. (1987), 'The preference for agreement and contiguity', in G. Button and J. R. E. Lee (eds), *Multilingual Matters*, Clevedon, PA.
Schank, G. (1987), 'Linguistische Konfliktanalyse', in G. Schank and J. Schwitalla (eds), *Linguistische Konflikte in Gespraechen*, Narr: Tübingen.
Schiffrin, D. (1984), 'Jewish argument as sociability', *Language in Society*, 3, 311-35.
Simmel, G. (1970), 'Geselligkeit', in *Grundfragen der Soziologie*, Goeschen: Stuttgart.
Spranz-Fogasy, T. (1986), '"Widersprechen": Zu Form und Funktion eines Aktivitaetstyps' in *schlichtungsgesprächen. Eine gesprächsanalytische Untersuchung*, Narr: Tübingen.
Toulmin, S. (1983), *The Uses of Argument*, Cambridge University Press: Cambridge.
Ulmer, B. (1988), 'Medienthemen in alltaglichen Gespraechen. Formen und Funktionen von Medienrekonstruktionen', unpublished manuscript.
Vuchinich, S. (1984), 'Sequencing and social structure in family conflict', *Social Psychology Quarterly*, 47, 217-34.

9 Dominance and asymmetries in *A Doll's House*[1]

Ragnar Rommetveit

Aim and scope: from conversation analysis to interpretation of a polyphonic literary text

The purpose of this study is to explore in a stepwise fashion and, it is hoped, in increasing depth and scope, patterns of dominance and asymmetry in conversation between the two main characters in Henrik Ibsen's *A Doll's House*. The text that I shall examine in some detail is a sequence of 62 turns from the very first conversation between Nora and Helmer in the first act. This sequence will be analysed with respect to gross (and in part quantifiable) interactional dynamics and compared with a smaller fragment of conversation between them toward the end of the play.

The two excerpts will be dealt with *as if they were transcripts of real-life face to face communication*, both in the initial assessment of interactional dominance and coherence and when, after a micro-analysis of interactional moves, I proceed to enquire into patterns of semantic and strategic dominance (Linell, 1990). Asymmetry between the two partners in the conversation will then be further explored in terms of control of intersubjectively endorsed perspectives on things and states of affairs they talk about, i.e. in terms of distribution of *epistemic responsibility* (Rommetveit, 1990; forthcoming). Dialogically displayed dominance will consequently be examined as potential manifestations of asymmetric interpersonal relations such as those dealt with by Martin Buber in his explication of *Ich-Es* (I-it) - as opposed to *Ich-Du* (I-you) variants of human self-other relationships (Buber, 1958).

However, *A Doll's House* is a modern work of fiction, a

realistic drama. And, as George Lucács maintains in his studies of European realism (Lucács, 1950, p. 8), 'The inner life of man, its essential traits and essential conflicts, can be portrayed only in organic connection with social and historic factors'. Nora and Torvald Helmer are Henrik Ibsen's 'dolls', and the inner and interpersonal conflicts reflected in their conversation are hence presumedly also social conflicts, portrayed 'from within' and by dramatic means. How, then, does Ibsen through Nora and Helmer try to unveil essential conflicts within the bourgeois society in which their fates are embedded? When – if at all – can we identify the reflective and critical voice of their creator in their conversation?

These are the kind of questions I want to pursue in a final enquiry into the text *qua* polyphonic fiction. But let us start out by listening to Nora and Helmer *as if* they were real persons and read Ibsen's stage directions as accounts of scenery and non-verbal components of a real-life dialogue.

Extract 9.1 Conversation between Nora and Helmer immediately after Nora has come home from her Christmas shopping (Ibsen, 1961, pp. 1–5)

Nora: (Shuts the door. She continues to laugh quietly and happily to herself as she takes off her things. She takes a bag of macaroons out of her pocket and eats one or two; then she walks steadily across and listens at her husband's door.)
Yes, he's in.
(She begins humming again as she walks over to the table, right.)

1 Helmer: (in his study) Is that my little skylark chirruping out there?
2 Nora: (busy opening some of the parcels) Yes, it is.
3 Helmer: Is that my little squirrel frisking about?
4 Nora: Yes!
5 Helmer: When did my little squirrel get home?
6 Nora: Just this minute. (She stuffs the bag of macaroons in her pocket and wipes her mouth.) Come out, Torvald, and see what I've bought.
7 Helmer: I don't want to be disturbed! (A moment later, he opens the door and looks out, his pen in his hand.) 'Bought', did you say? All that? Has my little spendthrift been out squandering money again?
8 Nora: But, Torvald, surely this year we can spread ourselves just a little. This is the first Christmas we haven't had to go carefully.
9 Helmer: Ah, but that doesn't mean we can afford to be extravagant, you know.
10 Nora: Oh yes, Torvald, surely we can afford to be just a little bit extravagant now, can't we? Just a teeny-weeny

Dominance and asymmetries in A Doll's House

bit. You are getting quite a good salary now, and you are going to earn lots and lots of money.

11 Helmer: Yes, after the New Year. But it's going to be three whole months before the first pay cheque comes in.

12 Nora: Pooh! We can always borrow in the meantime.

13 Helmer: Nora! (Crosses to her and takes her playfully by the ear.) Here we go again, you and your frivolous ideas! Suppose I went and borrowed a thousand crowns today, and you went and spent it all over Christmas, then on New Year's Eve a slate fell and hit me on the head and there I was . . .

14 Nora: (putting her hand over his mouth) Sh! Don't say such horrid things.

15 Helmer: Yes, but supposing something like that did happen . . . what then?

16 Nora: If anything as awful as that did happen, I wouldn't care if I owed anybody anything or not.

17 Helmer: Yes, but what about the people I'd borrowed from?

18 Nora: Them? Who cares about them! They are only strangers!

19 Helmer: Nora, Nora! Just like a woman! Seriously though, Nora, you know what I think about these things. No debts! Never borrow! There's always something inhibited, something unpleasant, about a home built on credit and borrowed money. We two have managed to stick it out so far, and that's the way we'll go on for the little time that remains.

20 Nora: (walks over to the stove) Very well, just as you say, Torvald.

21 Helmer: (following her) There, there! My little singing bird mustn't go drooping her wings, eh? Has it got the sulks, that little squirrel of mine? (Takes out his wallet.) Nora, what do you think I've got here?

22 Nora: (quickly turning round) Money!

23 Helmer: There! (He hands her some notes.) Good heavens, I know only too well how Christmas runs away with the housekeeping.

24. Nora: (counts) Ten, twenty, thirty, forty. Oh, thank you, thank you, Torvald! This will see me quite a long way.

25 Helmer: Yes, it'll have to.

26 Nora: Yes, yes, I'll see that it does. But come over here, I want to show you all the things I've bought. And so cheap! Look, some new clothes for Ivar . . . and a little sword. There's a horse and a trumpet for Bob. And a doll and a doll's cot for Emmy. They are not very grand but she'll have them all broken before long anyway. And I've got some dress material and some handkerchiefs for the maids. Though, really, dear old Anne Marie should have had something better.

27 Helmer: And what's in this parcel here?

28 Nora: (shrieking) No, Torvald! You mustn't see that till tonight!

29 Helmer: All right. But tell me now, what did my little spendthrift fancy for herself?
30 Nora: For me? Puh, I don't really want anything.
31 Helmer: Of course you do. Anything reasonable that you think you might like, just tell me.
32 Nora: Well, I don't really know. As a matter of fact, though, Torvald . . .
33 Helmer: Well?
34 Nora: (toying with his coat buttons, and without looking at him) If you did want to give me something, you could . . . you could always . . .
35 Helmer: Well, well, out with it!
36 Nora: (quickly) You could always give me money, Torvald. Only what you think you could spare. And then I could buy myself something with it later on.
37 Helmer: But Nora . . .
38 Nora: Oh, please, Torvald dear! Please! I beg you. Then I'd wrap the money up in some pretty gilt paper and hang it on the Christmas tree. Wouldn't that be fun?
39 Helmer: What do we call my pretty little pet when it runs away with all the money?
40 Nora: I know, I know, we call it a spendthrift. But please let's do what I said, Torvald. Then I'll have a bit of time to think about what I need most. Isn't that awfully sensible, now, eh?
41 Helmer: (smiling) Yes, it is indeed – that is, if only you could hold on to the money I gave you, and really did buy something for yourself with it. But it just gets mixed up with the housekeeping and frittered away on all sorts of useless things, and then I have to dig into my pocket all over again.
42 Nora: Oh but, Torvald . . .
43 Helmer: You can't deny it, Nora dear. (Puts his arm round her waist.) My pretty little pet is very sweet, but it runs away with an awful lot of money. It's incredible how expensive it is for a man to keep such a pet.
44 Nora: For shame! How can you say such a thing? As a matter of fact I save everything I can.
45 Helmer: (laughs) Yes, you are right there. Everything you *can*. But you simply can't.
46 Nora: (hums and smiles quietly and happily) Ah, if you only knew how many expenses the likes of us skylarks and squirrels have, Torvald!
47 Helmer: What a funny little one you are! Just like your father. Always on the look-out for money, wherever you can lay your hands on it; but as soon as you've got it, it just seems to slip through your fingers. You never seem to know what you've done with it. Well, one must accept you as you are. It's in the blood. Oh yes, it is, Nora. That sort of thing is hereditary.
48 Nora: Oh, I only wish I'd inherited a few more of Daddy's qualities.

49 Helmer: And I wouldn't want my pretty little song-bird to be the least bit different from what she is now. But come to think of it, you look rather ... rather ... how shall I put it? ... rather guilty today ...
50 Nora: Do I?
51 Helmer: Yes, you do indeed. Look me straight in the eye.
52 Nora: (looks at him.) Well?
53 Helmer: (wagging his finger at her) My little sweet-tooth surely didn't forget herself in town today?
54 Nora: No, whatever makes you think that?
55 Helmer: She didn't just pop into the confectioner's for a moment?
56 Nora: No, I assure you, Torvald ...!
57 Helmer: Didn't try sampling the preserves?
58 Nora: No, really I didn't.
59 Helmer: Didn't go nibbling a macaroon or two?
60 Nora: No, Torvald, honestly, you must believe me ...!
61 Helmer: All right then! It's really just my little joke ...
62 Nora: (Crosses to the table.) I would never dream of doing anything you didn't want me to.

Initiative-response analysis of the conversation: assessment of interactional dynamics, dominance and coherence

The conversation presented *in extenso* will first be examined with respect to interactional dynamics, and the coding system I shall apply is the categorization of conversational turns elaborated at the University of Linköping. This version of conversation analysis, initiative-response or IR analysis, has by now been applied across a wide range of social settings (Linell and Gustavsson, 1987; Linell, Gustavsson and Juvonen, 1988; Linell, 1990). Its key terms 'initiative' and 'response' are, despite their deceptively eclectic-behaviouristic flavour, truly dialogical terms with a built in commitment to a three-step analysis of individual contributions (Foppa, 1990; Marková, 1990).

Every single conversational turn in an IR assessment of interactional dynamics must therefore be interpreted from a dual perspective: as potentially context bound, attuned to preceding turn(s); and as potentially context constitutive, constraining and/or governing subsequent contribution(s). Helmer's first contributions to the conversation (his turns 1 and 3) are thus, in an IR assessment, pure and strong initiatives, whereas turns 8 and 9 are categorized as compounds of response and weak initiative. Strong initiatives are requests and questions, soliciting a response from the other, while weak initiatives are basically comments, not requiring (but often inviting) a response. The theoretical foundation of the IR system with its eighteen turn categories is presented and discussed in detail by Linell, Gustavsson and Juvonen (1988). In what follows I shall only comment briefly upon features of coding and quantification of particular relevance in subsequent assessment of interactional dominance and coherence in conversations in *A Doll's House*.

All conversational turns are mapped on to the eighteen categories, and the coding does not allow for double classification. Each turn must therefore be unequivocally categorized, and the eighteen turn categories are systematically evaluated and assigned a rank order from 1 to 6 with respect to interactional dominance. Minimal, communicationally inadequate turns (such as turns 32 and 34) are assigned the bottom rank, 1. Minimal but accepted and focally alter-linked responses such as turns 2 and 4 are assigned rank 2. Turns with features of both response and strong initiatives such as turns 6 and 7 are given the rank order 4, and strong initiatives devoid of any response features such as turns 1 and 3 are assigned the top rank 6 with respect to interactional dominance. Gross interactional dominance on the part of each conversation partner over a sequence of turns can hence be assessed as the median rank value of all her or his turns during that sequence.

Interactional coherence and thematic continuity are reflected in focally alter-linked response components across consecutive turns (such as turns 6 to 9). Turns linked to – and pursuing – something the interlocutor her- or himself has said rather than the partner's intermittent contribution (such as Helmer's turn 15), on the other hand, indicate insertion of monologic discourse. Non-focally linked responses to the other's contributions, moreover, may be said to indicate incapacity and/or unwillingness to attune one's own talk to the attunement of the other. Such non-focally linked responses may be metacommunicative, such as Nora's turn 14: 'Sh! Don't say such horrid things!' Or they may be thematically peripheral or evasive, such as Helmer's turn 39. The money he talks about in that turn is hardly the money wrapped up in pretty gilt paper referred to by Nora in her preceding turn.

Gross interactional dominance can hence, for each conversation partner, be quantified in terms of an IR index, as the median value of all her or his turns on the ordinal dominance scale. Asymmetry between them is accordingly assessed as the difference between their IR indices, the IR difference. Relative insertion of strongly alter-controlling interactional moves, moreover, is quantified as a solicitation coefficient, S. The latter is simply the percentage of turns entailing components of strong initiatives such as, e.g. direct questions (Helmer's turn 1) and directives (Nora's turn 6). And gross evasion and/or avoidance of attunement to the other's contributions is quantified as an obliqueness coefficient, O. The latter is calculated as the sum of self-linked and non-focally alter-linked turns in percentage of all turns.

Quantification of qualitatively analysed data is never more robust than its qualitative base, and IR categorization of written conversation is necessarily infected by presuppositions or conjectures with respect to prosody. Ibsen's stage directions in parentheses, however, are in part also prescriptions for performance and therefore impose definite constraints on the range of plausible prosodic variations of the text. Margins of uncertainty of categorization due to residual options concerning prosody and non-verbal expressive behaviours are, hence, not of an order which seriously affects IR assessment of gross interactional dynamics in the two excerpts.

The text of primary concern in the present study is the conversation presented *in extenso* above. The sequence from the last act will be examined and commented upon mainly for comparative purposes. What happens in between the two sequences of conversation is that Helmer learns about his wife's sinful, yet in her own view sacred, secret: that she once took the law into her own hands and committed fraud in order to get money to help him recover from a potentially fatal disease. Having experienced his condemnation instead of appreciative understanding of what she did long ago, Nora has become disillusioned and has decided to leave her husband. The conversation from the last act takes place after Helmer has noticed that Nora, whom he believed was in bed, has changed her clothes. It consists of 26 consecutive turns, starting with Nora's opening remark: 'Sit down, Helmer. We two have a lot to talk about' (Ibsen, 1961, p. 79).

IR indices, IR differences, S coefficients and O coefficients for each of the two excerpts are presented in Table 9.1. And what, then, does Table 9.1 tell us about interactional dominance and coherence in the first conversation we listened to between Nora and Helmer?

The IR indices for the excerpt from the first act yield a rather unequivocal picture of gross interactional dynamics. The interaction between wife and husband is clearly asymmetric, and

Table 9.1 IR measures of conversation between Nora and Helmer from the first and last acts of *A Doll's House*

	Helmer	Nora	Difference
		First act	
IR index	3.78	2.69	1.06
S coefficient	61	9	52
O coefficient	32	10	22
		Last act	
IR index	3.37	3.43	-0.06
S coefficient	15	31	- 16
O coefficient	31	38	- 7

Helmer is definitely the dominant agent in their interaction. But *how* asymmetric is the conversation, compared to real-life dialogues of various kinds? How shall we interpret the IR measures presented in Table 9.1 in the light of relevant empirical evidence on patterns of interactional dynamics in conversations outside *A Doll's House*?

Linell and Gustavsson (1987) and Linell, Gustavsson and Juvonen (1988) report results of IR analysis of dialogues across a wide range of social settings. The material they have analysed consists of tape-recorded sequences of everyday conversations in informal as well as institutionally defined situations. It includes, in addition to informal conversation between friends, colleagues and spouses and discussion between children, child-adult discussion, patient–doctor dialogue, police interrogation, and dialogue between lawyer and defendant in legal settings.

Let us first examine the IR difference between Nora and Helmer in their first conversation in the light of the measures from real-life dialogues in similar settings examined by Linell, Gustavsson and Juvonen. The IR differences they find in conversation between equals talking together in informal settings vary from 0.07 (two female colleagues, teachers) to 0.38 (two school boys, one Swedish born and the other an immigrant). The IR difference between Nora and Helmer is 1.06. Their conversation, in the light of samples of dialogues from similar real-life situations, is thus remarkably asymmetric and very different from the dinner conversation between spouses analysed by Linell, Gustavsson and Juvonen (1988, p. 425). The patterns of interactional dominance for the two conversations as assessed by the ordinal scale are visually portrayed in Figure 9.1.

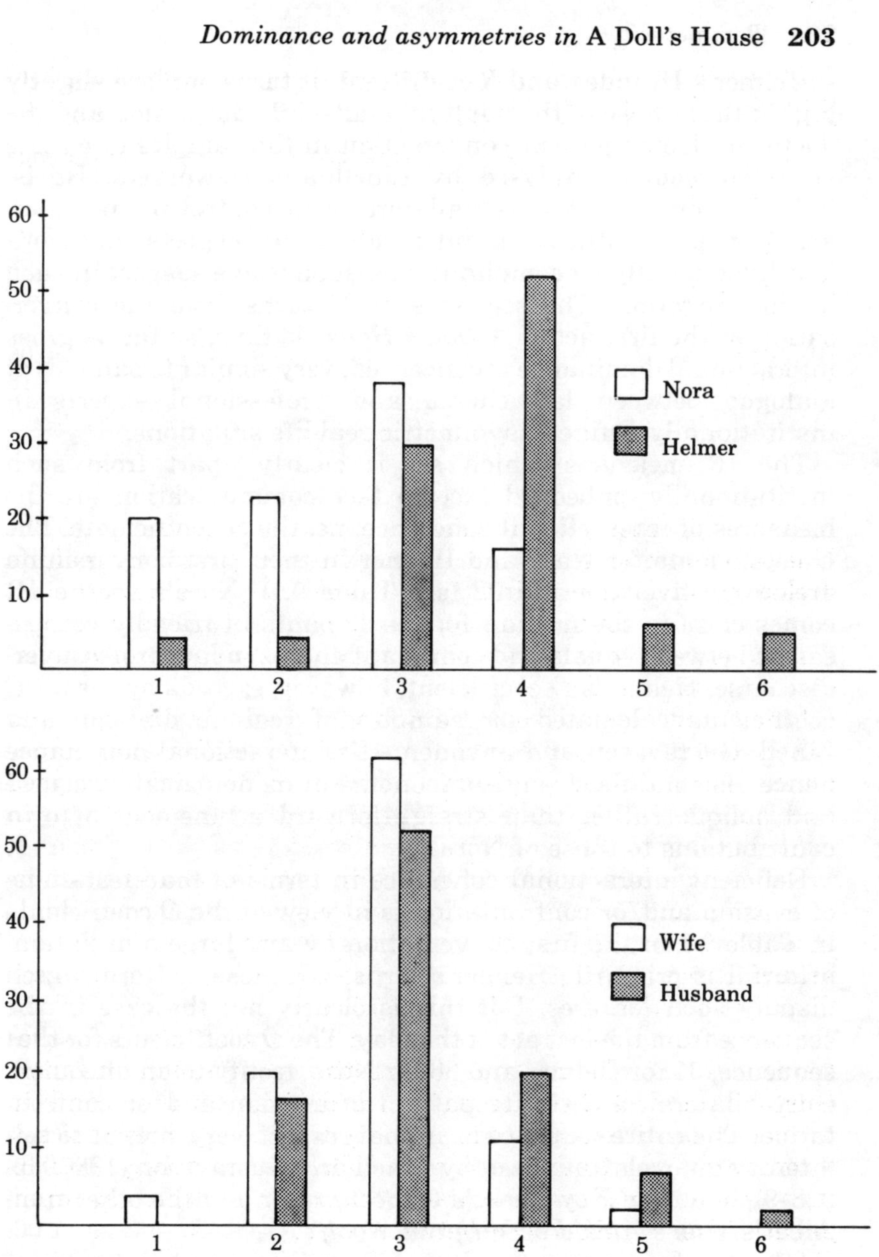

Figure 9.1. Distributions of turns on ordinal scale of interactional dominance. Nora and Helmer's first conversation and dinner conversation between wife and husband, from Linell, Gustavsson and Juvonen (1988, p. 425)

Helmer's IR index and S coefficient, it turns out, are slightly higher than those of the adult in adult-child discussion and the doctor in doctor-patient conversation in the samples of dyadic verbal discourse analysed by Linell and co-workers. He is, indeed, approximately as unilaterally in control of the interaction as police officials in interrogation of suspects, and Nora is interactionally as compliant as a submissive suspect in such an interrogation. The sequence of 62 turns from the conversation in the first act of *A Doll's House* is thus, as far as gross interactional dominance is concerned, very similar to samples of dialogue between lay clients and professional experts in institutionally defined asymmetric real-life situations.

The IR measures which set it clearly apart from such institutionally embedded face to face communication are the measures of interactional coherence, i.e. the O coefficients. The O coefficients for Nora and Helmer in their first conversation are, respectively, 9 and 32 (see Table 9.1). Nora's coefficient comes close to the median for participants in friendly conversation between equals and compliant clients in lay-professional discourse. Helmer's O coefficient, however, exceeds by far all O coefficients calculated for samples of real-life dialogues by Linell, Gustavsson and Juvonen. His interactional dominance hence also entails strong components of monological discourse and oblique rather than straightforward attunement of own contributions to those of Nora.

Deficient interactional coherence in terms of manifestations of evasion and/or confrontation is in view of the O coefficients in Table 9.1 in the first conversation by and large a unilateral affair: it is primarily Helmer's turns, not those of Nora, which display such features. But this is clearly not the case in the sequence from the last act of the play. The O coefficients for that sequence, 31 for Helmer and 38 for Nora, testify to an unequivocally bilateral and strong pattern of evasion and/or confrontation. The entire sequence is, in that respect, very similar to two 'literary quarrels' analysed by Linell and Gustavsson (1987, pp. 228-9), one from Key-Åberg's *O. Scenprator* and the other from Albee's *Who's Afraid of Virginia Woolf?*

In view of the quantification of gross interactional dynamics presented in Table 9.1, our IR analysis of the two excerpts from *A Doll's House* may thus be summarized as follows. The first conversation is strongly asymmetric, with Helmer as a dominant agent whose interactional moves testify to evasion and/or confrontation rather than attunement to the attunement of his wife, and with Nora as a cooperative and interactionally submissive partner who lets herself be controlled. The IR measures for the sequence from the last act do not at all portray such a pattern of interactional dominance. The Nora we encounter in this brief fragment of their conversation is *Helmer's equal*, and, perhaps, as judged from their S and O coefficients, even slightly superior opponent in an otherwise relatively symmetric quarrel.

On semantic dominance, setting and taking of perspectives, and distribution of epistemic responsibility

Linell and his co-workers (Linell and Gustavsson, 1987; Linell, Gustavsson and Juvonen, 1988, and Linell, 1990) emphasize again and again that IR analysis aims at interactional, not semantic, dominance and coherence. The micro-analysis upon which the IR measures rest is consistently and systematically myopic: every single turn is interpreted in its strictly local context, and categorization is in principle unaffected by hypotheses or presuppositions concerning genre, potential superordinate objectives of the dialogue and pervading major themes. IR categorization of conversational turns is hence also strictly proactive or 'objectively hermeneutic' (Övermann *et al.*, 1979) in the sense that assessment of response and initiative features of any single turn at any given stage of a dialogue is detached from information about continuation of that dialogue beyond the next, immediately adjacent turn.

It is therefore not possible to make plausible inferences concerning semantic content and communicative significance from IR categorization of single conversational turns. And, as Linell (1990, p. 21) maintains,

> there is no way of uncovering the ways actors use their turns to pursue their topics and perspectives by just looking at IR-measures (which simply reflect interactional functions in the local contexts). Topical perspectives are normally the emergent products of sequences of turns (or of long monological turns).

When Helmer asks Nora whether it is his little skylark who is chirruping and a police officer asks a suspect whether the latter had planned the crime, they are both interactionally manifesting *strong initiatives*. And nothing more is captured by IR categorization of their turns. The facts that Helmer is apparently engaged in innocent flirtation whereas the police officer's question does *not* fit into such a genre are not captured at all.

Categorization of conversational turns in terms of focally or non-focally alter-linked response components, however, presupposes judgement concerning thematic continuity across adjacent turns. Locally assessed interactional coherence is thus, when we examine it closely, actually semantically founded. And gross interactional coherence and cohesion (Halliday and Hasan, 1976) are composed of local constituents. Topical coherence across long sequences of turns is necessarily locally generated, and indeed primarily out of thematic continuity across adjacent turns. IR categorization, even though myopic and geared toward assessment of interactional functions, thus entails semantic analysis. Its key terms, 'initiative' and 'response', are also, in my view, semantically based dialogical terms.

Let us hence begin our enquiries into patterns of semantic and strategic dominance in the first conversation between Nora and Helmer by examining in some detail semantic features of pairs of adjacent turns which have already been categorized as interactionally linked in our initial IR analysis. The pairs I have chosen are four from the opening of the conversation. Only segments of the turns of unequivocal relevance in IR assessment of interactional coherence are presented below, and words and expressions of pivotal significance for thematic continuity across turns are underlined.

Extract 9.1a
1 Helmer: Is that my little skylark . . .?
2 Nora: . . . it is.

6 Nora: . . . see what I've bought.
7 Helmer: . . . 'Bought' . . .? . . . squandering money . . .?

7 Helmer: . . . 'Bought' . . .? . . . squandering money . . .?
8 Nora: . . . can spread ourselves . . . haven't to go carefully
            . . .

8 Nora: . . . can spread ourselves . . . haven't to go carefully
            . . .
9 Helmer: . . . (not) afford to be extravagant . . .

Turn 1, we remember, was categorized as a pure, strong initiative and turn 2 as a pure, focally alter-linked response. The interactional coherence is simple and unequivocal: the little skylark Helmer asks about is immediately identified by Nora (by the skylark herself!) and referred to by the pronoun 'it'. Thematic continuity is mediated by anaphoric deixis. The segment of turn 6 reproduced above entails also a strong initiative and turn 7 a compound of a focally alter-linked response and

Dominance and asymmetries in A Doll's House 207

another strong initiative. Thematic continuity across the two adjacent turns is established by Helmer's repetition of the word 'bought' from turn 6 in an interrogative tone, and continuity across response and initiative features within turn 7 by the semantic interface between 'bought' and 'squandering money'.

Nora's turn 8, having been categorized as a compound of a focally alter-linked response and a weak initiative, pursues via the expression 'spread ourselves' the theme of Helmer's initiative in turn 7, 'squandering money'. And Helmer's turn 9, we remember, belongs to the same IR category. It is in virtue of what is meant by '(not) afford to be extravagant' an interactionally coherent comment upon the initiative feature 'haven't to go carefully' (or the whole) of Nora's immediately preceding turn, and invites rather than demands her to continue.

Nora's effort to direct her husband's attention to the Christmas presents she has brought home is via the sequence bought - '-bought?' ... squandering money - can spread ourselves ... haven't to go carefully - (not) afford to be extravagant channelled into a debate about the family's financial predicament and Nora's - in Helmer's view, irresponsible - spending of money. And that sequence is merely the sequence of coherence-constitutive features of locally assessed interactional coherence. By extracting the semantic-topical contents of response and initiative features over three consecutive adjacency pairs, turn by turn, we have thus embarked upon an enquiry into semantic dominance and emergent topical perspectives. Let us now expand the scope and explore the topical development of, and options with respect to, perspectives on what Nora and Helmer are talking about.

Their dialogue is not, like dyadic discourse embedded within institutionally defined instrumental frames, predetermined or heavily constrained with respect to either topics or perspectives, but thematically 'locally sensitive' in the sense that it may at any stage be tagged on to objects and events attracting attention within the immediately perceived situation in which it takes place. It is thus, as far as genre is concerned, a fairly prototypical conversation (Luckmann, 1990; Bergmann, 1990). Which potential aspect(s) of immediately given and attended to objects will become intersubjectively endorsed topics in the dialogue between Nora and Helmer depends, therefore, upon their 'directed openness beyond the immediately given to potential experience' (Graumann, 1989, p. 97).

The issue of thematic control is, accordingly, to a large extent a matter of individual setting and taking of perspectives

(Graumann, 1989; 1990), of shifts of perspective across thematically connected adjacent turns, and control of such shifts. Nora's turn 6 is indeed, interactionally, a strong initiative: she tries to control Helmer's locomotion and gaze so as to attain convergence of attention on to what she has bought. And Helmer's turn 7 is clearly and focally alter-linked – when we disregard shifts of perspective and examine it within the restricted scope adopted in assessment of local, verbally manifested interactional and thematic coherence. Helmer lets himself – even though reluctantly – be disturbed. He puts his work aside and enters into conversation with his wife. But he does *not* leave his worries behind him. His perspective on the parcels on the table is pervaded by concern about the cost of those parcels rather than their contents.

Nora's opening remark, even though clearly aimed at joint attention toward the Christmas gifts inside the parcels, also allows for interactionally and thematically connected talk oriented toward bills, payment and future economic affairs beyond those immediately given and jointly attended to objects. And when Helmer in turn 7 exploits this option, she immediately adopts the perspective set by him. She does not at all try to pursue her own initiative in turn 6 by self-linked contributions such as, e.g. 'But wait a little, Torvald. See first what I have bought.' By arguing (*against* her husband) that they can spread themselves a little this year, she is in turn 8 *eo ipso* engaged in a debate about the parcels and her Christmas shopping on Helmer's premises. The strategically crucial interactional moves in the beginning of their conversation are thus turns 7 and 8. What happens across those thematically connected adjacent turns is that *Helmer sets and Nora takes a perspective clearly at variance with – and in some important respects contrary to – that of her opening remark.*

But what, more specifically and on empirical grounds, can we infer about *Nora's* perspective and interactional intention in turn 6? We have just seen her return from her shopping in a happy mood, humming and laughing 'quietly and happily to herself'. To the extent that her mood reflects interactional intentions and anticipations, we can thus safely infer that she neither intends nor anticipates a confrontation with her husband over reckless spending of money. What kind of conversation *she* hopes and expects to emerge out of joint attention to the parcels on the table is in part revealed in turn 26, when she once more makes an attempt at directing Helmer's attention to what she has bought. She wants to chat with him about the particular gifts she has bought for their three children and the maids, about a little sword, a trumpet, a doll, clothes and handkerchiefs. Prospective issues for discussion from her perspective are therefore issues of potentially joint concerns such as whether Ivar will like that little sword and whether she ought to have bought something better than the clothes and handkerchiefs for dear old Anne Marie.

This, however, is not what worries Helmer. He is, as far as attunement to her perspective is concerned, as evasive as when later on in turn 39, after having pushed Nora to tell him what she fancies for herself, he twists their conversation back into moral tutoring and debate about her alleged economic irresponsibility. Helmer's dominance is on both occasions inextricably fused with and contingent upon Nora's submission. He controls topics and perspectives because Nora lets herself be controlled. And this holds true also when Helmer, apprehending signs of guilt in her face, engages in a regular interrogation of her (turns 49-62). Nora lets herself be interrogated about her visit to the confectioner's and consumption of sweets. She is, like a fearful child who has misbehaved, lying about her misdemeanours, but not for a moment questioning her interrogator's moral authority and premisses for passing judgement.

The Nora we encounter in the fragment of conversation from the last act does not at all resemble a compliant child submitting to parental authority. The main topics of discourse are once more her conduct and style of life, but now expanded in time back to her childhood and in scope so as to encompass her entire life situation and previously not talked about and largely unacknowledged aspects of her marital life. This time it is Nora herself who, stubbornly groping for words of her own, wants to talk about such matters, and we remember from assessment of gross IR measures that the resultant dialogue seems to develop into a symmetrical quarrel. But the gross measures of confrontation and/or evasion for the two conversation partners, it turns out, are composed of different kinds of contributions. Nora's O coefficient (see Table 9.1) is composed of self-linked conversational contributions only, whereas Helmer's O coefficient is made up of exclusively alter-linked meta-communicative comments. What emerges out of their different kinds of oblique contributions, however, is a confrontation rather than the kind of evasive argumentative sequences observed by Knoblauch (this volume, chapter 8) in real-life family dinner-table talk.

Their conversation is thus, despite Nora's attempts to reach out toward Helmer and share her dawning insights with him, semantically asymmetric. Her attempts to establish intersubjectivity result in expressions her husband protests against and talk he does not understand. Her contributions hence turn into a monologue. This is particularly transparent when she, as in the following excerpt from the last act, is groping for novel words for her relationships to her father and to Helmer (Ibsen, 1961, p. 80):

> Extract 9.1b
> Nora: (shakes her head) You two never loved me. You only thought how nice it was to be in love with me.
> Helmer: But Nora, what's this you are saying?
> Nora: It's right, you know, Torvald. At home, Daddy used to tell me what he thought, then I thought the same. And if I thought differently, I kept quiet about it, because he wouldn't have liked it. He used to call me his baby doll, and he played with me as I used to play with my dolls. Then I came to live in your house ...
> Helmer: What way is that to talk about our marriage?
> Nora: (imperturbably) What I mean is: I passed out of Daddy's hands into yours. . . .

Such words and expressions are not spoken at all in the first dialogue in *A Doll's House*, when Helmer is in control. Meaningful expressions about his wife and her marital situation on his premises are 'my little skylark', 'my little squirrel', 'my little spendthrift', 'my little singing bird', and 'my little sweet-tooth' (see turns 1, 3, 5, 7, 21, 43, 49 and 53). And when Helmer talks meaningfully and efficiently *to* and *about* Nora in words such as 'skylark' and 'squirrel', it is of course because their meaning potentials exceed by far their conventional zoological reference. Such expressions constitute also potential drafts of contracts concerning categorization of persons (Rommetveit, 1974) and can be used to identify particular persons we address and/or talk about. But words such as 'skylark', 'squirrel' and 'spendthrift' become firmly and dialogically established pet names only when both partners have accepted and endorsed the categorizations entailed within them as means of unequivocal identifying reference.

When we start listening to the first conversation between Nora and Helmer we know nothing about their background and the doll-like childhood and marital life Nora talks about toward the end of the play. But we observe immediately that Helmer's expressions 'skylark', 'squirrel', etc., constitute a solidly and dialogically established vocabulary of pet names rather than improvised proposals for categorization. When in his very first turn he talks *to* and *about* her as 'my little skylark', she does not at all hesitate and say: 'What's this you are saying?' or 'What way is that to talk . . .?' Every time she is addressed by Helmer as, respectively, 'skylark', 'squirrel', 'spendthrift', etc., she responds as spontaneously and compliantly as a little child who has thoroughly accepted and learned to obey its pet name. And Nora once uses two of those words herself. When Helmer agrees that she saves everything she *can*, but adds that she simply can't, she says, smiling quietly and happily (turn 46): 'Ah, if you only knew how many expenses the likes of *us skylarks and squirrels* have, Torvald!'

The meaning potentials entailed within Torvald's rich vocabulary of pet names range all the way from delightful, chirruping skylarks via erratic squirrels to totally irresponsible spendthrifts. The vocabulary is for that reason exceptionally well-suited to the conversational fusion of flirtation and reproach. It allows Helmer to talk intermittently and at times simultaneously in two tongues, affectionately and reproachingly *to* and *about* his wife. And it makes it exceedingly difficult for Nora - and for us - to disentangle components of genuine affection from moral reproach in his contributions to the dialogue. Helmer's dominance, even though equal to that of a police officer in interrogation of a suspect as far as gross IR-measurements are concerned, is softened and veiled by reciprocal manifestations of emotional attachment. It is indeed at times so efficiently camouflaged that someone overhearing parts of their conversation may get an impression of nearly idyllic relations between the spouses.

Helmer's vocabulary of pet names thus, in a way, constitutes an intricate semiotic, cognitive-emotive net within which Nora is unknowingly kept a captive. It serves to fuse affection and moral reproach and hence also, it seems, to sustain *and* camouflage basic interpersonal asymmetries such as those dealt with by Martin Buber (1958) in his explication of *Ich-Es* as opposed to *Ich-Du* relations. Expressions and utterances with potentially intersubjective content can, in Buber's view, bring about authentic and immediate experiential communion only when embedded in *Ich-Du* interaction, i.e. only when one person utters them *to*, without any explicitly or tacitly conveyed comment *about*, an addressee. When what we say to the other is infiltrated by comments about her or him, on the other hand, we are approaching the other as an object in a world structured in terms of our own purposes and interests. We are thus, in such *Ich-Es* interaction, protecting our own 'life-world' (*Lebenswelt*) against intrusion from fellow human beings.

Distinctive features of *Ich-Du* interaction as opposed to *Ich-Es* interaction is immediacy as opposed to mediacy. Immediacy has to do with what Bakhtin (1973) in his literary studies refers to as 'the loophole of the consciousness and the word', with fusion of own perspective with that of one's conversation partner. And such Buberian notions have recently been pursued and further elaborated by Bråten (1988a; 1988b) in convergent cross-disciplinary explorations within social psychological theory, systems analysis and empirical research on 'proto-conversation' between infants and adult caretakers. *Ich-Du* interaction is, according to Buber (1958, p. 29 and p. 57) a prerequisite for development of human identity and own identity (*Eigenwesen*). The identity of a human being who has been persistently dealt with as an *'Es'* by her or his 'significant others' is bound to become a borrowed identity.

Helmer throughout their first dialogue protects his own *Lebenswelt* very efficiently against intrusion from Nora's interests and concerns, and his very efficient protection must, in view of Buber's reflections on basic features of human dialogicity, be interpreted in conjunction with the fact that his talk *to* her is inextricably fused with talk *about* her as 'skylark', 'squirrel', 'spendthrift', etc. Helmer's semantic dominance thus reflects a pervasive *Ich-Es* asymmetry in his relationship to his wife, and his control of intersubjectively accepted and endorsed perspectives may accordingly be further investigated in terms of distribution of epistemic responsibility among conversation partners.

Distribution of epistemic responsibility is not merely a matter of semantic dominance and thematic control, but has to do with verbally manifested transformation of human subjectivity into potentially shared social reality. Hans-Georg Gadamer (1975, p. 432) maintains that 'that which comes into language ... receives in the word its own definition.' A dialogue about yet-not-verbally identified states of affairs in a pluralistic social world is epistemically totally asymmetric if, and only if, one of the conversation partners unilaterally controls the words and expressions by which both of them topicalize those states of affairs and transform them into potentially shared social realities. And this may in principle be the case even if the partner deprived of epistemic responsibility is the one who establishes joint attention on to the things and events they talk about and hence, in a way, is in control of topics.

Deprivation of epistemic responsibility on the part of one of the conversation partners appears to be a recurrent feature across a variety of institutionally defined asymmetric conditions of discourse. A psychiatric patient, for instance, may have a minimal impact upon the way in which her or his personal problems are brought into language *qua* symptoms even though she or he is the one who has privileged access to those very problems (Käsermann, this volume, Chapter 5). The story about a suspect which in written form serves as the input in subsequent official legal procedures, moreover, is as a rule a story told from the professional stance of the police interrogator rather than from the individual suspect's outlooks and concerns (Linell and Jönsson, this volume, Chapter 4). And the fate of the allergic child in a multi-party pediatric setting, it appears, may become that of a quasi-partner and 'non-person' in discourse dominated by adult caretaker and medical expert (Aronsson, this volume, Chapter 3). Asymmetric allocation of epistemic responsibility is in such cases as a rule a reflection of patterns of socially acknowledged and presumably rationally grounded patterns of dependence and professional responsibility.

Nora and Helmer engage in conversation without any shared commitment to particular topics or perspectives. Events such as Nora's Christmas shopping and things such as the parcels towards which she directs her husband's attention may in principle become subjectively and potentially intersubjectively meaningful in infinitely many ways. They acquire subjective meaning and significance when experienced within life-worlds pervaded by human interests, concerns, and future-oriented projects. The parcels, for instance, may be imbued with significance from directed openness toward potential future experience of the children's excitement and joy when they open the parcels, from concern about 'dear old Anne Marie', and from worries about payment of bills and long-term economic calculations. In order to make plausible inferences concerning distribution of epistemic responsibility in a conversation about them we have also to take into account such options with respect to perspectives and topicalization, including options which after their conversation are 'lost possibilities' (von Wright, 1974, p. 34).

Thus Nora's remark (in turn 26) that Anne Marie should have had something better might obviously have been responded to by Helmer and pursued further by both of them. That remark might, for instance, in cooperation, have been expanded into a thematically connected sequence of turns about what the children and maids need and how the particular gifts will be appreciated by the recipients. Such an expansion would doubtless be more in line with what Nora hoped and intended when she engaged her husband in conversation about the parcels than the ensuing debate about budgetary issues we have witnessed. But it is, after their conversation, one of countless lost possibilities.

The tragic asymmetry in the first conversation in *A Doll's House*, it seems, is an asymmetry with respect to tacitly yet reciprocally shared social reality. Helmer lets himself be disturbed and engages in conversation with his wife, but he neither listens nor talks to her as an epistemically equal and co-responsible partner. Nora is a captive within his polysemous and ambiguous net of pet names and, in Buberian terms, an '*Es*' in *Ich-Es* interaction on his premisses. She smiles happily while talking about herself in words - 'skylarks and squirrels' - borrowed from her husband's vocabulary of pet names for her.

This is no longer the case when we encounter her in conversation with Helmer toward the end of the play. What has happened in between the two conversations has shaken her deeply and provoked her to reflect upon her previously efficiently camouflaged and unacknowledged imprisonment and borrowed identity.

Reflections on the conversation as a polyphonic literary text

Nora Helmer is a character in a realistic drama, a woman devised by Henrik Ibsen. Versions of her have for more than hundred years come alive on stages all over the world. And to the extent that the actress on the stage lends voice and flesh and blood to *Ibsen's* Nora, we are still puzzled and inclined to wonder about her borrowed identity and unredeemed *Eigenwesen* after having listened to her conversations with Helmer.

John Northam comments in his book *Ibsen's Dramatic Method* on the prelude to the first conversation in *A Doll's House* as follows (Northam, 1971, p. 16):

> when Ibsen makes Nora ... pop a couple of sweets into her mouth as soon as she comes in from shopping, and then takes pain to hide all signs of them as she hears her husband's voice, he tells us in a matter of seconds several things about Nora's character: it is childish; it goes in awe of authority; it is willing to deceive.

This may be true, but it is of course not the simple and whole truth about her. Ibsen's Nora loves sweets, but she also enjoys making other people happy. Her personal commitment does not extend to financial institutions and anonymous people from whom they have borrowed money (turn 18). However, she cares for her husband and children, loves buying Christmas presents, and shows real concern for their dear old maid. Such potential manifestations of her *Eigenwesen* do not penetrate and shape their conversation about her Christmas shopping in the same way that Helmer's foresight into economic problems and his instrumental rationality do. But they may, precisely for that reason *and* in view of her creator's reflections on the bourgeois society he tries to unveil in *A Doll's House*, be interpreted as manifestations of unredeemed female identity within that society.

Ibsen in the autumn of 1878 was working on a first draft of *A Doll's House*. His working title was *The Tragedy of Contemporary Society* (*Nutids-Tragedien*), and he writes in his notes about his dramatic project (Ibsen, 1878 in: Ibsen 1931, p. 368):

> There are two kinds of moral laws, two kinds of consciences, one in the man and an entirely different in the woman. They do not understand one another; but the woman is in practical life judged according to the man's law, as if she were not a woman, but a man. . . .
> A woman cannot be herself in contemporary society, which is an exclusively male society, with laws written by men and with accusations and passing of judgements concerning female conduct from a male position.

The Ibsen we encounter in these notes is an essayist engaged in social scientific reflections. Ibsen the dramatist, on the other hand, speaks through his characters. He is hence engaged in 'ventriloquation', i.e. in a semiotic activity 'whereby one voice speaks *through* another voice or voice type as found in social language' (Wertsch, 1991, Chapter 3, p. 11). The terms 'voice', 'voice type' and 'social language' convey notions developed by Bakhtin (1981) and further explicated by Wertsch (1991) in his *Voices of the Mind*, and a major objective in Bakhtinian analysis is to explore in depth patterns of intertextuality and social embeddedness of individual human voices. Wertsch maintains, about the implications of the approach for analysis of real-life conversations as well as of literary texts (Wertsch, 1991, Chapter 6, p. 23):

> Because utterances inevitably invoke a social language, it is no longer possible to view dialogue in terms of two localized voices . . . one must look to the social language that frames speaker's utterances in order to interpret what it is they have said and to identify who is doing the talking.

Who, then, is doing the talking in the first conversation we listen to in *A Doll's House*? - It is definitely not Ibsen the essayist we encountered in his notes from 1878. Neither Nora nor Helmer voices his views. Rather, what we hear in their conversation are voices from a cultural collectivity within which unresolved conflicts and patterns of suppression are very efficiently camouflaged. A major feat of Ibsen, the dramatist, in the first part of the play, it seems, is indeed to embed basic patterns of dominance and asymmetry in a dialogue conducted in 'the social language' of ordinary family conversation in such a way that we are going to be taken by surprise when those patterns are revealed later on.

Helmer's vocabulary of pet names is thus neither an arbitrary collection nor representative of the ways Ibsen has heard loving and authoritarian husbands address their wives, but a semiotic net designed by a master of words in such a way that Nora is kept a captive and at times even enjoys being imprisoned. The word in the original Norwegian text (Ibsen, 1879) which in my view epitomizes the entire vocabulary, the compound 'spille-fugl', is not listed in the 1986 standard dictionary of the Norwegian majority language at all. It is a word constructed by Ibsen himself for particular purposes, and it is used only four times in his entire collected works, once in each of the equivalents of turns 7 and 40 and twice in the equivalent of turn 43 in the original Norwegian edition of *A Doll's House* (see *Ibsen-Ordbok*, 1958, p. 894). The word is composed of 'spille' (play) and '*fugl*' (bird) and is alternatively translated as 'spend-thrift' (turns 7 and 40) and 'pet' (turn 43); but in Ibsen's use it is a rather ingenious semantic fusion of the English expressions 'singing bird' and 'person addicted to gambling'. As used in his original dramatic text, it is thus a conversational implementation of a 'double bind', allowing Helmer to talk *to* and *about* Nora simultaneously in two tongues, and in such a way that neither she, nor we who listen to the conversation, can disentangle deprivation of epistemic responsibility from genuine moral reproach, and condescending disregard from genuine affection.

Nora is in the original Norwegian text in the beginning of the play addressed and referred to by definite descriptions, i.e. by the expression '*lerkefuglen*' (the lark bird) rather than '*den lille lerkefuglen min*' (my little skylark) and by '*ekornet*' (the squirrel) rather than '*det lille ekornet mitt*' (my little squirrel), etc. Ibsen's Helmer uses the possessive in connection with the pet names only in turn 49: he would not want *his* little song bird the least bit different from what she is now. The possessives in turns 1, 3, 5, 7, 21, 43 and 53 have been introduced by McFarlane (Ibsen, 1961) who thereby makes Helmer repeatedly address his wife as *his* (little) property. Ibsen's consistent use of the definite article, on the other hand, foregrounds the taken-for-grantedness or *Als-bekannt-setzung* (Reichling, 1963) of Helmer's categorizations. The intrusion of talk *about* Nora in talk *to* her is thus linguistically more unequivocally mediated in the original Norwegian than in the standard English version of the play.

Ibsen's preparatory notes on *A Doll's House* in 1878 are written by an engaged and critical observer, and his insights into previously largly unacknowledged conflicts within his contemporary bourgeois society are attained by critical analysis of and reflections upon the society from the outside. His challenge as a dramatist and composer of conversations is to portray and unveil those camouflaged social conflicts and patterns of suppression from inside the society, as experienced and lived by persons embedded in it such as Nora and Torvald Helmer. And if we listen for relative unequivocal ventriloquation in *A Doll's House* on such assumptions, we may recognize the author's own voice through that of Nora in the excerpt from the last act of the play.

Bakhtin (1981, p. 293) maintains, 'The word ... becomes "one's own" only when the speaker populates it with his own intention, his own accent, when he appropriates it to his own semantic and expressive intention.' This, it seems, is precisely what Nora does with Ibsen's abstract and analytically couched words about the unredeemed female identity in a society in which women are deprived of epistemic responsibility. She is, after all, *his* beloved doll, designed to embody and later on reveal the predicament of women in a society ruled by men. His reflectively assessed insight into that predicament is converted into dawning self-insight in Nora and mediated to us in her confrontation with Helmer in the last act of the play. It is not surprising that Helmer is bewildered and asks: 'What way is that to talk . . .?' Nora's novel words about her relationships to her father and to Helmer do not fit into the frame of an ordinary family conversation in their home. We are actually listening to Ibsen's words, but appropriated to Nora's semantic and expressive intentions.

The fact that performances of *A Doll's House* still attract and engage audiences all over the world may be interpreted as a tribute to its author and/or as a sad sign of inertia as far as redemption of the female identity in our societies is concerned. The conflict between perspectives in the play as Ibsen construed it, however, is not merely a marital conflict *anno domini* 1879. It is also a conflict between reflective, calculating instrumental rationality and spontaneous, immanently meaningful human activity and intrinsically rewarding care for fellow human-beings. When modern versions of Ibsen's Nora come alive on the stage and engage modernized Helmers in conversation, they may hence also provoke us who listen to their conversations to ponder on our own possibilities for immanently meaningful and moral human life in a society pervaded by techno-economically oriented instrumental rationality. And Ibsen's statements in his notes on the first draft of *A Doll's House* are today, more than a hundred years after they were written, accepted in interrogative form as issues of central theoretical significance in social-scientific and humanistic research on the predicament of women in contemporary society.

The question whether 'there are two kinds of moral laws, two consciences, one in the man and one in the woman' is thus the superordinate and basic question in Carol Gilligan's empirical studies of moral development and female ethics of care (Gilligan, 1982). Nora, we remember, had, prior to her confrontation with Helmer, been judged and condemned by her husband for having committed fraud a long time ago in order to help him regain his health. Helmer's moral reaction in that situation is, in view of Gilligan's findings, a typically and unequivocally male moral reaction. She maintains that women by and large conceive of moral problems as problems of care and responsibility in relationships whereas men tend to conceive of them as problems of rights and rules. Thus (Gilligan, 1982, p. 100), 'The moral imperative that emerges repeatedly in interviews with women is an injunction to care, a responsibility to discern and alleviate the "real and recognizable trouble" of this world.'

Female ethics of care, however, is in Carol Gilligan's view as a rule not acknowledged as such, but is categorized as lack of male right-and-duty moral. And she presents evidence that 'the woman is . . . judged according to the man's law, as if she were not a woman but a man' even in Piaget-inspired psychological investigations of moral development (Kohlberg, 1968). The issues Ibsen dealt with in his preparatory notes and wanted to raise by his construction and unveiling of patterns of dominance and asymmetries in *A Doll's House* were thus moral issues, but moral issues which today also are being pursued and illuminated in empirical psychological research.

Note

1. My thanks to Krish Arnesen and Marianne Garte for help in coding of the texts and to Professor Per Linell for expert supervision and correction of our IR coding. I am also indebted to Professor Harold Noreng and Professor Magne Rommetveit for guidance concerning relevant Ibsen literature and lexicographical information.

References

Bakhtin, M. (1973), *Problems of Dostoevsky's Poetics*, translated and edited by C. Emerson, University of Minnesota Press, and Manchester University Press: Manchester.
Bakhtin, M. (1981), *The Dialogical Imagination: Four essays by M. M. Bakhtin*, University of Texas Press: Austin TX.
Bergmann, J. (1990), 'On the local sensitivity of conversation', in I. Marková and K. Foppa (eds) *The Dynamics of Dialogue*, Harvester Wheatsheaf: Hemel Hempstead.
Bråten, S. (1988a), 'Dialogical mind: the infant and the adult in protoconversation', in M. E. Carvallo (ed.), *Nature, Cognition and System*, Kluwer Academic Publishers: Dordrecht.
Bråten, S. (1988b), 'Between dialogical mind and monological reason: postulating the virtual other', in M. Campanelli (ed.), *Between Rationality and Cognition*, Meynier: Turin.
Buber, M. (1958), *Ich und Du*, Verlag Lambert Schneider: Heidelberg.
Foppa, K. L. (1990), 'Topical progression and intention', in I. Marková and K. Foppa (eds), *The Dynamics of Dialogue*. Harvester Wheatsheaf: Hemel Hempstead.
Gadamer, H. G. (1975), *Truth and Method*, edited by G. Barden and J. Cumming, Sheed and Ward: London.
Gilligan, C. (1982), *In a Different Voice: Psychological theory and women's development*, Harvard University Press: Cambridge, MA.
Graumann, C. F. (1989), 'Perspective setting and taking in verbal interaction', in R. Dietrich and C. F. Graumann (eds), *Language Processing in Social Context*. North Holland: Amsterdam.
Graumann, C. F. (1990), 'Perspective structure and dynamics in dialogues', in I. Marková and K. Foppa (eds), *The Dynamics of Dialogue*, Harvester Wheatsheaf: Hemel Hempstead.
Halliday, M. A. K. and Hasan, R. (1976), *Cohesion in English*, Longman: London.
Ibsen, H. (1879), *Et Dukkehjem*, (A Doll's House). Gyldendal: Copenhagen.
Ibsen, H. (1931), Samlede Verker. Hundreårsutgave, VIII. Gyldendal Norsk Forlag: Oslo.
Ibsen, H. (1961), *A Doll's House*, translated by James Walter McFarlane, *The Oxford Ibsen, V.*, Oxford University Press: London.
Ibsen-Ordbok, (Ibsen Dictionary). Ordforrådet i Henrik Ibsens samlede verker (1958). Gyldendal Norsk Forlag: Oslo.
Kohlberg, L. (1968), 'The child as a moral philosopher', *Psychology Today*, 2, 25-30.

Linell, P. (1990), 'The power of dialogue dynamics', in I. Marková and K. Foppa (eds), *The Dynamics of Dialogue*, Harvester Wheatsheaf: Hemel Hempstead.
Linell, P. and Gustavsson, L. (1987), *Initiativ och respons. Om dialogens dynamik, dominans og koherens*, Studies in Communication 15, University of Linköping.
Linell, P., Gustavsson, L., and Juvonen, P. (1988), 'Interactional dominance in dyadic communication: a presentation of initiative-response analysis'. *Linguistics*, 26, 415-42.
Lucács, G. (1950), *Studies in European Realism*, Hillway: London.
Luckmann, T. (1990), 'Social communication, dialogue, and conversation', in I. Marková and K. Foppa (eds), *The Dynamics of Dialogue*, Harvester Wheatsheaf: Hemel Hempstead.
Marková, I. (1990), 'A three-step process as a unit of analysis in dialogue,' in I. Marková and K. Foppa (eds), *The Dynamics of Dialogue*, Harvester Wheatsheaf: Hemel Hempstead.
Northam, J. (1971), *Ibsen's Dramatic Method. A study of the prose dramas*, Universitetsforlaget: Oslo.
Övermann, U., Tilman, A., Konau, E. and Krambeck, J. (1979), 'Die Methodologie einer "objektiven Hermeneutik" und ihre allgemeine forschungslogische Bedeutung in den Sozialwissenschaften', in H. G. Soeffner (ed.), *Interpreative Verfahren in den Sozial- und Textwissenschaften*, J. B. Metzensche Verlagsbuchhandlung: Stuttgart.
Reichling, A. (1963), 'Das Problem der Bedeutung in der Sprach-wissenschaft', *Innsbrucker Beiträge zur Kulturwissenschaft*, Sonderheft, (Special issue), 9.
Rommetveit, R. (1974), *On Message Structure: A framework for the study of language and communication*, Wiley: London.
Rommetveit, R. (1990), 'On axiomatic features of a dialogical approach to language and mind,' in I. Marková and K. Foppa (eds), *The Dynamics of Dialogue*, Harvester Wheatsheaf: Hemel Hempstead.
Rommetveit, R. (forthcoming) 'Outlines of a dialogically based social-cognitive approach to human cognition and communication', to appear in an anthology edited by Astri Heen Wold.
Wright, G. H. von (1974), *Causality and Determinism*, Columbia University Press: New York.
Wertsch, J. V. (1991), *Voices of the Mind: A sociocultural approach to mental action*, Harvester Wheatsheaf: Hemel Hempstead and Harvard University Press: Boston, MA.

10 | Asymmetries in group conversations between a tutor and people with learning difficulties

Ivana Marková

Many people with learning difficulties suffer from a language and communication deficiency. This deficiency may result from a variety of factors. It may be due to an underlying physiological or neurological defect, to the learning difficulty itself, to lack of practice in conversation, or to a combination of several of these and other factors. The non-handicapped, on their part, rarely have sufficient skills and sensitivity to communicate with people whose speech is impaired, who need a longer time to respond or who try to communicate non-verbally.

In several studies carried out in Scotland (Jahoda et al., 1988; Cattermole et al., 1990; Marková et al., forthcoming) it has repeatedly been found that people with learning difficulties who live either at home with their parents, or in hostels run by local authorities, have little communicative interaction with people outside the mental handicap world. Their main social activities are attending clubs for people with learning difficulties or participating in events with members of their own families or with other people with learning difficulties.

Leudar (1981) suggests that the social position of people with learning difficulties, even in the relatively non-institutional environment of Adult Training Centres where they spend their time working and learning various skills, is such that their experience of communication is one of being placed in a *non-reversible role*. He argues that they are not given equal opportunities to initiate and perpetuate discourse, to question anything, to make statements or to express their attitudes and feelings openly. As a result such people may develop active strategies to avoid communication (Leudar, Fraser and Jeeves, 1981; Leudar and Fraser, 1985). It appears that interactions between staff and persons with learning difficulties most often take the form of instructions or orders exhibiting a high degree of control (Prior et al., 1979; Marková et al., forthcoming). These various factors, each having an inhibiting effect on the speech and communication of a person with learning difficulties, interplay with each other, thus producing a multiple effect disadvantaging such a person even further.

What kinds of communicative asymmetries?

Probably all dialogues involve some kinds of asymmetry (Linell and Luckmann, this volume, Chapter 1). In a dialogue between a person with learning difficulties and a non-handicapped person, some of these asymmetries are established situationally because of the handicapped person's impaired speech and communication. Others arise from the fact that words have diagnoses and prognoses implicitly built into their meaning potentials (Marková, 1990a). Being socially shared, word meanings entail many of the societal unconscious, semi-conscious and conscious stereotypes and attitudes (Goffman, 1968; Moscovici, 1984). Finally, asymmetries in speech and communication result from explicit institutionally determined power relationships and the dominance of one party over the other in knowledge and abilities. Doctor-patient, adult-child, teacher-pupil and police-suspect are examples of relationships based on such explicit power.

Many asymmetries in interactions between staff and residents in a mental handicap hospital appear to stem from the institutional power relationships and automatized institutional routines. The nature of interactions between staff and residents with moderate/severe learning difficulties was explored in a study carried out in Scotland (Marková et al., forthcoming). One of the main findings was that most interactions initiated by hospital staff were related, in one way or other, to basic life necessities such as meals and toileting and to institutional rules and routines. Only in a minority of cases was it the purpose of the staff's initiated interactions to express interest in people with learning difficulties *qua* personal and social beings rather than as patients to be kept alive. For example, at mealtimes in the hospital dining room, the main reasons for staff-resident interactions was to remind residents how to hold cutlery, to hurry up with eating so that another group of residents could take lunch, and to control residents' table manners.

It was not only meals but also other kinds of interactions that were observed to be routinized to extremes. The following example is a write up of field notes of a 'shaving' event that occurred in a hospital and involved a resident with learning difficulties, Brian, and a member of the hospital staff:

> Brian saw the nurses walking to the toilets and immediately rose to join the group of residents waiting for a shave. When his turn came, Brian sat in one of the three chairs lined up facing the washbasins. No words passed between Brian and the busy staff member as shaving foam was routinely slapped on his face and the rapid shave began. Staff did talk among themselves, however, about their diets. The shave took 1 1/2 minutes and once over, Brian went to the washbasin, washed his face with water, and dried it with a communal towel. Staff rinsed the razor with hot water, and began shaving the next resident. (from Marková et al., forthcoming).

It could be argued, of course, that talking to the resident during shaving could lead to a razor injury. However, the point of the described situation is that the resident was not, at any stage of this interaction, i.e. even before or after the shaving, acknowledged by the staff as a fellow human-being. The member of staff who was shaving the resident while talking to another member of staff could just as well have been polishing a table or washing up dishes.

These examples thus show that interpersonal interactions in institutions can become automatized routines in which the relationships between persons are reduced to those existing between persons and physical objects, i.e. to sheer *Ich-Es* relationships (Rommetveit, this volume, Chapter 9; Farr, Chapter 11). Thus, in a very real sense people with learning difficulties live in a world apart.

It was also found (Marková et al., forthcoming) that, in hospital, 83 per cent of all interactions between staff and residents lasted less than one minute and only 2 per cent of all interactions were conversations lasting longer than ten minutes. Clearly, the brevity of these interactions could hardly provide the basis for any meaningful communicative exchanges. They did not allow a discussion topic to be developed or emotional bonds between interactants to be formed; their brisk and superficial nature did not encourage people with no or few verbal skills to communicate their needs, wishes and feelings.

Until recently, speech therapy for people with learning difficulties was based on a medical deficit model. This meant that a person with learning difficulties was, and sometimes still is, regarded as a patient having a speech disorder and therefore requiring treatment in order to approach or achieve a level of normal functioning. Assessment of language and communication skills based on this ideology tends to be a fault-finding procedure to identify problems in the person's performance with a view to remediation (Rogers-Warren et al., 1983; Robertson, Richardson and Youngson, 1984; Marková, 1990b). Thus this deficit model, by its very nature, focuses only on the speech and communicative problems of a person with a learning difficulty rather than on the problems arising in a situation in which two people, one with and one without a speech deficiency, try to establish communication. More recently, however, speech therapists have argued for a more dialogical approach in speech therapy (Jenkins, 1990; Calculator, 1988). According to this approach, both the persons with learning difficulties and their interlocutors take responsibility for the outcome in communication and both require training. However, such an approach is still in its infancy. In order to develop a dialogical approach, it is important, first, to identify the sources of dialogical asymmetries and second, their implications for the dynamics of dialogue.

The analysis of group discussions of people with mild learning difficulties

Method and procedure

The reported study was part of a bigger project concerned with social skills training of people with mild learning difficulties which was carried out over twelve weeks. The data reported in this chapter were obtained during the course of conversations of four discussion groups formed in the first week of this project. Participants were selected from those people with mild learning difficulties who came daily to one Adult Training Centre in central Scotland either from a mental handicap hospital or from a parental home. The aim of the discussion groups was to explore spontaneous participation of people with mild learning difficulties in a group situation, their ability to express opinions, to listen to others, to respond to what other people said, and to pursue a topic (for details see Cattermole, 1988).

The setting

As pointed out above, people with learning difficulties in institutions almost always find themselves in non-reversible roles when talking to the non-handicapped. This perpetuates a vicious circle: being placed into roles in which they are responding rather than initiating agents, they conform to the role of respondents and in turn thus confirm the presuppositions on the basis of which such roles are defined.

It was the purpose of the reported study to break this vicious circle. We intended to create social settings that would be conducive to conversation and that would give people with learning difficulties an opportunity to interact with the non-handicapped as relatively equal conversational partners. It was decided to establish discussion groups consisting of five to six people with mild learning difficulties and a tutor. Two tutors were involved in the discussion groups, both of them working for the self-advocacy movement of people with learning difficulties and actively participating in the effort of the movement to improve their quality of life. The tutors were well known to the participants with learning difficulties and had friendly and informal relationships with them.

Discussion group sessions took place in the speech therapy unit, away from the hospital buildings and from the Adult Training Centre and they were video-taped for subsequent analysis. A daily newspaper was passed round and used to start a group discussion. While few participants could read more than a few words, several exploited the abilities they did have, using newspapers for finding out whether TV programmes they liked were on, looking up football results, and so on. Therefore, newspapers were not unfamiliar or threatening to them. The paper used was the *Daily Record*, a tabloid published in Scotland, selected because of its familiarity to the participants and the large number of pictures it contained. The pictures and headlines were used by the tutors to prompt a discussion based on a news story, a TV programme liked by participants, sports or subjects frequently occurring in the news, such as the royal family.

The tutor's task was to create a social setting in which *conversation* rather than *training* would take place. The tutor himself was to participate in group discussion in the same way as the other participants. He would run the discussion group, but in such a way as to avoid taking an 'expert role', providing direction to the discussion only when this was necessary, e.g.

should the conversation dry up. Although each of the tutors was well prepared for his task, the situation inevitably suffered from substantial inbuilt difficulty. The tutor was more knowledgeable than other members of the group, had a higher social status, was responsible for the smooth running of the discussion group and was supposed to intervene when the discussion came to a halt. Moreover, it was he who brought the newspaper and who set the task for the group. Discussion groups lasted about an hour and the material to be analysed came from the video-tapes of the first five minutes of the four discussion groups.

Analysis of the discussion groups

Given the asymmetries of knowledge and status between tutors and group participants, the purpose of the analysis of the group discussions was, first, to explore the pattern of dialogical asymmetries. Sinclair and Coulthard's (1975) analysis of communicative acts was adapted for direct coding from videotapes. This analysis was based on frequency counts of the following six kinds of communicative acts, most typical of asymmetric teacher–pupil interaction in the classroom: information, elicitation, direction, evaluation, reply (verbal) and reaction (non-verbal). The analysis showed a highly asymmetric pattern of interactions in all four discussion groups, with the tutors largely using elicitations, directions and evaluations, while the participants with learning difficulties largely used replies and reactions (Cattermole, 1988). The data so obtained were very similar to those reported by Sinclair and Coulthard (1975) on teacher–pupil interaction.

The subsequent interview with the tutors revealed that they were genuinely surprised by the results of the analysis, having been totally unaware, until they learned the results of the analysis, of their highly dominant role in the discussion groups. It was thus apparent that in spite of their determination to establish conversations, the discussion groups could more appropriately be called highly asymmetric dialogues.

In the Sinclair and Coulthard (1975) type of analysis the system of categories of communicative acts is mutually exclusive. In other words, each communicative act is assigned one function only. For example, an act can be categorized either as elicitation, or as a response or as something else, but it cannot have two different functions at the same time. Moreover, while sometimes categorization of the specific speech act cannot be made without taking context into consideration, e.g. deciding whether the act is an initiative or a follow up, in general, each act is categorized independently of those of others. Consequently, this kind of analysis could be misleading. First, it does not allow for the possibility that the speaker's communicative action may fulfil several functions at the same time and second, utterances in a dialogue are mutually interdependent rather than independent of each other.

In contrast to the assumptions on which either-or kinds of categorization procedures are based, according to the dialogical approach, individual turns and/or utterances have several functions at the same time (Mukařovský, 1977; Bakhtin, 1981; Marková and Foppa, 1990). Which of these functions is or are foregrounded is largely situationally determined. Each turn and utterance, according to this view, is taken to be only a part in a dialogical chain (Vološinov, 1973). Moreover, the dialogical point of view presupposes that individual turns in a dialogue and conversation are Janus-like (Linell, 1990), i.e. they are *both* context constituting and context renewing. They are also both past and future oriented; they are both stable and dynamic. They are oriented towards the speaker's own perspective and also towards the other's perspective. In general, turns and utterances are Janus-like in many different ways. These Janus-like characteristics, such as past and future orientation of a turn, self- and other-perspectivity, stability and dynamics, are not, therefore, assumed to be mutually exclusive. Instead, they are part of the same dialogically defined dimension. This means, for example, that each turn, rather than being categorized as either elicitation or response, is conceptualized as involving both some elicitation and some response although, in extreme cases, one or the other may be missing. Each turn and utterance can thus be viewed in terms of dialogical logic as the outcome of such two interacting characteristics and analysed as a three-step process (Marková, 1990a). Initiative–response (IR) analysis (Linell *et al.*, 1988), is based on these conceptual prerequisites.

In order to explore dialogical asymmetries in the above discussion groups, IR analysis has been applied. IR analysis, assigning each conversational turn to one of eighteen categories based on Janus-like assumptions, was originally developed for the study of interactional dominance and topic coherence in dyadic conversations (Linell, Gustavsson and Juvonen, 1988; for a brief account of IR analysis see Rommetveit, this volume, Chapter 9). In IR analysis the various indices of asymmetry are calculated for each of the two interlocutors separately and are then compared. In a group situation, similarly, the indices of asymmetry can be calculated for each participant separately, and then compared with those for the group as a whole. An initiative in a group discussion may be directed at a group as a whole or at a particular individual; in either case an initiative can result not only in the response of a particular individual but also in responses of other participants. For example:

Extract 10.1
T: Jean, do you ever watch it?
J: Yes, I watch it.
A: I watch it.
B: I watch it too.
C: I watch *Starsky and Hutch*.

Moreover, while an initiative may be directed at a particular individual someone else may steal the turn and respond instead. In addition, the speaker may be looking at and/or speaking to one member but intending the message to reach someone else or the whole group (see also Aronsson, this volume, Chapter 3).

As mentioned above, preliminary analysis of our discussion groups (Sinclair and Coulthard, 1975) indicated a highly dominant role for the tutors. It was therefore decided to apply IR analysis in a particular way. First, the group discussion was considered as if basically dyadic with the tutor treated as one participant and the remainder of the group as the other. Second, there were instances of group discussions in which the tutor did not participate. Examples of such interactions were examined separately (see pp. 234-5).

In addition to the fact that the present study was concerned with group rather than two-person discussions, there were several other features that were not present in the studies by Linell and his colleagues. First, our participants were people with impaired speech and learning difficulties who often did not comprehend what the other interlocutor had said. Second, conversations were video-taped rather than audio-taped, this enabling coding of non-verbal initiatory and response gestures. Consequently, these features had to be reflected in codings.

Each turn may, to varying degrees, be both a response to preceding turns and an initiation of a new topic. Linell *et al.* (1988) therefore ordered turns, falling into each of their eighteen categories, on a six-point ordinal scale from those which were strongly initiatory and weakly responsive, scoring 6, to the most strongly responsive and weakest from an initiatory point of view, scoring 2 and 1. In the present study the following categories were added to the existing eighteen and their interactional strength was scored on the six-point scale as follows:

- a non-verbal gesture used as an initiative: 3
- a non-verbal gesture used as a response: 2
- a response based on a miscomprehension: 1

Although we are dealing with group rather than with two-person conversations, it was not necessary to introduce other categories for them because it had been decided to treat the group discussions dyadically, i.e. the tutor as one half of the dyad, and those with learning difficulties as the other. For example, if one participant with learning difficulties responded on behalf of the other(s) or if he or she stole a turn, such responses and initiatives would count towards the pool of initiatives and responses of all the participants with learning difficulties. As mentioned above, the decision to treat all participants with learning difficulties as one side and the tutor as the other side of a dyad, and to make codings accordingly, was due only to the enormous asymmetry between the tutor's contributions on the one hand and those of the other participants on the other. Figure 10.1 shows the IR profile, i.e. the mean values of interactional strength measured on the six-point scale for each of the 21 categories. The higher numbers on the scale represent greater initiatory strength. One can see that the frequency of the tutor's contributions to the dyad was relatively greater in the categories that scored highest, i.e. 6, 5, and 4, on the scale. These categories indicate stronger initiatives. In contrast, the participants with learning difficulties (remember that these are group and not individual scores) scored higher in categories indicating stronger contribution of responses or miscomprehension. Similar results to those in Figure 10.1 were obtained in the other three discussion groups. Taking all four discussion groups together, the results showed that the tutors' scores on the IR indices ranged from 3.84 to 5.33 in the four groups. In contrast, IR indices of people with learning difficulties ranged from 2.0 to 3.2.

Table 10.1 shows IR index (mean values) and other measures of conversational interaction (proportions) taken from one discussion group, namely balance (B), solicitation (S), fragmentation (F) and obliqueness (O) coefficients (Linell et al., 1988).

The balance coefficient, B, is defined as the proportion of expanded responses. In order to obtain balance scores, the interlocutor must respond to the immediately preceding

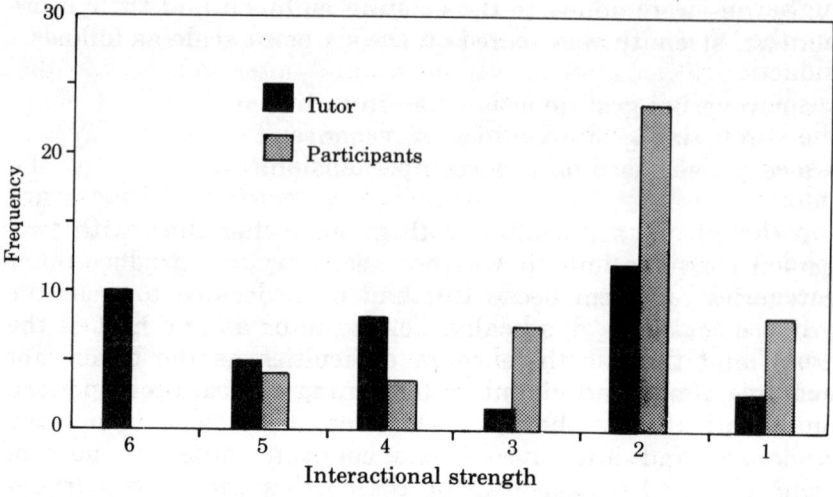

Figure 10.1 Frequency and category of tutor and participant interaction.

Table 10.1 IR index and other coefficients of conversational interaction

	IR	B	S	F	O
Tutor	3.84	0%	61%	39%	21%
Participants	2.5	13%	6.5%	8.6%	2.1%

contribution from his or her conversational partner. Thus the score of 0 per cent for the tutor on B coefficient indicates that he did not expand on the participants' immediately preceding turns. Similarly, Gustavsson (1988) found that in teacher–pupil educational dialogues it was rare for the teacher to score high on the B coefficient. The teacher's task is to ask questions, correct and evaluate the pupil. In a similar way, in our study the solicitation coefficient, S, which includes questions and other strong initiatives, comprised over 61 per cent of all of the tutor's contributions. The fragmentation coefficient, F, expressing the proportion of unconnected or non-locally connected initiatives or responses, and the obliqueness coefficient, O, expressing the proportion of turns avoiding a link up with the main content of the interlocutor's adjacent turns, were also very high for the tutor.

Gustavsson (1988) predicted that the F coefficient would be higher in lessons than in conversations. The tutor's high score on the F coefficient therefore indicates that he adopted a didactic, rather than a conversational approach in the discussion group. It means that the tutor, rather than developing the discussed topic, fragmented conversations by turning to issues which were not, locally, the focus of talk. Finally, the tutor's relatively high O coefficient indicates that he did not contribute to the smooth and fluent conversation. Rather, he tended to return to his own, previous initiatives that were not successfully followed up by the others.

It was apparent that the tutor found it difficult to maintain the group's conversation, and in his effort to do so he frequently nominated an individual to make a contribution. If the individual did not respond 'adequately', the tutor nominated another participant. The following extract illustrates the problem. Here the tutor nominated one individual, Andy, to contribute to the discussion and having failed to obtain an adequate response, he appealed to the rest of the group to see if anyone else was interested in speaking about the topic in the newspaper.

Extract 10.2
Tutor: Is there any football on, Andy?
A: Aye.
T: What? The Celtic match?
A: What . . . eh? . . . What about the Celtic tonight?
T: Who are Celtic playing then, Andy?
Who are Celtic playing tonight?
Does anyone else want a look at the paper?
B: Aye, I do.
T: Do you want to give the paper to Catherine, Andy?

It is important to draw attention to the context-boundedness of codings. That an initiative is considered by the researcher as unrelated or only obliquely related to the main topic is determined by his or her definition of the situation and by the communicative context in which the turn is placed. Consider, for example, an excerpt from police interrogation (quoted in Linell, 1990: 159–60):

P: Sven Erik Anderson . . . it was Erik you said, wasn't it?
S: Yes
P: (9 sec) 55-07-11 (5 sec) 5386 (civil registration number which P takes from his file) (4 sec) occupation, what do I write there?
S: Officer-of-state
P: What?
S: Officer-of-state
P: Oh yes (13 sec) In which parish are you registered?
S: um . . . St Nicholas

P: OK (7 sec) Married or single?
S: Single

This interview is based on a questionnaire in which the policeman collects demographic information from the suspect, such as his name, address, occupation, marital status and so on. In this particular context, all these apparently different issues are coded as part of the same topic, namely, obtaining demographic information (Linell, personal communication). However, one can easily think of a dialogue in which questions of this kind would be treated as attempts to initiate new topics, and therefore as instances of increasing fragmentation and obliqueness of the dialogue. For example, in a dialogue concerning the participants' occupations a sudden question by one of them about the other's marital status or an inquiry about the other's address might not only constitute a switch to another topic but could also be felt as an intrusion into a person's privacy. Thus it is clear that coding of turns is not context free and what would be considered a strong new initiative in one social setting would not be so in another setting.

The development of topic

Although this study was set up to encourage people with learning difficulties to get involved in conversation the tutors assiduously pursued the classroom technique. They asked questions, insisted on answers to their questions and if they did not consider answers adequate they pursued them further. As was pointed out in the previous section, didactic techniques are not conducive to conversation. Solicitation, obliqueness and fragmentation, none of which facilitates conversation, were very high in the tutor's score for asymmetry. In contrast, the balance-coefficient, indicating the proportion of expanded responses to one's interlocutor, was 0 per cent for the tutor.

We shall now turn to the balance coefficient in order to consider possible reasons for the tutor's 0 per cent score. Let us take the following example.

Extract 10.3
T: Can you talk about some news . . . Grace . . . Can you talk about something you've seen in the paper?
P1: (Grace passes the newspaper to P2): I read the paper every day.
T: Aye. Is there anything there you would like to talk about?
P1: Eh, well the teachers going on strike.
T: Right. Was it there in the paper?

T: Why are they on strike?
P3: It's the Union, they belong to a Union or something.
T: Why did the teachers go on strike?
P3: To get more money, I think, and to get better education.
T: Do you think they are right to go on strike?
P3: They shouldnae strike, they shouldnae strike.
T: (speaks to P1) What do you think Grace?

As can be seen, in this example all of the tutor's contributions were direct questions in which he followed up his own goal of encouraging conversation 'about the news'. It is significant that the tutor did not, himself, contribute to the topic progression. Even if the participant did respond to his question, the tutor, rather than expanding on the topic, turned his attention to the next participant, asking her what she thought about the teachers' strike.

The tutor's question 'Why did the teachers go on strike?' is embedded in its relevant 'outside'. There are several aspects of the embeddedness of this question to consider. The first concerns the quality of the response. In the above case the participant P3 had already explained that the strike had something to do with the unions. However, the tutor asked the same question again, apparently not satisfied with the answer he had been given.

This question, therefore, was again a strong initiative. An alternative to this strong initiative could have been to expand on what the participant had said already. It was possible, for example, for the tutor to develop the idea that the unions had a strong influence, and perhaps to offer some more information about this influence.

The second aspect of the embeddedness of the question, 'Why did the teachers go on strike?' concerns its meaning potential and its particular meaning in the given context. The meaning potential of this question *in vacuo* is 'request for information'. Yet the context in which the question was asked made it clear that the tutor did not request information. He did not really want to know why the teachers had gone on strike but was testing the participant. More precisely, in using this pseudo-question the tutor was not testing the participant's knowledge about that particular strike or about strikes in general, but was testing his speaking and communicative ability.

The third aspect of the question's embeddedness concerns the joint construction of meaning, essential to any conversation. At the local level, i.e. at the level of an individual turn, the meaning of the question was decided largely on the tutor's terms. The other interlocutor was only given the chance of accepting the tutor's perspective, not that of constructing the meaning of the question on a more equal basis, as would be typical of conversation. However, it is apparent that even in such a highly asymmetrical situation as this one, the meaning of a turn is still constructed jointly by both participants, even if only at a very basic level. Although the tutor dismissed the content of the other interlocutor's message and responded by initiating a new topic, the dialogue could continue only because he or she accepted the tutor's perspective, either by validating it silently or by topicalizing it.

By verbalizing his strategic intentions the tutor distorted the neutral local coherence that normally characterizes informal conversations. According to Foppa (1990), the principle of neutral local coherence states that speakers make additions to, comment on and expand the interlocutor's turn so that the conversational flow from one turn to the other is maintained. Ignoring an interlocutor's turn, whether because of strategic intention or from some other reason, distorts neutral local coherence and fragments conversation. Strategic intentions infringe on the local continuation of a topic. Since the tutor adopted a didactic approach in group discussions and had decided beforehand what counted and what did not count as an adequate contribution and interpreted what the participant had said according to his own intentions, the result was more like a monological dialogue than a conversation. A monological dialogue is an obstruction to the real development of a topic, as Foppa (1990) has observed.

At a more global level, again, the joint construction of meaning in terms of the topic was achieved largely on the tutor's terms. The tutor set the perspective by deciding what counted as a valid contribution to the dialogue. Contributions that did not count as valid were not responded to and therefore were cancelled out and treated as off the record.

Group conversations without a tutor

There were spells in these conversations during which the tutor either left the scene, for example, looked out of the window, or when participants with learning difficulties temporarily interacted fluently among themselves without him. For example, there was an instance, in one of the dialogues, in which they were trying, mostly non-verbally, to make a decision as to what to talk about. A non-verbal, joking suggestion by one of them was to talk about 'page 3', i.e. the page with sex stories and pictures of half-naked young women. When the tutor was not looking, the initiator showed the page to the others and they expressed their agreement with laughter, nodding their heads and with pointing gestures or disagreement by hand gestures or by a monosyllabic 'no'. While the tutor was not part of this decision-making because he was looking out of the window, the participants watched his reactions to see whether he paid them any attention. Their mutual interactions were spontaneous and were interrupted only by the tutor returning to the group.

Another fluent episode without contributions from the tutor encompassed thirty-two verbal and gestural contributions in a conversation about the American TV series *Dallas*. The participants were keen to express their views about the series, and evaluated individual actors. They tried to solicit responses from other interlocutors to their own suggestions. The episode was only interrupted by the tutor's 'Who wants to look at the paper?' and a succeeding nomination 'Bob, what's your favourite page in the paper?'

Non-reversible roles and the joint construction of meaning

It was pointed out at the beginning of this chapter that people with learning difficulties are usually placed in non-reversible roles when communicating with others. However, roles in dyads like adult–child, doctor–patient, teacher–pupil, police–suspect and, more generally, professional–client, are also, in some sense, non-reversible. In such dyads there is a culturally in-built implicit and institutional legitimacy with respect to the non-reversibility of roles. This legitimacy is commonly recognized by both parties. It is imparted by power relationships and by asymmetries of knowledge and status. Yet one can observe different kinds of non-reversibility in professional–client roles according to whether the client is a person with or without learning difficulties. In the latter case, although the roles of professional and client are non-reversible, it is considered essential by the general public and the client that the professional treat him or her seriously. For example, although a patient mainly only responds to the doctor's questions, his or her answers are entered into the doctor's notes and may play an important function in the doctor's diagnosis of the patient's illness. In police–suspect interrogations the suspect's responses are written down and treated as evidence of the suspect's deed. The pupil's performance is assessed on the basis of his or her responses to the teacher's questions.

Interactions in adult–child dyads are usually more flexible than those between professional and client, and the degree of their non-reversibility is dependent both on the adult's and the child's individual differences and on cultural differences and custom. After all, the child will, in due course, become an adult, which will automatically abolish the 'child role'. Moreover, as time progresses, the roles between adult and child may actually be reversed, even with respect to the same individuals. An elderly parent may get into a dependent role with respect to his or her child; a successful 'child' may become a boss to the 'adult'; and so on.

In contrast, non-reversibility of roles between a professional and a person with a learning difficulty is different in kind. First, there is a stigma, in our culture, concerning subnormal cognitive capacities. People with learning difficulties are often perceived by others as not only having subnormal cognitive capacities but also as being socially unskilled, linguistically incompetent and emotionally impoverished (Brewer and Yearley, 1989; Jahoda et al., 1988). As a result, the non-handicapped often change their communicative style once they realize that their interlocutor has learning difficulties (Aloia and MacMillan, 1983; Kernan et al., 1986; Sabsay and Platt, 1985). Even more important, research studies have shown that staff in mental handicap institutions are often non-responsive to communicative attempts of people with learning difficulties (Cullen et al. 1983; Marková et al., forthcoming). A response, even if a negative one, is a kind of confirmation of the speaker. In contrast, a non-response is perceived by people as equivalent to disconfirmation of the speaker (Watzlawick et al., 1967; Marková, 1987, pp. 69–71). People therefore strive for acknowledgement of their communicative contributions. If they do not receive attention from other interlocutors, they often try again (Knoblauch, this volume, Chapter 8). If the person does not repeat his or her communicative effort the implication is that he or she accepts the status of non-existence. In this vein, a person with learning difficulties whose communicative contributions are not responded to is reduced to an *Ich-Es* relationship with the non-respondent.

It thus appears that there are both exogenous and endogenous factors with respect to non-reversibility of roles in dialogues concerning people with learning difficulties. As was pointed out at the beginning of this chapter, the exogenous factors are due, first, to learning and communicative disabilities incapacitating people, and second, to institutional routines and the stigma attached to learning difficulties. The endogenous factors concern asymmetries in communication due to learning difficulties, impaired speech and lack of communicative skills. In the present study we were hoping to minimize these endogenous factors by changing the setting in which conversation takes place and instructing tutors not to use didactic styles. However, despite the tutors' best intentions of treating people with learning difficulties as conversational partners, the old didactic patterns of communication and of non-responding to a person kept reappearing. Moreover, since the participants with learning difficulties did not initiate conversation and were not forceful in any other ways, the tutors, in order to keep interactions going, made their own moves. In this manner, asymmetries were perpetuated and reconstructed again and again during the course of conversation.

Our data suggest, however, that when the tutor was temporarily excluded from discussions, the participants with learning difficulties could enjoy genuine conversations. When neither exogenous nor endogenous sources of asymmetries were present, their brief group discussions became more like those of true conversations.

Communicative awareness

Given the presence of both the exogenous and endogenous factors in group discussions, it was not so surprising that tutors were highly dominant. There are, however, two issues that are more significant. First, tutors were not aware of their dominant role. Second, they were unaware of their unresponsiveness to their group parties and of their use of didactic, rather than conversational techniques.

Treating a person with a handicap 'just like anybody else' is a dictum one now hears both from professionals and from laypeople. It is a laudable goal but, as the present study has indicated, it is more difficult to achieve than might appear.

The results of the present study suggest that it is not enough, if the existing pattern of interactions is to be changed, that the non-handicapped simply have the intention of establishing an equal relationship in conversations with people with learning difficulties. What individuals actually 'give off' (Farr, this volume, Chapter 11) in conversation in terms of their verbal and non-verbal gestures is only the tip of the iceberg. Communication is embedded in social and cultural activities that are automatized, semi-conscious and unconscious. These activities necessarily affect our expressions and, since they are habitual and unreflexively, socially shared, they are difficult to change. Our social representations and language concerning phenomena such as mental illness, mental handicap, physical disabilities and stereotypes are so powerful and so resistant to change because we are so little aware of their effect.

It thus follows that one way of affecting these underlying cultural stereotypes, social representations of mental handicap and their linguistic expressions, would be to make the professionals more aware of their communicative patterns. If a person has learning difficulties and speech impairment, it is likely that he or she will always be on the responding end. However, the conversational patterns between the professional and a person with learning difficulties could be altered to some degree by increasing the balance coefficients and by decreasing the proportions of solicitations, fragmentations and obliqueness on the part of the professional by responding to what the interlocutor has said.

Increasing communicative awareness and the change of dialogical dynamics in the direction of conversational rather than didactic patterns could be part of professional training. Of course, at present there is no evidence to indicate that such training actually would improve the quality of communication between the professional and the person with learning difficulties. However, there are two things that such professional training certainly would lead to. First, it would result in more epistemic responsibility being given to those with learning difficulties and speech impairment. Second, and for the first time, it would not *only* be the person with learning difficulties and speech impairment whose communicative skills were to be improved through training. Training the professional in the skills of setting and taking perspectives and in becoming more aware of his or her communicative actions would re-affirm the claim that dialogical mutuality involves contributions from both, and not just one, of the participants.

References

Aloia, G. F. and MacMillan, D. L. (1983), 'Influence of the EMR label on initial expectations of regular-classroom teachers', *American Journal of Mental Deficiency*, **88**, 255-62.

Bakhtin, M. M. (1981) *The Dialogic Imagination: Four essays by M. M. Bakhtin*, edited by M. Holquist, translated by C. Emerson and M. Holquist, University of Texas Press: Austin, TX.

Brewer, J. D. and Yearley, S. (1989), 'Stigma and conversational competence: a conversational analytic study of the mentally handicapped', *Human Studies*, **12**, 97-115.

Calculator, S. (1988), 'Exploring the language of adults with mental retardation', in J. Bedrosian and S. Calculator (eds), *Communication Assessment and Intervention for Adults with Mental Retardation*, Taylor and Francis: Boston, MA.

Cattermole, M. (1988), *Social Skills Training for People with a Mental Handicap*, MSc thesis, University of Stirling.

Cattermole, M., Jahoda, A. and Marková I. (1990), 'Quality of life of people with learning difficulties moving to community houses', *Disability, Handicap and Society*, **5**, 137-52.

Cullen, C., Burton, M., Watts, S. and Thomas, M. (1983). 'A preliminary report on the nature of interactions in a mental-handicap institution', *Behaviour Research and Therapy*, **21**, 579-93.

Foppa, K. (1990), 'Topic progression and intention', in I. Marková and K. Foppa (eds), *The Dynamics of Dialogue*, Harvester Wheatsheaf: Hemel Hempstead.

Goffman, E. (1968), *Stigma*, Penguin: Harmondsworth.

Gustavsson, L. (1988), *Language Taught and Language Used*, Linköping Studies in Arts and Science 18, University of Linköping.

Jahoda, A., Marková, I. and Cattermole, M. (1988), 'Stigma and the self-concept of people with a mild mental handicap', *Journal of Mental Deficiency Research*, **32**, 103-15.

Jenkins, P. (1990), 'Communication with people with learning difficulties: a problem for all'. Paper presented at the Annual Meeting of the British Association, 20-24 August.

Kernan, K. T., Sabsay, S. and Rein, R. P. (1986), 'Aspects of verbal behaviour cited by listeners in judging speakers as retarded or not retarded', *The Mental Retardation and Learning Disabilities Bulletin*, **14**, 24-43.

Leudar, I. (1981), 'Strategic communication in mental retardation', in W. I. Fraser and R. Grieve (eds), *Communication with Normal and Retarded Children*, John Wright and Sons: Bristol.

Leudar, I. and Fraser, W. I. (1985), 'How to keep quiet: some withdrawal strategies in mentally handicapped adults', *Journal of Mental Deficiency Research*, **29**, 315-30.

Leudar, I., Fraser, W. I. and Jeeves, M. A. (1981), 'Social familiarity and communication in Down's Syndrome', *Journal of Mental Deficiency Research*, **25**, 133.

Linell, P. (personal communication).

Linell, P. (1990), 'The power of dialogue dynamics', in I. Marková and K. Foppa (eds), *The Dynamics of Dialogue*, Harvester Wheatsheaf: Hemel Hempstead.

Linell, P., Gustavsson, L. and Juvonen, P. (1988), 'Interactional dominance in dyadic communication: a presentation of initiative-response analysis', *Linguistics*, **26**, 415-42.
Marková, I. (1987), *Human Awareness*, Hutchinson: London.
Marková, I. (1990a), 'A three-step process as a unit of analysis in dialogue', in I. Marková and K. Foppa (eds), *The Dynamics of Dialogue*, Harvester Wheatsheaf: Hemel Hempstead.
Marková, I. (1990b), 'Language and communication in mental handicaps', in H. Giles and W. P. Robinson (eds), *Handbook of Language and Social Psychology*, Chichester and New York: Wiley.
Marková, I. and Foppa, K. (1990), *The Dynamics of Dialogue*, Harvester Wheatsheaf: Hemel Hempstead.
Marková, I., Jahoda, A., Cattermole, M. and Woodward, D. (forthcoming), 'Living in hospital and hostel: the pattern of interactions of people with learning difficulties', *Journal of Mental Deficiency Research*.
Moscovici, S. (1984), 'The phenomenon of social representations', in R. M. Farr and S. Moscovici, *Social Representations*, Cambridge University Press: Cambridge and New York: and Editions de la Maison des Sciences de l'Homme, Paris.
Mukařovský, (1977), 'Two studies of dialogue', in J. Burbank and P. Steiner (eds), *The Word and Verbal Art*, Yale University Press: New Haven and London.
Prior, M., Minnes, P., Coyne, T., Golding, B., Hendy, J. and McGillivary, J. (1979), 'Verbal interactions between staff and residents in an institution for the young mentally retarded', *Mental Retardation*, **17**, 65-9.
Robertson, I., Richardson, A. M. and Youngson, S. C. (1984), 'Social skills training with mentally handicapped people: a review', *British Journal of Clinical Psychology*, **23**, 241-64.
Rogers-Warren, A. K., Warren, S. F. and Baer, D. M. (1983), 'Interactional basis of language learning', in K. T. Kernan, M. J. Begab and R. B. Edgerton (eds), *Environments and Behavior*, University Park Press: Baltimore, M.D.
Sabsay, S. and Platt, M. (1985), 'Weaving the cloak of competence: a paradox in the management of trouble in conversation between retarded and non-retarded interlocutors', in M. Platt and S. Sabsay (eds), *Social Setting, Stigma, and Communicative Competence: Explorations of the conversational interactions of retarded adults*, John Benjamin: Amsterdam and Philadelphia.
Sinclair, M. McH. and Coulthard, R. M. (1975), *Towards an Analysis of Discourse*, Open University Press: London.
Vološinov, V. N. (1973), *Marxism and the Philosophy of Language*, translated by L. Matejka and I. R. Titunik, Seminar Press: New York and London.
Watzlawick, P., Bearin, J. H. and Jackson, D. D. (1967), *Pragmatics of Human Communication*, Norton: New York.

11 | Bodies and voices in dialogue
Rob Farr

In this chapter I wish to consider the implications, for the dynamics of dialogue, of a fundamental form of asymmetry that, so far in this volume, has remained largely implicit. It is the asymmetry between self and others. Moreover, it is important to appreciate the different roles of vision and of speech in relation to both the emergence and the development of a sense of self in humans. The self needs to be understood in terms of both its phylogeny and its ontogeny before its role in dialogue can be adequately understood. An understanding of the nature of the self in humans is also a necessary pre-requisite for understanding those mutualities in dialogue that will be the topic of the next volume in this series.

Sources of symmetry and of asymmetry in the relations between self and others

The face as a source of asymmetry

The source of the asymmetry between self and others in dialogue is visual rather than vocal. It is to be located in the human face rather than in the human voice. If this distinction between vision and voice holds then important differences ought to emerge in the dynamics of face to face encounters compared to encounters which are either more remote or less immediate. This distinction is also the one between embodied and disembodied forms of speech. The face that lies at the inter-face between self and others is the participant's own. The lack of symmetry occurs because the face that identifies self to others also separates self from others. Self and others are on opposite sides of that face.

When participants converse face to face each faces the same problem. There are as many inter-faces as there are faces. It is, therefore, as far as participants are concerned, a symmetrical form of asymmetry. The asymmetry is not *between* participants – in terms of either their status or their knowledge, as elsewhere in this volume – but rather *within* each. The experience is common to all provided they are of normal hearing and vision. The form of their isolation, however, is unique to each. It is what makes self different from others.

The body as a source of asymmetry

Since each participant in a face to face dialogue is an object to the others who are present each, by interacting with these others, becomes an object to him- or herself, i.e. becomes self-conscious. Each is most tangibly present in terms of his or her own body. We perceive others; but, usually, we can only be conscious of ourselves. There is a basic asymmetry here between my perception of others and my conception of myself. My eyes are vital in regard to the former; they are of only limited significance in regard to the latter. It is the eyes of others who are present which helps to determine, in large measure, the extent to which I become conscious of myself. We do not see ourselves as others see us. This is the root of the asymmetry between self and others.

Heider (1958) has brilliantly portrayed the divergence in perspective between self and others in his monograph *The Psychology of Interpersonal Relations*. The distinction, for Heider, is between P (i.e. the perceiver) and O (i.e. the other). O is visually salient in the eyes of P. What is most salient about O in the eyes of P is O's body. P is only very occasionally an object in his or her own visual field. The consciousness, on the part of P, that he or she is an object in the visual world of O considered as a P, i.e. as a perceiver, is a form of self-consciousness. The self of which P is here conscious is a bodily self. In terms of Heider's perspective, which is a highly visual one, we have a dialogue between two bodies, i.e. those of P and of O. The former is experienced, the latter is perceived. This is true for both participants.

Speech as a source of symmetry

Heider did not relate the divergence in perspective between P and O, (or between self and others) to the dynamics of dialogue.

Heider was a highly visual thinker. He was, after all, an artist *manqué*. We need, now, to relate Heider's divergence in perspective between P and O to the dynamics of dialogue. This should also enable us to gain a better appreciation of the role of vision in relation to speech.

The divergence in perspective between speaker and listener (Farr and Anderson, 1983) is much less sharp than that between perceiver (P) and others (O). When we speak we also hear ourselves speak. There is no asymmetry between what we hear when we speak and what others hear provided, of course, that we share with them a common language and culture and that neither we nor they are deaf. This is why, in the social psychology of Mead (1934), language is the key to understanding the peculiar, self-reflexive, nature of human intelligence.

In speech the face is no longer the barrier between self and others that it is in vision. Deafness is the only barrier between speaking and listening. We are concerned here with the relation between output (speech) and input (listening). If a person is deaf there is a barrier between output and input since he or she cannot hear him- or herself speak. When a person speaks he or she influences him- or herself as well as others. The relation between output and input is thus different in speech to what it is in vision. This is why, as a species, we are more self-reflexive in the auditory modality than we are in the visual (Mead, 1934; Farr, 1987). Self-reflexivity, in the present context, is a form of symmetry.

Embodied versus disembodied dialogue

I wish, in the present section, to distinguish between embodied and disembodied dialogue. It is probably best to conceive of them as falling along a continuum, rather than as forming a dichotomy, with bodies and voices acting as anchors at the two ends. The dialogue between Helmer and Nora in Ibsen's play *A Doll's House* is an example of a dialogue between two voices (see Rommetveit, this volume, Chapter 9). The voices are those of the dramatist. They remain silent until a couple of actors enact the parts in a particular performance of the play. The performance is then an embodiment of a dialogue that originated in the mind of the playwright.

At the other end of the continuum is what Mead (1934) described as 'a conversation of gestures', i.e. two, or more, bodies talking. Some conversations, though possibly only fictional ones, might occupy varying locations along the continuum from embodied to disembodied speech at different stages in the course of the same conversation. This would apply, for example, to the grin on the face of the Cheshire cat, with whom Alice was conversing, who, much to Alice's annoyance, kept on appearing and disappearing in the course of their conversation.

My primary interest is in the study of embodied dialogue. This is because vision is as important as speech in determining the dynamics of such dialogues. The role of vision in relation to speech is a comparatively neglected topic of research in the study of dialogue. When vision plays a significant role in determining the dynamics of a dialogue the potential for misunderstanding is much greater than when its role is insignificant. This is because the asymmetries in dialogue identified in the previous section of this chapter are more closely associated with vision than they are with speech. Simmel (1908) noted a further reason:

> the majority of the stimuli which the face represents are puzzling: in general, what we see of a man will be interpreted by what we hear from him, while the opposite is more unusual. Therefore the one who sees, without hearing, is much more perplexed, puzzled, and worried, than the one who hears without seeing (Simmel, 1908; quoted from 1969 edn., p. 360).

Dialogue versus conversation

Luckmann (1990) distinguishes between dialogue and conversation. He defines dialogue in the following terms:

> dialogue is sign-bound face-to-face communication which involves that high degree of immediacy and reciprocity which occurs when the streams of consciousness of the participants in social communication are fully synchronised. (Luckmann, 1990, p. 56)

This, from my point of view, is a perfect description of a truly embodied dialogue. The visual component is explicit since the participants communicate 'face-to-face'. Vision may also play an important role in ensuring that the streams of consciousness of the participants are fully synchronized. Here the role of non-verbal communication is likely to be decisive (Argyle, 1969; 1975). Many of the most important channels of non-verbal communication are visual in nature. The 'signs' referred to in Luckmann's definitions of dialogue could be visual as well as vocal.

Luckmann (1990) defines conversation as 'a historical subspecies of dialogue in which a relatively high degree of specifically communicative symmetry, typically experienced as equality, prevails' (Luckmann, 1990, pp. 57, 58). The distinctive feature, for Luckmann, of conversation, in contrast to dialogue, is its symmetry. This accords well with the view being advanced here that asymmetry is an important component of dialogue, especially when it is defined in the way that Luckmann defines it.

It is clear, from the findings reported by Marková (this volume, Chapter 10), that vision played an important role in the interactions between the tutor and his clients. This, in part, was a function of the limited linguistic skills of the persons whom the tutor was seeking to help. In part also it was a function of the task the tutor set for the group. It was the tutor, rather than his clients, who introduced the tabloid press and who decided that the group would talk about something they were reading in the papers. The activities of the group included reading as well as talking. In the tabloid press in the United Kingdom there is an extremely high ratio of images to text in comparison to the broadsheets. It is also clear that photographs featured prominently in the group's conversation. The 'suggestion' on the part of the group that they might discuss the nude model on page 3 was mediated non-verbally rather than being raised, vocally. The individuals in this particular group read the papers mainly to find out what was on television and whether their favourite football team had won or lost.

The tutor's task, in Marková's study, was to engage the group in conversation rather than to conduct a dialogue. This is no mean task given the nature of the institutional context in which the discussion took place, i.e. a long-stay hospital for the mentally handicapped. Despite the commitment of the tutor to the notion of equality there was precious little evidence in the transcripts of the symmetry that Luckmann takes to be the hallmark of conversation. It reads more like a dialogue than a conversation. This is also borne out in the statistical analysis of the data.

Intrinsic versus extrinsic forms of asymmetry

The asymmetry between self and others that I am proposing, especially in the visual modality, is intrinsic to the nature of dialogue rather than extrinsic (Linell and Luckmann, this volume, Chapter 1). In this it differs from exogenous forms of asymmetry such as differences between the participants in terms of their status and their knowledge. Most of the studies in the present volume are of this latter nature. The difference, however, may be more apparent than real.

In Linell's terms, the asymmetry I propose could be local, as in the alternation between self and others in turn-taking, or it could be global, with one interactant being dominant over the others. Linell (1990) uses the term 'global' to refer to the dialogue considered as a whole. This is the unit of analysis he uses. The interface between self and others, however, is both cause and consequence of interacting with others in the course of everyday life. It is only through interacting with others in everyday life that human beings become objects to themselves and, hence, acquire a sense of their own selfhood. The interface, of which I speak, between self and others is as much a consequence as it is a cause of these interactions (Farr, 1990).

It is mainly through speech that this sense of self is achieved *across* dialogues rather than being formed in the course of any one. The self, then, is more than merely global in Linell's use of the term. It has to be trans-global. The unit of analysis is no longer that of a single dialogue. No dialogue is hermetically sealed off from those that came before it or from those that will follow after. This is where the asymmetries of status and of knowledge within the wider society enter into and become operative within a particular dialogue, i.e. through the selves of the participants. The self, in this trans-global sense, is a prerequisite for the mutualities in dialogue that will be the topic of the next volume in this series.

Perspectival theory

The position outlined in this chapter is both an elaboration and a refinement of Graumann's perspectival theory (Graumann, 1990). We are both interested in what is going on between participants in the course of a dialogue. In a disembodied dialogue precious little, I would claim, goes on between participants, i.e. there are voices but no bodies. Embodied dialogue, however, involves both vision and speech: there are bodies as well as voices. Bodies are not only objects in other people's social world; they are the locations in space/time of unique perspectives. What is happening visually as well as what is being said in the course of a dialogue needs to be taken into account. This is why I believe the prefix 'inter' is of crucial importance (Farr, 1990). It is a locative. It indicates where to look in order to find the critical elements that need to be explained, i.e. look in the space between participants. It is not the action so much as the interaction that is important; there would be no space if there were no bodies. Within and between voices there are only pauses, no spaces. In speech, the temporal dimension is important; in vision the spatial dimension. A perspective, according to Mead (1934), is a point in space/time from which events are viewed.

I agree with Graumann (1990) that it is not helpful to distinguish between the partners in a dialogue in terms of their being either speakers or listeners. This is because speakers are also listeners and listeners become speakers. It makes sense, I believe, to distinguish between self and others and then go on to note how the relation between self and others in speech is quite different from what it is in vision (Farr and Anderson, 1983). It is probably not an exaggeration to claim that pronouns are a device for handling problems of reference in inter-personal space. They are a linguistic device for switching the attention of one's interlocutors. The first, second and third persons are all bodies. Somebody is talking to somebody, usually about somebody else. Deictic words, such as pronouns, are a linguistic response to problems of an essentially visual nature. They might not be needed in a species without vision.

Vision and speech

Vision is the sensory modality *par excellence* for the perception, at a distance, of both people and objects. People can see each other a long way off but, usually, they can only hear each other talk at more intimate distances. In terms of its evolutionary significance vision, initially, was more important than speech. People have to be close to each other in order to converse – or at least they had to be before the invention of the telephone. The human voice does not carry very far – especially in noisy environments. Many significant events in life are expressed in words and conveyed through speech. This, perhaps, is why humans spend so much time talking to each other. From a purely visual perspective, however, it is easy to underestimate the significance of speech. This, I believe, is what happened in the history of psychology. The most powerful illusions are visual.

The social group as a form of visual illusion

Philosophers, ever since Aristotle, have noted that a human being is a social animal. Humans tend to congregate in small groups. This is a distinctive feature of life in society. Cartwright and Zander (1954) in their introduction to the study of groups noted the ubiquity and importance of groups in the social life of humans:

> If it were possible for the overworked hypothetical man from Mars to take a fresh view of the people of Earth, he would probably be impressed by the amount of time they spend doing things together in groups. He would note that most people cluster into relatively small groups, with the members residing together in the same dwelling, satisfying their basic biological needs within the group, depending upon the same source for economic support, rearing children, and mutually caring for the health of one another. He would observe that the education and socialisation of children tends to occur in other, usually larger, groups in churches, schools, or other social institutions. He would see that much of the work of the world is carried out by people who perform their activities in close inter-dependence within relatively enduring associations. He would perhaps be saddened to find groups of men engaged in warfare, gaining courage and morale from pride in their unit and a knowledge that they can depend on their buddies. He might be gladdened to see groups of people enjoying themselves in recreations and sports of various kinds. Finally he might be puzzled why so many people spend so much time in little groups talking, planning, and being 'in conference'. Surely he would conclude that if he wanted to understand much about what is happening on Earth he would have to examine rather carefully the ways in which groups form, function and dissolve. (Cartwright and Zander, 1954, p. 3).

The Martian could just as easily have concluded, on the basis of the same evidence, that it was important to study dialogue if he was ever to understand humans. It is a visual illusion that groups are an important feature of human life. An illusion is some sort of mismatch between appearances and reality. Things are not quite as they appear to be. The observation that people stand or sit close to each other is trivial in comparison to what happens when they do so. Groups may appear, visually, to be important; the reality behind the illusion is that dialogue is even more important. This is why I believe it is important to study the relation between vision and speech. Vision may even trick us into underestimating the significance of speech. The size of groups and the settings in which they meet are often determined by the natural range of the unamplified human voice. A human being, besides being a social animal, is also *Homo loquens* (Fry,

1977; Farr, 1980a). Indeed he or she is the former largely because he or she is the latter.

The Martian was perfectly correct to note what he did. This after all, is what he saw. He may, of course, have been deaf, in which case the significance of human speech may have eluded him. It is more likely, however, that, due to the extra-terrestrial distances involved, he had never been close enough to any group of humans to learn their language. We should beware, in our treatment of the Martian, not to repeat Itard's mistake with the wild boy of Aveyron, i.e. the danger of assuming that because he does not talk he cannot hear. This error led Itard to assign the wild boy to an institute for deaf-mutes (Lane, 1977). Our visitor from Mars may have heard human speech, but its significance eluded him. The mistake the Martian made was to conclude that 'if he wanted to understand much about what is happening on Earth he would have to examine rather carefully the ways in which groups form, function and dissolve' (Cartwright and Zander, 1954, p. 3). He should have decided, instead, that it was important for him to learn a human language and to engage in dialogue. It is an easy mistake for a Martian to make. There is no need for humans to repeat it. The reason why groups appear to be important is because they enable humans to converse with each other.

Vision and speech in evolutionary context

Let us move now from the level of the group to that of society. Humans have long been impressed by the division of labour to be found in the beehive and the ant colony. Mead (1934) compared and contrasted the societies of ants and of other insects with those of humans. From a careful reading of the scientific evidence then available to him Mead came to the conclusion, remarkable at the time, that it was probably odour and the sense of smell that was responsible for the social order to be observed in societies of insects. He, himself, believed that, in human societies, it was speech and the sense of hearing that were responsible for social order. Two quite distinct sensory orders, then, underlie the societies of insects and of humans. The contrast is between chemistry and language. The division of labour within the ant colony, according to Mead, is chemical and physiological; within human societies it is linguistic and cultural. Dialogue and conversation help to determine the division of labour.

The phylogenetic gap between the societies of ants and those of humans is enormous. For Mead there were two developments in the evolution of the human species that set it apart from all other species.

The relation between vision and touch

The first development was the emergence of a close relationship between the hand and the development of the central nervous system. This development is common to man and the higher primates. Important here is the opposable thumb that enables humans and other primates to grasp objects and to use them as tools. This, in turn, enables humans to develop the notion of an 'object'. Mead's doctoral studies at Berlin, which he never successfully completed, were concerned with the relationship between vision and touch. They were carried out between 1890 and 1892. His supervisor was the philosopher Dilthey. As a result of contact with physical objects humans build up a three-dimensional representation of the world. Our experience of physical contact with objects is a necessary prerequisite to our later experience of ourselves as objects in the social world of other people (Joas, 1985). I agree with Joas's reading of Mead on this point. We are objects in the social world of others. As a result of interacting with those others we become objects to ourselves, i.e. we become self-conscious. The self of which we are conscious is a bodily self. Humans are able to act towards themselves as objects. This makes them different from other organisms. They are, as Mead said, minded organisms. This capacity for self-reflection is rooted in human social experience and is the basis on which the intelligence that is unique to humans develops. The self of which we are conscious is the self that we are to others. According to William James (1890) we have as many different selves as there are groups of people to whom we are important.

Speech and language

The second development was the evolution of the vocal gesture in the direction of speech and language. Language is the key to the development of human intelligence. We also use language in relating to others just as others use it in relating to us. Our contact with objects is physical in form; our contact with people is primarily dialogical and social in form. Vision and touch are vital to us in threading our way through physical space. Speech and listening are more important to us in moving through social space. A different sort of vision is required of us when we relate to others. This vision controls our speech rather than our movements. We have to watch what we say rather than what we do. It is others who watch what we do to see if it is consistent with what we say. This is part of the asymmetry between vision and speech to which I wish to draw attention. We perceive depth in the physical world; we maintain our distance in the social world. The ways in which we approach and avoid objects are different from the ways in which we approach and avoid people. These activities involve two quite different sets of skills. We handle objects and address people. If we 'handle' people we do so metaphorically rather than literally.

Speech and vision in historical perspective

The relationship between vision and speech changes over time. In the course of evolution vision, as the principal source of information about events at a distance, was vital to human survival. Nowadays, what the pilot of a supersonic jet can see through his or her windscreen is highly marginal in terms of survival – survival depends, instead, on other things and on other people, while vision is mainly of use for reading the instruments within the aircraft. We noted above, following Mead (1934), how vision in relation to touch was crucial (in both phylogeny and ontogeny) to the development of a conception of physical objects. This in turn, is an essential prerequisite (Joas, 1985) to the notion of the body as an object and of the self as a body.

I need this notion of the self in order to be able to distinguish between embodied and disembodied speech. We also noted above, again following Mead, the distinctive role of speech and of language in the evolution of the human species. Speech became even more important than vision in the development of human intelligence. This started in the prehistory of the human species. When it comes to recorded history further significant shifts occurred in the balance between vision and speech.

A significant shift in the balance between vision and speech occurred with the invention of the printing press and the advent, in many cultures, of mass literacy. This was preceded by the Renaissance which, in its turn, gave birth to the Reformation. Both of these major events in Europe were formative influences in the development of individualism (Farr, 1991). The written word became at least as important as the spoken word. Reading became as important as speaking. Individuals, through reading, were able to free themselves from the restrictions and limitations of their local cultures (in terms of both space and time). They were also able to challenge authority and to come to their own conclusions. These developments enabled individuals to think for themselves. They sharpened the divergence in perspective between self and others.

While the world of the printed page is not directly related to the dynamics of dialogue there is an indirect link. Reading is a much less immediate activity than talking. Immediacy is an integral element in our definition of dialogue (Luckmann, 1990). Reading as an activity changes the nature of the relationship between self and others. Dialogues occurring in literate cultures are likely to be significantly different from dialogues occurring in preliterate cultures.

While reading depends on the possession of linguistic skills it is a highly visual activity. The vocabulary that one uses in dialogue is likely to be greatly enriched through reading. The speech utterances, in dialogue, of the literate are more likely to be grammatical than the utterances of the illiterate. Riesman (1950; 1954), in his writings on individualism, refers to the individual trying on new roles for herself within the circle of light cast by her own reading lamp. Our ability to imagine ourselves being other than we are is profoundly influenced by what we read. It is also influenced by what we see in terms of films and television. Vision does play a role that affects the dynamics of dialogue. We often anticipate encounters in our imagination before we confront them in reality. As Goffman said 'Many crucial facts lie beyond the time and place of interaction, or lie concealed within it' (1956, p. 1). Many of these facts are acquired through reading and viewing.

It is not appropriate, here, in an article on dialogue, to deal with literacy except to note that it is part, though only part, of the story that relates vision to speech in human affairs. Reading aloud is an activity whereby the printed word is converted into speech. Speech here is disembodied for the voice of the author blends with that of the reader and only one of the two is present in any corporal sense. Most reading, however, is subvocal and so fails to qualify as a form of dialogue even if the words of the author evoke a response in the minds of readers.

Objects and persons

As autonomous agents persons are less controllable and predictable than inanimate objects. The perception of persons is a form of social psychology (Heider, 1958), the perception of objects is not. Heider showed how our perception of others is nested within our perception of objects. The perception of objects, however, is of primary significance. We need to have a conception of what an object is before we can conceive of our body as an object and of our self as a body. I have derived this, above, from the social psychology of G. H. Mead. Mead was more concerned with awareness of self whereas Heider was more concerned with awareness of others. We need both to understand the dynamics of dialogue.

Other persons are objects, I would argue, because the skin is such a compelling boundary from a visual perspective. This is a theme to which I shall return when I consider dialogue as a form of social encounter. The self that I am in the eyes of others is also a bodily self. Without those other eyes the self might be just a voice rather than a body. This is why it is important to distinguish between embodied and disembodied speech. In face to face encounters we become conscious of being objects in the social world of those we encounter in everyday life, i.e. we become conscious of our own bodies. If the encounter is not face to face then the self is not necessarily an embodied self in the full sense of the term.

In the perception of others the skin is an important boundary; in our awareness of ourselves it is ordinarily not. We become self-conscious when others look at us or when we hear ourselves speak. This is why the chronically shy are ill at ease in the presence of others (Zimbardo, 1977). If we become too self-conscious then we blush and our skin conveys a visual signal to others. It is not our intention to reveal to others what we have in mind. In the terminology of Goffman impressions are 'given off' as well as managed. The communication is inadvertent. We are not, on such occasions, in control of our own bodies. The skin, here, forms the boundary between self and others. We are not, ordinarily, conscious of it until it suddenly reddens. Darwin (1872), in Chapter 13 of *The Expression of the Emotions in Man and Animals*, vividly described the uniquely human emotions of self-attention such as embarrassment and shame (Farr, 1980b). It is not possible, Darwin claimed, to identify the stimulus that causes the blush since it is the mind rather than the body that is affected when we blush. Persons are objects with a mind of their own.

Heider spelled out the rules of inference whereby we go beyond the evidence available to us visually when we attribute various motives, goals, intentions, etc., to others. This is the field of attribution theory. Here the skin clearly is an important boundary between self and others. Attributions are inferences in the mind of P that enable P to anticipate, and perhaps to control, the behaviour of O. Heider showed how these inferences are nested within the causal attributions we make concerning the movements of objects in the physical environment. We do not normally attribute motives, intentions, etc., to objects – only to persons. This is a part of Heider's distinction between objects and persons.

There is also a moral dimension to the distinction between objects and persons. The basic dichotomy between the world of objects and the world of persons is comparable to Buber's distinction between *Ich-Es* and *Ich-Du* relationships (Buber, 1937). We can, of course, treat people as though they were objects. This, indeed, is the whole point of Buber's moral philosophy as it had been that of Kant. Rommetweit (this volume, Chapter 9) uses Buber's distinction in order to explore asymmetries in the relation between Helmer and Nora in Ibsen's play *A Doll's House*. Dolls are not autonomous moral agents. Wives, as Helmer was to find out, are. Dolls, according to Rommetweit, are epistemically irresponsible. They can be dressed or undressed either by children or by fully grown men. They can be passed from one owner to the next as Nora was from her father to her husband. They can be transported from one house (the parental home) to another (the matrimonial home). They do not move, of their own accord, between houses. Birds and squirrels, however, can do so. The asymmetry between Helmer and Nora is one of status – that between men and women in the final quarter of the nineteenth century.

Dialogue as a form of social encounter

Goffman was interested in describing what happens when people come within sight and sound of each other. Such encounters usually occur face to face. Dialogue can be considered as a form of social encounter. In the encounter the visual aspects of the interaction are salient; in the dialogue the vocal and linguistic aspects are salient. It is important to study both. Goffman's account of the social encounter can serve as a frame for identifying the visual components in the study of dialogue.

Goffman (1956) in his participant observational studies of life on the Shetland Islands, noted how the crofters, from within the privacy of their own homes, could observe, other islanders passing by outside. If one of those being observed should approach the crofter's cottage, Goffman noted, the whole demeanour of the observer would change in anticipation of the impending encounter. At the door the encounter is face to face and hence, is highly social in character. Both, now, are within sight and sound of each other. He noted similar changes in the demeanours of waitresses as they pushed open the door separating them and the staff in the kitchen, from members of the public seated in the dining room of the local hotel.

Goffman wrote much on the micro-sociology of social encounters that is highly germane to an understanding of dialogue. His writings are particularly rich in the depiction of visual aspects of face to face encounters. Vision is crucial to understanding the many subtle distinctions Goffman made between the public and private dimensions of such encounters. He was also particularly good at describing the settings in which these encounters occur and the effect of the setting on the form of the encounter. Talk occurs within these settings. It is nested within the wider social and physical setting. The lecture is dramatically different from the radio broadcast (Goffman, 1981).

The actor, in Goffman's sense, is in no position to read off the impressions forming in the minds of others. This is because, visually, there is a divergence in perspective between self and other. Just as the observer has no direct access to the intentions of the actor, so the actor has no direct access to the impressions forming in the minds of observers. The skin here, is an important boundary. Impressions are based on that segment of the act that is visible from the perspective of an observer. The direction of causality, here, is *from* the act, i.e. the expressive behaviour of the actor, to impressions forming in the minds of observing others. Goffman provides us with a model of the actor; Heider provides us with a model of the observer. We need to be able to fit the two together in order to understand the dynamics of social encounters. Goffman is concerned with the conception that others have of self; Heider with the conception that self has of others.

Elsewhere (Farr, 1990) I have shown how Ichheiser's (1949) suggestion about the importance of distinguishing between expression and impression was taken up and elaborated by Goffman in *The Presentation of Self in Everyday Life*. There is no need, here, to repeat that account. It is necessary, however, in the light of the distinction between vision and speech, to differentiate between two forms of expressive behaviour. For both Darwin (1872) and Goffman (1956) the expressive behaviour of one organism causes impressions to form in the minds of observing and listening others. Most of these signals and signs are mediated visually. This is why embodied speech is different from disembodied speech. In dialogue as a form of social encounter there is an asymmetry between self and others in the visual modality. Speech, however, is also a form of expressive behaviour. When we speak those who listen include the self. The relationship between self and others is quite different in the oral/aural modality to what it is in the visual modality. Speech is a form of expressive behaviour that creates impressions in our own minds that are comparable to the impressions our words create in the minds of other listeners. The dynamics of speech are different from the dynamics of visually mediated communication. Dialogue, as a form of social encounter, includes both. Skinner, in a pun on his own name, claimed that 'The skin is not that important as a boundary' (Skinner, 1964, p. 84). It is a particularly compelling boundary, visually, for the reasons identified earlier. It is not, however, an important boundary when it comes to the analysis of dialogues that are not face to face encounters.

The role of vision in dialogue

Bergmann (1990) has drawn attention to the importance of local sensitivity in conversation. He uses the term 'local sensitivity': 'to capture the tendency inbuilt in every topic talk to focus on elements of the encounter's context which are situated or occur in the participants' field of perception but have not been topicalised so far' (Bergmann, 1990, p. 207). He cites as an example the change of topic in the family discussion around the dining table when Hugo, the canary, flies into the room. Vision here plays an important role in topic progression. The importance of local sensitivities in the analysis of conversation has been ignored up until the publication of Bergmann's article. The classic work in the field of conversation analysis involves the analysis of telephone conversations. The telephone, however, greatly restricts the scope for purely local sensitivities to affect the topic progression. Rutter (1984, 1987), in his theory of 'cuelessness', shows how impoverished a conversation by telephone is in comparison to a face-to-face encounter.

What I have tried to do in this chapter is to indicate where, I believe, vision may be of importance in relation to the dynamics of dialogue. I have done this by seeking to distinguish between embodied and disembodied speech. I have treated the relation between self and others as a source of asymmetry in the visual modality and as a source of symmetry in the oral/aural modality. I have also sought to contrast encounters and dialogues, though the latter is a case of the former. I have used Goffman's account of the encounter as a frame for the study of dialogue. This enables me to be more explicit about the role of vision in relation to the dynamics of dialogue. It is the asymmetry between self and others, especially in the visual modality, that generates differences of opinion, some of which may be resolved in the course of conversation.

References

Argyle, M. (1969), *Social Interaction*, Methuen: London.
Argyle, M. (1975), *Bodily Communication*, Methuen: London.
Bergmann, J. R. (1990), 'On the local sensitivity of conversation', in I. Marková and K. Foppa (eds), *The Dynamics of Dialogue*, Harvester Wheatsheaf: Hemel Hempstead.
Buber, M. (1937), *I and Thou*, translated by Ronald Gregor Smith, T. T. Clark: Edinburgh.
Cartwright, D. and Zander, A. (eds), (1954), *Group Dynamics: research and theory*, Tavistock: London.
Darwin, C. (1872), *The Expressions of the Emotions in Man and Animals*, Appleton: London.
Farr, R. M. (1980a), 'Homo loquens in social psychological perspective', in H. Giles, W. P. Robinson and P. M. Smith (eds) *Language: Social psychological and perspectives*, Pergamon: Oxford.
Farr, R. M. (1980b), 'On reading Darwin and discovering social psychology', in R. Gilmour and S. Duck (eds), *The Development of Social Psychology*, Academic Press: London.
Farr, R. M. (1987), 'The science of mental life: a social psychological perspective', *Bulletin the British Psychological Society*, 40, 2-17.
Farr, R. M. (1990), 'The social psychology of the prefix "inter": a prologue to the study of dialogue', in I. Marková and K. Foppa (eds), *The Dynamics of Dialogue*, Harvester Wheatsheaf: Hemel Hempstead.
Farr, R. M. (1991), 'Individualism as a collective representation', in V. Aebrocher, J. P. Deconchy and E. M. Lipionsky (eds), *Idéologies et Représentations Sociales*, Delval: Cousset, Switzerland.
Farr, R. M. and Anderson, A. (1983), 'Beyond actor/observer differences in perspective', in M. Hewstone (ed.), *Attribution Theory: Social and functional extensions*, Blackwell: Oxford.
Fry, D. (1977), *Homo Loquens: man as a talking animal*, Cambridge University Press: Cambridge.
Goffman, E. (1956), *The Presentation of Self in Everyday Life*, University of Edinburgh Social Science Research Centre, Monograph No. 2.

Goffman, E. (1981), *Forms of Talk*, Blackwell: Oxford.
Graumann, C. F. (1990), 'Perspectival structure and dynamics in dialogues', in I. Marková and K. Foppa (eds), *The Dynamics of Dialogue*, Harvester Wheatsheaf: Hemel Hempstead.
Heider, F. (1958), *The Psychology of Interpersonal Relations*, Wiley: New York.
Ichheiser, G. (1949) 'Misunderstandings in human relations: a study in false social perception', *American Journal of Sociology*, LV, Special Supplement, pp. 1-72.
James, W. (1890), *The Principles of Psychology*, 2 vols, Holt: New York.
Joas, H. (1985), *G. H. Mead: A contemporary re-examination of his thought*, Polity Press: Oxford, (translated from the original German edition of 1980 by Raymond Meyer).
Lane, H. (1977), *The Wild Boy of Aveyron*, George Allen and Unwin: London.
Linell, P. (1990), 'The power of dialogue dynamics', in I. Marková and K. Foppa (eds), *The Dynamics of Dialogue*, Harvester Wheatsheaf: Hemel Hempstead.
Luckmann, T. (1990), 'Social communication, dialogue and conversation', in I. Marková and K. Foppa (eds), *The Dynamics of Dialogue*, Harvester Wheatsheaf: Hemel Hempstead.
Mead, G. H. (1934) *Mind, Self and Society: From the standpoint of a social behaviourist*, edited, with an introduction, by C. W. Morris, Chicago University Press: Chicago, IL.
Riesman, D. (1950), *The Lonely Crowd*, Doubleday: New York.
Riesman, D. (1954), *Individualism Reconsidered*, The Free Press: Glencoe, IL.
Rutter, D. R. (1984), *Looking and Seeing: The role of visual communication in social interaction*, Wiley: Chichester.
Rutter, D. R. (1987), *Communicating by Telephone*, Pergamon: Oxford.
Simmel, G. (1908), 'Sociology of the senses: Visual interaction', in R. E. Park and E. W. Burgess (eds), *Introduction to the Science of Sociology*, (3rd edition, revised) (1969) University of Chicago Press: Chicago and London.
Skinner, B. F. (1964), 'Behaviourism at fifty', in T. W. Wann (ed.), *Behaviorism and Phenomenology: Contrasting bases for modern psychology*, University of Chicago Press: Chicago, IL.
Zimbardo, P. G. (1977), *Shyness: What it is, what to do about it*, Addison-Wesley: Reading, MA.

Conclusion

Ivana Marková and Klaus Foppa

The dynamics of dialogue

In Volume 1 (*The Dynamics of Dialogue*, Marková and Foppa, 1990) of this series, two different yet complementary senses of dialogism were explored. Dialogism was examined, first, as an epistemology of mind and language, and second, in terms of specific aspects of dialogue, i.e. of face to face symbolic interaction between people.

Dialogism in the former sense is conceived to be a *perspectival* epistemology and it conceives of language as a *dynamic* phenomenon in its *socio-historical-cultural* contexts. It presupposes a dyadic view of language. This means that language and its relevant 'outside', e.g. cultural, socio-historical or situational contexts, form an unbreakable dyad. Accordingly, the study of language also involves a study of its relevant 'outside', just as in the case of figure and ground. Consequently, by definition, any language change also implies a change in the relevant 'outside' (in whatever way that outside may be defined).

The second, a more narrow sense of dialogism examined in Volume 1, pertained to the study of dialogue as face to face symbolic interaction. In particular, it focused on mutuality and perspectivity in topic maintenance and change and on some aspects of dominance and asymmetry in dialogical dynamics. These latter aspects, i.e. asymmetry and dominance, are the subject of specific exploration in this second volume.

As already implied in the previous volume, asymmetries are omnipresent characteristics of dialogues. While dialogues must, by definition, be reciprocal, interlocutors differ in their control of the content, quality and quantity of their dialogical contributions and, consequently, equality or symmetricity between them is exceptional. Even in a very informal conversation one can point to different kinds of asymmetries. In a trivial sense, the fact that one interlocutor introduces a particular topic into a conversation imposes a kind of asymmetry between the interlocutors. As the dialogue unfolds, one participant may say more than the other; or one participant may cut the subject short and introduce another topic into the discussion, and so on. As interlocutors set and take perspectives, mutually construct the meaning of what they say, develop intersubjective relationships and impart knowledge, they reduce certain dialogical asymmetries while establishing others. In this sense asymmetries are inherent in the dynamics of dialogue.

In saying that two parties have a dialogue or that they continue to have a dialogue one usually implies that they strive to reduce certain kinds of asymmetries in their social encounters, positions, perspectives, knowledge or whatever is at stake. In fact, the effort to establish what can broadly be called *equality or symmetry of the relationships* between people has characterized much of the dynamics of social change in Western culture for centuries. For example, there has been a long struggle in the Western world to establish equality among people in terms of their civil rights and obligations; in terms of equality of opportunities; in expressing opinions – the list of such issues in which to establish equality or symmetricity would be endless. Equality is often seen as an ideal towards which society at large strives. Since humankind is still far away from this 'ideal', we may, at this stage, dispense with worries about the possible consequences of such a total harmony and equality and perhaps of the resulting general inertia. What we may say, though, is that while acknowledging symmetry as a value to strive for, the driving forces of progress and of social change are the existing states of asymmetries, inequalities, imbalances and disharmony. It is apparent that many asymmetries pertaining to dialogue as such are determined by exogenous inequalities existing between interacting people. Indeed, as Linell and Luckmann (Chapter 1) say, if we were equal in knowledge, experience and relationships, there would hardly be any reasons to communicate.

In Greek philosophy, dialogue was a form of discourse by which to impart knowledge, clarify concepts and argue about things. For example, in a Socratic dialogue the concept of a particular phenomenon was explored and more precisely defined through questions, answers and arguments. Thus, a Socratic dialogue was by its nature an asymmetric form of discourse. The party that was either more knowledgeable or more experienced, through critical questioning and through instruction, not only determined the topic to be discussed but led the less knowledgeable and less experienced party to a particular kind of answer and to a particular way of thinking. As the pupil became educated through dialogue, the asymmetry in knowledge between the two interlocutors was progressively reduced.

The subject of asymmetries of knowledge and of status is of particular interest to the authors of this volume. While most chapters examine empirical problems of asymmetries of knowledge and status, certain conceptual issues are taken up in other chapters (Linell and Luckmann, Chapter 1; Farr, Chapter 11), or treated in combination with the study of empirical material (e.g. Rommetveit, Chapter 9).

The main themes of this volume

The concept of asymmetry

The term 'asymmetry' is used in this volume in a variety of ways and at different levels of conceptualization and of analysis of dialogue. Perhaps one should rather use the dyadic term 'symmetricity-asymmetricity' to point to the nature of this complex concept. A particular dialogue can be said to be symmetrical with respect to, say, the number of initiatives and responses of each of the participants and still be asymmetrical with respect to who determines the topic. Or a dialogue as a whole can be symmetrical with respect to the number of words that each speaker has used overall, yet asymmetrical if quantity of speech is analysed at more local levels.

Linell and Luckmann (Chapter 1) provide an exposition of the terms and concepts that are used in this volume. Since this volume 'focuses on the interactional environments and consequences of asymmetries' (p. 2) the authors draw attention to general assumptions about the nature of asymmetries in dialogue and to the meanings of different kinds of dialogical inequivalences. That a dialogue is asymmetrical as such does not tell us whether or not communication will be successful, whatever success and failure may mean in a given context. Rather, as Linell (1990) maintains, asymmetry is a concept which is *neutral* with respect to success and failure in communication. Specific kinds of asymmetries in specific contexts, however, may lead to breakdown in communication. For example,

Käsermann (Chapter 5) shows that asymmetries, induced by lack of communicative cooperation in therapeutic dialogue, can lead to communicative failure.

In the concluding chapter of this volume, Farr addresses another fundamental form of asymmetry, that between self and others. Farr calls it 'a symmetrical form of asymmetry' (Chapter 11, p. 242). He draws attention to the implications of the fact that while both participants in a dialogue can *see* the other (unless of course they are blind), they do not see themselves, and therefore to a large extent are ignorant of the visual impact they make on the other participant. So while the self is in a *symmetrical* position with respect to other selves, there is an *asymmetry* for each self in the sense that 'we do not see ourselves as others see us' (Chapter 11, p. 242). While this asymmetry holds in the visual modality, it does not exist in the oral/aural modality since the self can listen to its own voice just as it can to those of others. Thus the asymmetry between voice and vision has important consequences for the study of self as *speaker* and self as *listener*.

Knoblauch (Chapter 8) maintains that family talk is often characterized by the avoidance of asymmetries because they might lead to conflict. He shows that speakers in family argumentative talk produce disagreement collaboratively in a way which evades dominance, especially by 'avoiding both the abyss of conflict talk and the byway of instruction' (pp. 166–7). He points out that argumentation, keeping harmonious balance of well-tempered disagreement, is a pleasurable pastime and it can be upheld only if individual members avoid the temptation to dominate the scene. We have to be clear, however, about several issues. As Linell and Luckmann (Chapter 1) argue, asymmetries are to be found both at *local* and *global* levels. While *dominance* refers to a more global property of a dialogue, one can identify various other kinds of asymmetries at local levels. In other words, avoiding asymmetries at one level does not mean avoiding them totally. Second, the argumentative conversations of the kind described by Knoblauch require a certain cultural milieu, for example, among polite, middle-class, democratic and well-behaved people in some, temporarily unproblematic, situations. It would therefore be useful to explore the relationships between argumentation and its cultural embeddedness in different social milieux.

The context for dialogue

An essential feature of this volume is the implicit presupposition of all the authors that an utterance *in vacuo* is but a potentiality for meaning. This presupposition is stated explicitly in Käsermann's (Chapter 5) claim that one cannot decide about an utterance *in vacuo* whether or not it is a communicative obstruction. To describe something as an obstruction one needs to consider the context in which such an utterance appears. Wintermantel (Chapter 6) shows that the meaning of simple instructions is dependent on their position in sequences of more complex, hierarchically organized interactions between interlocutors. The expert has a choice with respect to the manner and detail in which to instruct the novice.

Just as utterances are *context bound* they are also *context constitutive*. By choosing a particular utterance the speaker determines what does and does not count as a legitimate follow up of the previous contribution. For example, Käsermann (Chapter 5) shows that the client in a psychotherapeutic session gradually changes his performance, both qualitatively and quantitatively, as a result of the therapist's moves. This happens if the client has difficulty in responding to such moves because they do not fit into the expected pattern of communicative exchanges (however, see also the section of epistemic responsibility).

Just as utterances often determine the kinds and quality of dialogical asymmetries, so does the setting in which a dialogue takes place. Institutional dialogues often reflect the dominating perspective (see next section) of the professional as in Aronsson's (Chapter 3) and in Linell and Jönsson's (Chapter 4) studies. Settings also define the legitimacy of particular kinds of dialogical activities. For example, while in instructional settings (Wintermantel, Chapter 6) teaching dialogues are taken for granted, imparting knowledge or 'teaching' in informal conversation can be a delicate matter. Although certain asymmetries in knowledge often become interactively relevant and cannot be ignored if a dialogue is to proceed, in informal discussions such 'teachers-to-be' 'must carefully prepare the ground before launching into "teaching" on their own initiative' (Keppler and Luckmann, Chapter 7, p. 160).

The setting and the dialogical contributions, therefore, both have two functions. First, they are context bound, functioning as a communicative resource or as a potentiality for different meanings to be established. Second, the setting and the dialogical contributions are also context constitutive, functioning as a constraint on a dialogue. Relatively stable socio-cultural contexts for dialogue exist as potentialities. However, they are not only *accomplishments* of the past but they also become *reaccomplishments* of the actual dialogical process (Linell and Luckmann, Chapter 1). Moreover, both the resource and the constraint functions of the setting and language are themselves culturally and socio-historically determined.

Perspectivity and the joint construction of meaning

As in *The Dynamics of Dialogue* so in the present volume, *perspective-setting* and *perspective-taking* (Graumann, 1989; 1990) are considered to be defining features of dialogicity. The focus of Linell and Jönsson's (Chapter 4) study is the subject of perspective-setting in discourse. By perspective the authors mean an orientation adopted by one or jointly by several participants. Depending on the adopted orientation, one and the same story can be told in different ways, yielding different narratives. This is so because different aspects of the story can be foregrounded and thus acquire a different relevance in the narrative. Analysing police/suspect interviews, Linell and Jönsson show that the police are interested in facts and technical details. The suspect, on the other hand, wants to tell his or her own story, often giving details about the background to a petty crime, provides justifications and excuses, and tries to re-establish his or her self-respect. In reports constructed by the police on the basis of these interviews, it is the policeman's perspective that manifests itself, the dialogicality being largely hidden (Linell and Jönsson, Chapter 4, p. 76). Such reports often take the form of monologues rather than of dialogical constructions.

The meaning of the term 'perspective', however, is difficult to pinpoint exactly and may refer to different things. At one extreme, by perspective could be meant no more than something holding a dialogue together like, say, the notes of the suspect's responses which the policeman wrote in his report (Linell and Jönsson, Chapter 4) or the articles or photographs in the newspaper passed round among people with learning difficulties in a group discussion (Marková, Chapter 10). At the other extreme, by 'perspective' one can mean the anonymized and monological attitude with which the police officer asks questions. One can also point to the egocentrically oriented 'perspective' of a suspect, referring to his or her marginalization in society, depression and unhappy life circumstances (Linell, 1990). Such different 'perspectives' reveal themselves also in the different meanings that a policeman's question, such as 'why did you do that?', has for the speaker and for the suspect.

Several chapters in this volume show that even in highly asymmetric dialogues the meaning (or, one could say, perspective) of the dialogue is constructed jointly by all the participants. For example, in instructional dialogues between expert and novice in which the participants 'start from different points with different purposes ... they have to come together by co-ordinating their individual perspectives' (Wintermantel, Chapter 6, p. 130). She shows that instructing someone is more than just the transfer of information. It is a dialogical situation in which both partners must take the perspectives of each other's position with respect to the subject matter. The expert is influenced by the novice's questions but at the same time follows his or her intentions.

The very definition of informal discussion entails that goals or problems to be solved are not given in advance. Precisely the opposite; Knoblauch (Chapter 8) points out that informal discussions can be the processes by which problems are constructed. He shows that in argumentative dialogues the problem is constructed jointly, and he discusses some of the building blocks of jointly constructed disagreements, such as different kinds of contradictions and rhetorical or redundant statements. In contrast to Wintermantel's instructional dialogue, the purpose of which is to solve a problem, an argumentative dialogue is a game, the purpose of which is to argue for its own sake. Knoblauch makes it plain, just as Käsermann (Chapter 5) and Wintermantel (Chapter 6) do, that an utterance on its own is only a potentiality and that it obtains its particular meaning only through the following and preceding utterances. In argumentative discussions, disagreements may crop up anywhere in a conversation (Knoblauch, Chapter 8). However, speakers are usually careful not to start real conflict talk. They avoid such a danger by re-establishing reciprocity and complementarity and expanding on what was said previously.

In the case described by Marková (Chapter 10), while meanings of utterances are constructed jointly by a tutor and people with learning difficulties, it is the perspective of the professional that comes to the fore. Yet, at least a minimal acceptance of the tutor's perspective is required for group discussions to proceed.

Epistemic responsibility

Epistemic responsibility (Rommetveit, forthcoming) concerns the question 'of *control* of intersubjectively endorsed perspectives on things and states of affairs' [italics added] (Rommetveit, Chapter 9, p. 195) that are the subject of dialogue. In institutional dialogues it is largely the professional who has such a privilege. Institutional dialogues have pre-set agendas and topics, are goal driven and have a pre-determined dictionary. In informal discussions, on the contrary, one would expect control over what is talked about and from what point of view to be more equally shared. Rommetveit (Chapter 9, p. 212) maintains that distribution of epistemic responsibility is more than just 'a matter of semantic dominance and thematic control'. Since language forms a part of our thinking environment, the control of word meanings and topics of concern directly affects our shared social reality. Asymmetries in epistemic responsibility thus have both endogeneous (dialogical) and exogeneous (contextual) sources.

In his analysis of Ibsen's *A Doll's House*, Rommetveit shows that Nora is made both irresponsible as a person and also epistemically non-responsible. The two meanings are conflated in Ibsen's drama. First, she is thought, by her husband, to be irresponsible because she is a 'spendthrift'. In the first part of the drama she does not question the moral authority of her husband to control her actions and she lies 'like a fearful child who has misbehaved' (Rommetveit, Chapter 9, p. 209). Thus she is in a similar situation to that of a suspect (Linell and Jönsson, Chapter 4), who looks for excuses for his or her misdemeanours when the policeman sets the agenda for interrogation. Second, Nora is made epistemically non-responsible by not being allowed to topicalize her own new conversational initiatives. She topicalizes, however, her husband's expressions, accepting her new identity as a 'squirrel' and 'skylark'. Such unilateral control of the words that *one* participant introduces but *both* participants topicalize signifies, according to Rommetveit, the most extreme form of asymmetry in epistemic responsibility.

Although the subject of epistemic responsibility is explicitly discussed by Rommetveit, it also pervades other chapters. It takes a special form in Aronsson's (Chapter 3) analysis of multi-party talks between doctor, parent and child in a pediatric surgery. Multi-party talks always provide potentialities for the formation of temporary alliances to express hidden agendas and unexpressed conflicts. Aronsson reveals the ways in which conflicting goals may shape adult discourse, showing that for such purposes the child's participant status can be gradually transformed from that of a dialogue partner to that of a nonpartner, i.e. someone with no epistemic responsibility. The two adults, the doctor and the mother, talk to each other *through* the child, in order to preserve their own, professional or parental, authority. Although the child is actually an addressee he only gives minimal responses without any attempt to topicalize whatever is going on. Social distance between the doctor and child is artificially upheld by the mother, who intervenes as soon as she fears that her parental authority could be undermined. Moreover, the child, in this multi-party talk, is often addressed as 'he' rather than 'you' both by the doctor and by his mother.

The asymmetric distribution of epistemic responsibility in professional–client interaction is also highlighted in Marková's (Chapter 10) analysis of group discussions between a tutor and people with learning difficulties. This study shows that while at one level people with learning difficulties are partners in a discussion, at another level they are treated as non-persons because their contributions are not topicalized at all by the dominant party, i.e. by the professional. Similarly, the psychiatric patient in Käsermann's (Chapter 5) study is not treated as epistemically responsible when the therapist responds uncooperatively and obliquely to what the patient says. One should be aware, however, of potential problems arising from the analysis of therapeutic dialogues out of context of the overall therapy. Käsermann herself points to this issue when she says that her analysis of cooperative and uncooperative moves is concerned with a *local*, and not the *global*, level of dialogue. She recognizes that lack of cooperation on the part of therapist may be a strategy to achieve a particular therapeutic goal.

Asymmetric distribution of epistemic responsibility amounts to depriving dialogical participants of their humanity and treating them as physical objects rather than fellow human beings, as *Ich-Es*, rather than *Ich-Du* (Rommetveit, Chapter 9). Farr (Chapter 11) draws attention to the distinction between objects and persons in the broader context of the social psychology of perception (Heider, 1958). He implies that there is a threat to sustaining one's self if one is treated as an *Ich-Es* rather than as an autonomous moral agent. Nora was deprived of her autonomy by her husband Torvald who listened to her through filters of his image of her, and responded to her through his model of her. However, isn't it the case that not listening, and responding to others through one's filters, is more common than we would wish to admit?

Asymmetries in knowledge

As Drew (Chapter 2) says, sheer differences in knowledge among the participants in a dialogue may be the least interesting kind of dialogical inequality. He maintains that more interesting are cases where the individual either has knowledge but not the legitimacy to use it, or where the individual knows something at one level but does not know it as another level, thus being caught in a dilemma or facing embarrassment. In other words, it is the *interactional* consequences of asymmetries of knowledge to which Drew turns his attention. He points to different perspectives of self and others (see also Farr, Chapter 11) and shows that asymmetry between interlocutors does not simply arise from their 'having' different knowledge. Rather, the asymmetry could be occasioned by the interactions in which they are engaged in challenging each other's versions of the story in question (Drew, Chapter 2, p. 30). In this case asymmetry arises from their having different perspectives of the issue in question, and they use interactional strategies to challenge asymmetries by attacking each other's accounts. A similar point of view is also expressed by Farr (Chapter 11) when he shows that asymmetries in knowledge, while they can have an objective basis, may also be due to the fact that the speaker has different access to what is said than the listener.

The question of the legitimacy of showing one's knowledge, to which Drew (Chapter 2) draws attention, is taken up by Keppler and Luckmann (Chapter 7) and by Knoblauch (Chapter 8). Keppler and Luckmann analyse instances of teaching carried out not by institutionally defined instructors but by situationally selected 'teachers' in informal discussions. While asymmetries of knowledge are a universal part of human social life and of everyday conversations, specific asymmetries of knowledge often become interactively relevant; indeed, they may become communicative obstacles unless the direction of conversation is changed from its original course. In contrast to institutional teaching, the 'teaching' that takes place in conversations is based on particular dialogical rules as to how to start it, how to end it and how long it should take place. In conversations nobody has a pre-set legitimacy to be a teacher, and teachers-to-be must conform to the interactional etiquette in order not to overstate their case.

Knoblauch maintains that in informal discussions 'teaching' can start from disagreement. Being involved in a series of argumentative sequences, however, speakers try to avoid establishing the implied asymmetries of knowledge. If one speaker assumes the role of teacher too often, the right to disagree is endangered and other speakers would be degraded to recipients of the teacher's knowledge. The establishment of new topics in argumentative sequences helps to prevent this.

It would be interesting to examine, in a more systematic manner, the different kinds of 'teachings' in the family conversations analysed in this volume. Thus we have here a conversation between Nora and Torvald in *A Doll's House* and family conversations in Keppler and Luckmann's and Knoblauch's studies. In the conversation between Nora and Torvald in the first act of Ibsen's drama, the nineteenth century patriarchal hierarchy and clear subordination of Nora penetrates both the form and the content of what is said. In contrast, in the latter two cases family members avoid hierarchical relationships, being well aware of the implicit rules in a modern and democratic family that dominance of one person over others infringes on good manners and the right of the individual. It is likely that one could find, even in the Norway and Germany of today, an Ibsenian kind of family conversation with implicit rules as to who is and who is not allowed to teach. But the issue that concerned Ibsen was the societal nature of asymmetrical relationships, with the unquestioned dominance and status of the male over the female family members. In today's European families, too, interactional etiquette might play a trifling role and power hierarchy by one family member over another could prevail. This, however, would be viewed, presumably, as a more local or an interpersonal matter rather than as a societal matter. Consequently, it would be well worth exploring linguistic manifestations of such interpersonally based, rather than societally based, dialogical asymmetries in family conversations.

Methodological issues

While *The Dynamics of Dialogue*, the first volume of the series, dealt mainly with the conceptual foundations of *dialogism* (Marková, 1990, p. 4), in this volume the empirical aspects of dialogism are much more prominent. With the exception of Linell and Luckmann (Chapter 1), who are concerned with conceptual issues and the meanings of terms like 'asymmetry' and 'dominance', and Farr's (Chapter 11) discussion on the self as an inherent but mostly neglected source of asymmetry in dialogue, all the chapters refer to the results of some sort of empirical analysis of dialogue processes. Therefore, in a certain way this second volume brings the claims of *dialogism*, which were exposed in Volume 1, to the test. This volume is thus of interest for several reasons. First, it is a demonstration of the empirical fruitfulness of the dialogical approach to verbal communication. Second, it shows that three-step analysis, which may be seen as part of the dialogical conceptual framework (Marková, 1990), has implications for empirical data and can be applied at different levels (Marková, Chapter 10). However, it still has to be proved that these different levels of analysis are also conceptually equivalent.

A closer look at the individual contributions reveals that there are several kinds of methodological procedures within a common dialogical framework. In the chapters by Rommetveit and Marková the results of initiative–response (IR) analyses (see Linell, 1990) are reported. Rommetveit extends the IR analysis of Linell *et al.* (1988) to capture semantic and topical features in dialogue. He argues and shows that 'locally assessed interactional coherence is semantically founded' (p. 206) and maintains that the terms 'initiative' and 'response' are semantically based dialogical terms. Marková extends IR analysis to the study of group discussions involving people with learning difficulties.

Other empirical chapters may be seen as applications of ethnomethodological (Drew) and conversation-analysis kinds of procedures (Aronsson, Käsermann); still others, while inspired by conversation-analysis, apply phenomenologically-oriented analysis (Linell and Jönsson, Keppler and Luckmann, Knoblauch). In all these approaches the corpus of data relate to particular genres. By repeatedly examining the data the researcher seeks to find out patterns in them. He or she works inductively, assembling features of particular phenomena, selects examples with such features and analyses them in detail.

Wintermantel directs attention to an interesting and, as far as we can see, as yet unsolved problem. The problem concerns the question of the suitability of experimental procedures for the analysis of dialogues. Wintermantel's interest is focused on instructional dialogues between experts and novices which are not only asymmetrical with respect to knowledge but also 'artificial', even *in vivo*. However, in contrast to problem-solving experiments as traditionally treated by information-processing and individual cognitive psychologists, Wintermantel takes a dynamic and social approach to problem-solving. She views it, in a similar way to Mead (1934), as a speaking and listening activity. Moreover, she takes a perspectival and phenomenological approach to discussing the socio-interactional aspect of problem-solving dialogue. In this way her approach is reminiscent of that of Grossen (1988) who has studied intersubjectivity in Piagetian tasks such as conservation, and that of Rubinstein (1958; 1959) and his school, concerned with the role of instruction in problem-solving.

The methodological differences between more 'strictly dialogically' oriented analysis and that of conversation analysis will no doubt be of future interest. For example, one may wonder in what ways the two approaches would tackle the problem of the influence of the relevant interlocutors' knowledge differences on topic development and maintenance. However, in the present volume the methodological differences between the 'strictly dialogical' contributors and those inspired by conversation analysis are of more immediate importance. In some ways both approaches rest on a three-step assumption (although some authors do not use this terminology). However, while IR analysis presupposes the conceptual perspective of co-genetic or dialogical logic (Rommetveit, Chapter 9; Marková, Chapter 10), which means identifying a phenomenon in terms of *both* what it is *and* in terms of its *relevant* outside, ethnomethodological and conversation analysis do not rest on explicit conceptual presuppositions. Instead, they are oriented towards concrete sequences or communicative events as manifestations of certain underlying rules of communicative action. Both approaches are dialogical in essence, but possibly in a somewhat different way. While the conceptually grounded view of dialogicity is firmly rooted in the history of philosophy and linguistics (e.g. Hegel, 1816; Humboldt, 1836), the other view is more 'realistic' in the sense that no theoretical decisions are made in advance. Presumably both perspectives are necessary ingredients of a more complete form of empirical analysis of dialogical processes. Furthermore, it might even turn out that a closer look at the processes 'within' the individual subject will sometimes be a necessary supplement to an adequate understanding of dialogic behaviour.

Towards mutualities in dialogue

This volume has focused on asymmetries as inherent characteristics of dialogue. Yet it has been shown that while asymmetries are driving forces of communication in attempting to impart knowledge, exert power, persuade others and provide a platform for self-expression, dialogue can take place only if some basic commonalities of perspectives are established between the participants. In other words, although asymmetries are inherent characteristics of dialogue, their dynamics are dependent on the participants' *mutual* communicative efforts. While in some cases only a basic commonality in knowledge or experience is sufficient to establish rapport between participants, in other cases reciprocity of exchanges in terms of give-and-take is required for dialogue. 'Perspective-setting' and 'perspective-taking', 'intersubjectivity', 'complementarity in mutual actions' and 'self- and other- perspectivity' are examples of terms for the expression of different kinds of mutualities in dialogue. Moreover, mutualities often imply obligations or contracts binding the participants to take a particular perspective in their temporarily shared social world. The analysis of issues pertaining to mutualities in dialogue will be the subject of the next volume in this series.

References

Graumann, C. F. (1989) 'Perspective setting and taking in verbal interaction', in R. Dietrich and C. F. Graumann (eds), *Language Processing in Social Context*, North Holland: Amsterdam.
Graumann, C. F. (1990) 'Perspective structure and dynamics in dialogue', in I. Marková and K. Foppa (eds), *The Dynamics of Dialogue*, Harvester Wheatsheaf: Hemel Hempstead.
Grossen, M. (1988), *La construction sociale de l'inter-subjectivité entre adulte et enfant en situation de test*, Delval: Fribourg.
Hegel, G. W. F. (1812–16) *Science of Logic*, trans. A. V. Miller, George Allen & Unwin: London, 1969; Humanities Press: New York, 1976.
Heider, F. (1958), *The Psychology of Interpersonal Relations*, Wiley: London and New York.
Humboldt, W. von (1836–9) *Über die Kawi-Sprache auf der Insel Java*, I–III, Berlin: Königliche Akadamie der Wissenschaften.
Linell, P. (1990), 'The power of dialogue dynamics', in I. Marková and K. Foppa (eds), *The Dynamics of Dialogue*, Harvester Wheatsheaf: Hemel Hempstead.
Linell, P., Gustavsson, L. and Juvonen, P. (1988), 'Interactional dominance in dyadic communication: a presentation of initiative–response analysis', *Linguistics*, 26, 415–42.
Marková, I. (1990), 'A three-step process as a unit of analysis in dialogue', in I. Marková and K. Foppa (eds), *The Dynamics of Dialogue*, Harvester Wheatsheaf: Hemel Hempstead.
Marková, I. and Foppa, K. (1990), (eds), *The Dynamics of Dialogue*, Harvester Wheatsheaf: Hemel Hempstead.
Mead, G. H. (1934), *Mind, Self and Society*, University of Chicago Press: Chicago, IL and London.

Rommetveit, R. (1990), 'On axiomatic features of a dialogical approach to language and mind', in I. Marková and K. Foppa (eds), *The Dynamics of Dialogue*, Harvester Wheatsheaf: Hemel Hempstead.

Rommetveit, R. (forthcoming), 'Outlines of a dialogically based social-cognitive approach to human cognition and communication', in A. Heen Wold (ed.), *Festschrift for Ragnar Rommetveit*.

Rubinstein, S. L. (1958), *O Myshlenii i Putyach yego Issledovaniya* (On Thought and its Investigation), Izdavatelstvo Akademii Nauk USSR: Moscow.

Rubinstein, S. L. (1959), *Principi i Puty i Razvitiya Psikhologii*, (The Principles and Methods of the Development of Psychology), Izdavatelstvo Akademii Nauk USSR: Moscow.

Appendix

The transcription of conversation follows the conventions developed by Sacks, Schegloff and Jefferson (1974, pp. 731 ff.).

[	begin of overlapping talk of two or more speakers
]	end of overlaps
=	words directly connected, no interval between words
(1.0)	pauses that are longer than one second are indicated in length (seconds)
(- -)	pauses shorter than one second; '(-)' means a pause of 0.25 second, '(--)' a pause of 0.5 second, etc.
:::	prolonged pronunciation of a vowel or a consonant
°yes°	soft
YES	loud
yes	stressed
°hh	breathing in
hh	breathing out
,	upward intonational contour
?	strong upward contour
;	downward intonational contour
.	strong downward contour
whe-	utterance cut off
(and)	single parentheses indicate that the transcriber was uncertain; also used to
(Carl)	mark doubt about the speaker's identification
( )	empty parentheses indicate incomprehensible passages; also used when the speaker is not identified
((cough))	double parentheses indicate paralinguistic events

Name index

Adelswärd, V. 78, 98n
Agar, M. 11, 19n
Albee, Edward 204
Aloia, G. F. 236, 239
Altorfer, A. 101, 103, 123
Anderson, A. 243, 247
Apeltauer, E. 179, 193n
Argyle, M. 244, 257
Aronsson, Karin 22, 24, 49-74, 78,
    98n, 228, 266-7, 270
  on epistemic responsibility 266-7
  methodology 270
  on participant roles 6, 213
  on perspectives 263
  on voices 9
Atkinson, M. 1, 19n, 48, 106, 123, 165,
    194

Bakhtin, M. M. 5, 212, 217
  on turns 227
  on voices 9, 77, 98n, 215
Berenz, Norine 186
Berger, P. 163n
Bergmann, J. 98, 163n, 167, 186,
    193n, 207, 219n, 256-7
Bernstein, B. 77
Berthold, H. 186
Boggs, S. T. 180
Bråten, S. 212
Brenneis, D. L. 180
Brewer, J. D. 236
Brown, P. 50-2, 55-6, 68-9, 72,
    criticism of model 60
Bruzelius, A. 97
Buber, Martin 195, 211, 212, 214, 254
Burton, M. 236, 239

Caesar-Wolf, B. 77, 78, 96

Calculator, S. 224
Cartwright, D. 248, 249
Caspar, F. 107
Cattermole, M. 221, 224, 226, 236, 239,
    240
Cicourel, A. V. 1, 25, 26, 77, 96
Clark, H. 3, 75
Clayman, S. E. 45n
Cody, M. J. 78
Cole, P. 123, 142
Conley, J. M. 23-4, 48, 78, 193n
Corsaro, W. 1
Coulter, J. 169, 173-4, 193n
Coulthard, R. M. 226, 228
Coupland, J. and N. 60
Coyne, T. 222, 240
Craig, R. T. 60
Cranach, M. von 132
Cullen C. 236

Darwin, Charles 253, 255
Dietrich, R. 99, 219n, 271
Dijk, T. A. van 129, 141
Dilthey, W. 250
Dörner, D. 133
Drew, Paul 4, 5, 8, 17, 21-48, 163n
  on dominance 6, 9, 125, 166
  on knowledge asymmetries 267, 268
  methodology 269
Duncker, K. 133, 141

Emerson, C. 19, 99, 239
Erickson, F. 43, 47n
Etzioni, A. 98n, 99

Farr, Rob 4, 6, 7, 223, 238, 241-57,
    261-9
  on automatized interaction 223

methodology 269
 on self and others 262, 267
Fisher, S. 47n, 48
Foppa, Klaus 6, 227, 234, 259-73
 on contexts 1
 on methodology 102, 107, 122, 199
 on participation 104
Frankenberg, H. 192n
Fraser, W. I. 221
Fry, D. 248, 257

Gadamer, Hans-Georg 212, 219n
Garfinkel, H. 106, 123
Garnham, A. 129
Genette, G. 98n
Giles, H. 20, 240, 257
Gilligan, Carol 218, 219n
Goffman, Erving 163n, 222, 252, 253, 256
 on encounters 254-5, 257
 on form of talk 167
 on recepient design 49
 on speaker role 9
Golding, B. 222, 240
Goodman, N. 75, 76
Goodwin, C. 7, 11, 17, 46n
Grainger, K. 60, 74
Graumann, C. F. 2, 77, 103, 130, 247
 on language 126
 on perspectives 75-6, 207-8, 246, 264
Grawe, K. 107, 123
Grice, H. P. 116, 123
Grossen, M. 270
Gugler, B. 132, 141
Gumperz, John 43, 186, 189
Gustavsson, L. 199, 200, 202-3, 204, 230, 240, 272

Habermas, J. 8, 166, 170, 193n
Halliday, M. A. K. 206, 219n
Hasan, R. 206
Heath, C. 12
Hegel, G. W. F. 271
Heider, F. 242-3, 253, 254, 255, 267
Hendy, J. 22, 240
Heritage, John 1, 11, 17, 19n, 44, 47n, 106, 123, 165
Holquist, M. 19, 99, 239
Holt, E. 29
Humboldt, W. von 271, 272
Husserl, 75, 77

Ibsen, Henrik 195-220, 243, 254, 266, 268
Ichheiser, G. 255
Indermühle 132, 141

Jackson, S. 170, 178, 193n
Jacobs, S. 170, 178, 193n
Jaeger, K. H. 192n
Jahoda, A. 221, 236, 240
James, William 250
Jeeves, M. A. 221
Jefferson, G. 22-3, 53, 164n, 272-3
Jenkins, P. 224
Joas, H. 250, 251
Johnson-Laird, P. N. 129
Jönsson, Linda 5, 6, 8, 10, 12, 75-100
 on dominance 166
 on epistemic responsibility 213, 266
 methodology 270
 on perspectives 163n, 263, 264
Juvonen, P. 199, 200, 202, 204, 227

Kant, I. 254
Kalbermatten, 132, 141
Käsermann, Marie-Louise 22, 101-23, 163n, 213, 265
 on communicative failure 8, 262
 methodology 270
 on obstruction 46n, 263
Keppler, Angela 4, 5, 6, 121, 143-65, 164n
 on argumentative sequences 186
 on knowledge asymmetries 268
 methodology 270
 on teaching 182, 263
Kernan, K. T. 236
Key-Åberg, S. 204
Kintsch, W. 129
Klein, W. 190n
Knoblauch, Hubert 5, 166-94, 209, 236, 268
 on avoidance of asymmetry 262
 methdology 270
 on problems 265
Koerfer, A. 175
Kohlberg, L. 219
Konau, E. 205, 220
Kopperschmidt, J. 190n
Krambeck, J. 205, 220
Kühn, R. 165, 193n

Labov, W. 86, 87
Lane, H. 249
Lee, J. 22-3
Lein, L. 180
Leudar, I. 221
Levelt, W. J. M. 130
Levinson, S. 27, 50-2, 55-6, 61, 68-9, 72
 criticism of model 60
 on speaker role 49
Linell, Per 32, 73n, 204, 213, 231-2, 260

on argumentation 168
on dominance 101, 15, 203
methodology 199, 200, 202, 229, 269, 270
on nature of asymmetry 1-20, 21, 24, 28, 245-6
  domain 24, 125
  local and global 30, 122, 166, 262
  as neutral 261
on perspectives 75-100, 163n, 263
on socio-cultural contexts 264
on turns 227, 228
Litt, T. 163n
Loveday, L. 176
Lucacs, George 196
Luckmann, Thomas 32, 121, 186, 207, 260
  on conversation 244-5
  dialogue defined 2, 244, 252
  on knowledge asymmetries 268
  methodology 269, 270
  on mutuality of perspectives 95, 96
  on nature of asymmetry 1-20, 21
  local and global 30, 122, 166, 262
  on socio-cultural contexts 264
  on teaching 143-65, 182, 263
Lyman, S. 78

Maas, U. 190n
McFarlane, James W. 217
McGillivary, J. 222, 240
McLaughlin, M. L. 78
MacMillan, D. L. 236
Marková, Ivana 1, 6, 221-40, 259-73
  on language 71
  methodology 9, 199, 269, 270
  on vision 245
Marshall, C. R. 3
Maynard, D. 12, 122
Mead, G. H. 75, 243, 247, 249-50, 251, 253
  on problem-solving 270
Meehan, A. J. 46-7n
Miller, M. 169
Mischler, E. 77, 98n
Moesch, K. 107
Moscovici, S. 222
Mukařovský, J. 227

Newell, A. 133
Northam, J. 214
Northdurft, W. 191n

O'Barr, W. 23-4, 78
Olbrechts-Tyteca, L. 168, 185, 190n
Övermann, U. 205, 220

Paget, M. A. 25

Parsons, T. 11, 98n
Penman, R. 60
Petelman, C. 168, 175, 185, 190n
Perzold, H. G. 165, 193n
Piaget, J. 218, 270
Platt, M 236
Pomerantz, A. 40, 46n, 164n, 170
Prior, M. 222

Quasthoff, U. 190n

Reichling, A. 217
Riesman, D. 252
Richardson, A. M. 224
Rimmon-Kenan, S. 98n
Robertson, I 224
Robinson, W. P. 240, 257
Rogers-Warren, A. K. 224
Rommetveit, Ragnar 6, 8, 9, 49, 223
  on *A Doll's House* 195-220, 254
  on ambiguity 72
  on complementarity 166
  on context 75
  on epistemic responsibility 5, 266
  on language 52
  methodology 9, 227, 261, 269, 270
  on perspectives 76
Rorty, R. 52, 72
Rubinstein, S. L. 270
Rundström, Bengt 50, 52, 53, 73n
  on joking 51
  on parental control 54, 56, 59, 68
Rutter, D. R. 256

Sabsay, S. 236
Sacks, Harvey 18, 21, 40, 46n, 77, 164n, 190n
Sarfatti-Larsson, M. 98n
Sätterlund-Larsson, U. 56, 58
Schaefer, E. F. 75
Schank, G. 169
Schegloff, E. A. 33, 46n, 130, 164n
  on context 1, 18
  on greetings 30, 34
  on misunderstanding 26
Schenkein, J. 53
Schonbach, P. 78
Schutz, A. 15, 163n
Scott, M. 78
Sefi, S. 47n
Sharrock, W. 37
Shultz, J. 43
Siegerstetter, J. 135
Silverman, D. 24, 46n, 77
Simmel, G. 189, 244
Simon, H. 133
Sinclair, M. McH. 226, 228

Skinner, B. F. 256
Soeffner, H. G. 77, 97
Sommer, C. M. 103
Spencer, W. 77, 78
Spisak, F. 60
Spranz-Fogasy, T. 173
Stalnaker, R. C. 125
Suchman, L. A. 128, 134

Tannen, D. 24
Thelin, K. 97
Thomas, M. 236, 239
Tilman, A. 205, 220
Toolan, M. 86, 98n
Torode, B. 77
Toulmin, S. 168, 185, 190n
Tracy, K. 60

Ulmer, B. 164n, 186

Vallacher, R. R. 131
Vološinov, V. N. 227
Vuchinich, S. 174

Wald, B. 165n
Waletzky, J. 86
Wallat, C. 24
Warren, S. F. 224, 240
Watson, R. 78
Watts, S. 236, 239
Watzlawick, P. 236
Wegner, D. M. 131
Wertsch, J. V. 9, 65, 71, 77, 93, 215
Wintermantel, Margaret 5, 6, 8, 22,
    41, 124–42
  on instruction 263
  and perspectives 265
  methodology 270
Wittgenstein, L. 77
Wold, A. Heen. 74, 100, 220, 272
Wright, G. H. von 213

Yearley, S. 236
Youngson, S. C. 224

Zander, A. 248, 249
Zimbardo, P. G. 253

Subject index

accounts, 78
action knowledge, 130, 131-2, 134, 135, 138-9
adjacency pairs, 4, 173, 206, 207, 208
　and local asymmetries, 30
adult-child discourse, 45, 49, 204
　on non-reversible roles, 235, 236
advantage and access to knowledge, 32-3
　see also disadvantage
advice, 105, 106-7, 117-18
　from experts, 42-3, 47n
　and family life, 65, 68
　see also expert-novice; knowledge; teaching
agreement markers, 184
alliances, 52, 266
　conflicting, 72
　doctor-child, 50, 51, 59, 60, 64, 65, 71
　doctor-parent, 50, 51, 60, 64, 71, 267
　parent-child, 50, 51, 59, 60, 61, 65
ambiguity, 72-3
ambulance service example, 22-3
anaphors, 176
anticipated dialogues, 65-8, 71
argumentation, 166, 167
　and conflict, 187-9, 188-9
　　avoidance, 265
　and culture, 189, 192n, 262
　ending, 191n
　on fringe of instruction, 181-4
　generation through disagreement, 178
　institutional settings, 168
　institutionalized, 169
　natural, 190n
　phases of, 190n

and problem, 168-9
　sequences, 172-3, 181, 182-3
　and conflict, 184
　and teaching, 182-4
　and topics, 187, 188, 188-9
　tree of arguments, 168, 169
　and turn-taking, 169, 172-3, 179-81
　see also conflict; disagreement
assertion, 178, 192n
assumptions of common ground, 2-3
asymmetry/asymmetries
　avoidance of, 166-93, 262
　and communication failures, 261-2
　consequences of, 267
　and control, 41-3
　defined, 2, 27
　and dominance, 41
　global, 246, 262
　individual and social factors, 9-10
　intrinsic and extrinsic, 245-6
　as intrinsic feature of dialogue, 7-8, 259
　inverse, 105
　knowledge, 5-6, 21-47
　local, 246, 262
　as multi-faceted and heterogenous, 8-9
　necessary, 8
　and people with learning difficulties, 221-38
　reduction of, 124-41, 144-5, 260, 261
　self and others, 241-57
　as socially constructed, 11-12
　sources, 24
　　self as, 241-57
　of status, 254, 261
authority
　medical, 50

278

parental, 50, 59, 67, 70
  see also control; doctor-patient; power
avoidance
  of asymmetry, 166-93, 262
  of communication, 221
awareness
  communicative, 237-8
  of self and others, 252-3

background
  knowledge, 75, 96, 131
  of narratives, 86, 87
balance, 229, 230
behavioural tokens, 164n
body
  as source of asymmetry, 242
  and voices, 241-57
Boris Becker argument, 171-3, 174, 176-7, 181-2, 183, 192n

caller-called, 30-2, 45, 46n
car mechanic study, 136-8
caretakers, adult, 212
child
  degrading by parent, 59
  participant status, 71, 72-3, 267
    regulation of, 54-7, 60, 65
  role, 35-6, 37, 46n, 50, 73
  talk, 71
classrooms, 11
  turn-taking, 22
cliche, 29, 30
coalitions, 184
  see also alliances
coherence, 26, 206, 207
commonalities
  common ground, 2-3, 125-6
  of knowledge, 2-3
  of perspectives, 271
  see also mutuality
communication
  avoidance strategies, 221
  failures, 261-2
communicative
  aggregate, 167
    informal discussion as, 184-7
  awareness, 237-8
  cultures, 189
  difficulties, 26
  disruptive behaviour, 102, 104
  exchange, model of, 102-3
  genres, 171, 186
  see also learning difficulties, groups
competence, 101, 103, 105, 105-6, 121
complementarity, 166, 168, 181, 184, 265, 271

of disagreement, 170
conditional relevance, 7, 173, 174
  expansion, 178
conflict
  in *A Doll's House*, 196, 217-18
  and argumentation, 184, 187-9
  in pediatric consultations, 66-7
  social, 217
  talk, 166, 191n, 262, 265
    avoidance of, 180-1, 188-9, 265
    children's 180
    ping-pong rule, 179-81, 187, 190n-1n
context
  of asymmetries, 12-14
  bound, 263
  coding of turns, 231, 232
  constitutive, 199, 263-4
  cultural, 2
  for dialogue, 263-4
  social realities, 18
  see also institutional settings; multi-party; perspective/ perpectives
continuers, 164n
contradiction, 172, 173-5
contributions, oblique, 209
control
  and asymmetry, 41-3
  and disadvantage, 41
  and facework, 49-73
conversation
  analysis, 17, 19n, 269-70
  between spouses, 202-3
  defined, 163n, 244-5
  and dialogue, 244-5
  etiquette, 149
  prototypical, 207
  teaching, 143-63
  see also I-R analysis
cooperation, 103, 104-5
  example, 109-10
  see also obstruction; participation
corrections, 102-3, 106-7
  in psychotherapeutic sessions, 111-12, 114-15, 117, 119-20, 121-2
courts, 11
  and knowledge asymmetries, 23-4, 25
turn-taking, 22
culture, 9
  argumentative, 189, 192n
  and language, 259

dependence, 7-8, 213
detailing, level of, 125, 133, 134-9, 141
dialectical relation, 184-5
dialogicity, 271

280   Index

dialogism, 259, 269
dialogue
  asymmetry as intrinsic feature, 7–8, 259
  and contexts, 1
  definitions, 2, 244, 252
  see also language; perspective/perspectives; speech; turns
disembodied dialogue, 246
disadvantage, 32
  and control, 41
  and exogenous identities, 30–7
disagreed aspect, 175
disagreement, 166, 167, 168, 174
  and argument, 178
  building blocks of, 172–3
  ending of, 185–7
  and expansion, 191n
  rhetoric of, 175–8
  and teaching, 182–3
  tokens, 173, 180–1
  use of, 170
discrepant relevancies, 93–5
disembodied dialogue, 241, 243–4, 257
doctor-patient consultations, 11, 12, 38–9, 41, 45, 96, 204
  inverse asymmetry, 105
  and knowledge asymmetries, 24, 25
  and non-reversible roles, 235, 236
  pediatric, 57–9
  turn-taking, 22
Doll's House, A, 195–218, 243, 254, 266, 268
  I-R analysis, 206–14
dominance, 4, 5, 8–9, 10–11, 14, 96
  and asymmetry, 41
  in *A Doll's House*, 195–218
  avoidance of, 166
  and competence, 103
  defined, 19n, 101
  interactional, 9, 200–1, 202–3, 227
  and knowledge superiority, 125, 126
  and obstruction, 101–23
  quantitative, 9
  semantic, 9, 205–14
  strategic, 9, 195

embodied dialogue, 246–7, 256, 257
encounters
  face to face, 241–2
  family discussion, 186
  social, 189
  context of, 18
  dialogue as form of, 254–6, 257
endogenous asymmetry, 8, 10–11
epistemic responsibility, 195, 205–14, 238, 263, 266–7
  and asymmetry, 5

and women, 216, 217
equality, 2, 260
etiquette, conversational, 149
exogenous
  factors, 8, 10–11
  and knowledge asymmetries, 25
  identities, 45
  and disadvantage, 30–7
expansion, 178, 179, 180, 182, 213, 229–30, 232
  conflict avoidance, 265
  and disagreement, 181, 191n
expert-novice interaction 6, 11, 122, 124–41, 163n, 263, 265, 270
  advice from, 42–3, 47n
  turn-taking, 22
  and uncooperative exchanges, 114–15

face as source of asymmetry, 241
facework, 49–73
  hierarchy, 50–1
  model, 50–1
  self-orientated, 60
  threats and third parties, 68–71
family life, 50, 52
  and medical advice, 65, 68
family talk, 148, 163n, 171, 190n, 216
  and argumentation, 166, 177, 189, 209, 262
  as ideal, 170
  legitimized by parent, 71
  and teaching, 268
  topics, 256
filter, external, on information exchange, 81
form of talk, 167, 170
fragmentation, 229, 230–1, 232, 238
future dialogues, 65–8, 71

garage mechanics, 22, 136–8
Gienger argument, 171–3, 174, 185, 188, 192n
global asymmetries, 4–5, 8, 122, 262
greetings, 30–2, 33–5, 46n
groups
  discussion, 221–32
  without tutor, 234–5
  importance of, 248–9
  see also multi-party; social

health visitor study, 42–3, 47n
hidden dissent, 174

I-R analysis, 9, 227–32, 269
  A Doll's House, 199–205
Ich-Du relations, 6, 195, 211, 212, 214, 254

Ich-Es relations, 6, 195, 211, 212, 214, 254, 267
  and learning difficulties, 223, 237
identity *see Ich-Es* relations
idioms, 29, 30
immediacy, 212
impediments, 104
individual factors, 9-10
inequality, 3-4, 5
informal discussion
  avoidance of asymmetry, 166-93
  as communicative aggregate, 184-7
initiative-response *see* I-R analysis
institutional settings, 95-6, 163n
  argumentation, 168
  epistemic responsibility, 213, 266
  and knowledge asymmetries, 24-5, 43
  and perspectives, 263
  turn-taking, 22
  see also learning difficulties, people with; police interrogations
instructional exchanges, 124-41
  and argumentation, 181-4
  character of, 128
  defined, 126
  design of, 130-1
  instructor and recipient contributions, 127, 132-4
  pre-knowledge, 129, 130
  prerequisites, 126-7
  producing and understanding discourse, 127-31
instrumental utterances, 102, 105
inter-faces, 242
interactional
  coherence, 206, 207
  dominance, 9, 200-1, 202-3, 227
  dynamics, 29-37, 195, 199-205
  embeddedness and multi-party talk, 71-3
  interactions and learning difficulties, 221-3
intimate-stranger set, 32

joking, 51, 59, 65, 68
  and argumentation, 177

knowledge
  access to, 5, 6, 25
  authoritative, 27-30, 40-1, 45
  action, 130, 131-2, 134, 135, 138-9
  asymmetries, 5-6, 8, 21-47, 260-1, 267-9
    reduction of, 124-41, 144-5
  background, 75, 96, 131
  distribution, 105, 107
  inequality in, 16

  medical, 38-40
  normative entitlements to, 37-41
  ownership of, 37
  shared, 2-3
  social distribution, 4, 15-17, 45
  social stock of, 13-14, 142
  socio-cultural, 43, 44, 45n
  special, 15, 16-17
  technical, 22, 25, 40, 41, 43
  transmission of, 16-17, 124, 132-4
    conversational, 143-63
    and recipient, 153
    social, 14
    and wisdom, 158-63
  see also doctor-patient consultations; teaching, conversational

language, 16, 52
  as ambiguous, 72-3
  and dialogism, 259
  evolutionary context, 248-9
  social, 77, 215, 216
  and speech, 250-1
  written, 91-3
learning difficulties, people with, 245
  group discussions, 221-38
    analysis of, 226-32
  I-R analysis, 269
  and perspectives, 264, 265
  staff, 255-6
    interactions with, 221-3
legal system, 11-12, 77
  perspectives, 81
  see also police interrogations
life world (*Lebenswelt*), 211, 212, 213
literacy, 251-2
local asymmetries, 4-5, 8, 166, 262

medical consultations, 11, 12, 38-9, 46-7n
  see also doctor
mental model, 129
methodology, 17-18
miscommunication, 63
misunderstanding/misinterpretation, 25, 26, 112, 116-17, 129, 135, 229
  and vision, 244
monological dialogue, 234
moral issues, 215, 218
  objects and persons, 254
multi-party talk, 6
  conflicts, 52-3, 54-5, 60-3
  facework and control, 49-73
  and interactional embeddedness, 71-3
  negotiations in, 73

and threat, 68
multi-voicedness, 63, 65, 98n
mutuality, 96, 238
  of assumptions, 2-3
  dialogical, 238, 241, 259, 271
  of knowledge, 2-3

narrative, 76, 264
  and story, 98n
  structure of oral, 86-7
  theory, 86-90
  see also perspective/perspectives;
    police interrogations
natural argumentation, 190n
negated parallelism, 175, 176
negations, 174, 175
non-reversible roles, 221, 225
  and joint construction of meaning,
    235-7
non-verbal communication, 238, 244,
  245

object building, 138-9, 140
obliqueness, 209, 229, 230, 232, 238
obstruction and dominance, 101-23
off-record strategies, 52, 72
oppositions, 184
out-louds, 49

parents/parental
  authority, 67, 70
  authority of, 51
  domination, 102
  high-control, 53, 59, 71
  knowledge asymmetry, 57
  low-control, 53, 65, 73n
  repair work, 71, 72
  participation
    reduced, 101-7, 116, 118, 119, 121
    rights, 21-2
      equal, 19n
    status, 6, 8
pediatric encounters, 24, 50-73
  conflicts, 52-3
  and epistemic responsibility, 213
perception of self and others, 252-3
perspectival theory, 246-7
perspective/perspectives, 259
  in A Doll's House, 205-14
  commonalities, 271
  conflicts, 90-2, 93-5
  defined, 75, 264
  in institutional settings, 25
  instructional exchanges, 139, 141
  and joint construction of meaning,
    264-5
  mutuality, 75, 95, 96, 102
  in pediatric consultations, 63

police and suspects, 78, 81, 82-5
  reprocity of, 143, 149
  self and other, 27, 227, 242
  setting, 75-98, 264
  taking, 75-6, 264
persuasive techniques, 168
ping-pong rule, 179-81, 187, 190n-1n
police interrogations, 11, 12, 76, 78-
  86, 89-92, 93-7, 98n
  and context, 231-2
  and epistemic responsibility, 213
  I-R analysis, 204
  and non-reversible roles, 235, 236
  perspectives, 84-6, 163n, 264-5
  setting, 80-4
politeness, 149
  negative, 51
  positive, 51, 68
polyphonic text see Doll's House, A;
  voice
positive politeness, 51, 68
power, 10, 12, 14, 96
  defined, 19n
  and facework, 68
  relationships, 235
  social, 10-11
problem solving, 104-5, 109-10, 123
  as information-processing, 133
  instructional dialogue as, 134-8,
    139
  and knowledge transfer, 132, 133-8
  problems and argumentation, 169
professionalization, 16
proverbs, 29, 30
psychotherapeutic dialogue, 46n, 107,
  109-23, 163n, 263
  silence in, 46n, 111, 112, 116, 117,
    119, 121
  turn-taking, 22

quaestio, 169, 172, 185
quantitative dominance, 9
questioning, 27
  calling in question, 174
  instructional exchanges, 129, 138-9

recipient
  acknowledgement, 155, 156, 157,
    159-60, 162-3
  design, 49, 176
  and knowledge asymmetries, 124-6,
    128-30
  and knowledge transfer, 153
  participation, 164n
  signals, 155
  in teaching, 146
reciprocity, 3-5, 265
  and disagreement, 180

rectification, 182
reduced participation, 101-7, 116, 118, 119, 121
redundancy, 175-6, 177
reformulations, 191n
relevant outsides, 1, 233, 259
religious conversation, 164n, 181
   see also wisdom
repair work, 26, 63
   and conversational teaching, 149
   parental, 55-6, 57, 71, 72
repetition, 103, 174, 179
reports, 79-80, 81, 82, 83, 85-6, 91-3, 236
   and perspectives, 96-7, 163n
   space allotted, 89-90
resolution of asymmetry, 31, 32
responsibility
   epistemic, 238
   professional, 213
routinized interactions, 223

schizophrenic, 102
self
   consciousness of, 250, 253
   and others, 45, 252-4, 255, 262, 271
   as source of asymmetry, 241-57
self-reflexivity, 243
semantic dominance, 9, 205-14
silence, 103, 163
   in psychotherapeutic sessions, 46n, 111, 112, 116, 117, 119, 121
situation model, 129
skin, importance of, 253-4, 255, 256
sociability, 187, 189
social
   change, 260
   conflicts, 217
   distance, 56, 59, 267
   distribution of knowledge, 15-17
   encounters, 186, 189
   factors, 9-10
   interaction and past accomplishments, 13-14
   language, 77, 215, 216
   life of humans, 248
   power, 10-11
   roles, 71
   stock of knowledge, 13-14, 142
   individual and, 14
   structures, 9
Socrates/Socratic dialogue, 260-1
solicitation, 229, 230, 232, 238
speakers, 130, 247
   identity, 32-3
   role, 9, 49
speech
   disembodied, 241, 243-4, 257
   embodied, 241, 243-4, 256, 257
   and language, 250-1
   significance of, 248-9
   as source of symmetry, 242-3
   and vision, 242-3, 244, 245, 247-50, 252
   evolutionary context, 249-52
   historical perspective, 251-2
speech therapy, 223-4
   dialogical approach, 224
   medical deficit model, 223-4
spouses, conversation between, 202-3
status asymmetries, 254, 261
story-telling see narrative
strategic dominance, 9, 195
suspect stories, 75-98
symmetry, 2, 5, 21

T-scheme, 168
talk, organization of, 184
teaching, 6
   conversational, 5, 143-63, 268
      change of style, 145-6, 153
      and disagreement, 182-4
      opening sequences, 147-53
         pupil initiatives, 147-9, 160
         teacher initiatives, 149-53
      pupil-candidate, 149, 182
         selection, 146
      recipient of knowledge, 153, 155, 156, 157, 159-60, 162-3
      structure of, 145-58
      teacher-to-be, 149, 182
         selection, 146
      terminations of, 155-8, 159
      turn-taking, 154-5, 159
      and wisdom, 158-63
   legitimacy for, 267-8
   and non-reversible roles, 235, 236
technical knowledge, 22, 25, 40, 41, 43
telephone conversations, 30-2, 46n, 247, 256
testing, 34-5, 36
thematic continuity, 206-7, 208
thematic control, 207-8, 266
theoretization, 16
timing of ignition study, 136-8
topic
   and argumentation, 187, 188, 188-9
   development, 5, 232-4, 270
   and informal discussion, 167, 186
   maintenance, 259, 270
topicalization, 213
touch and vision, 250, 251
tree of arguments, 168, 169
try-marking, 164n
turns
   equal rights, 21-2

as Janus-like, 227
meaning of, 233-4
turn-taking
  and argumentation, 169, 172-3, 179-81
  and control, 43
  and conversational teaching, 154-5, 159
  in institutional settings, 45n
  in pediatric consultations, 54-7
  see also I-R analysis

uncooperative exchanges, 46n, 101-23
  direct violation, 110-15
  indirect violation, 115-20

validity claim, 169, 170, 174, 178, 187
ventriloquation, 215
violation of expectations *see* uncooperative exchanges
vision
  role of, 256-7
  and speech, 242-3, 244, 245, 247-50, 252
  evolutionary context, 249-52
  historical perspective, 251-2
  and touch, 250, 251
  and voice, 262
voice/voices, 9, 76, 215
  and bodies, 241-57
  defined, 77
  multi-voicedness, 63, 65
  and vision, 262

wisdom transmission, 145, 158-63, 164n
  and argumentative sequences, 186
women
  epistemic responsibility, 216, 217
  and moral problems, 218
  status asymmetry, 254
written text, 91-3, 213
  see also reports

'Yes-but', 175